BANKING AND FINANCIAL INSTITUTIONS LAW

IN A NUTSHELL®

TENTH EDITION

MICHAEL P. MALLOY
Distinguished Professor
University of the Pacific
McGeorge School of Law
Sacramento, California

WEST ACADEMIC

860 Blue Gentian Road, Suite 350
Eagan, MN 55121
1-877-888-1330

Published in the United States of America

ISBN: 978-1-68561-235-1

PREFACE

This book is intended for lawyers, law students, economists, bankers, and business people seeking to understand recent developments in banking and financial institutions law and policy.

Major changes have occurred. Broader rivalry developed over the last generation among banks, thrift institutions, securities firms, mutual funds, insurance companies, pension funds, and various retirement and investment accounts. Considerable deregulation was achieved; yet the next steps remain controversial. Unfortunately, a costly wave of U.S. bank and thrift failures came in the late 1980s and early 1990s. This led to tougher laws in 1989 and 1991, and substantial bailout and restructuring efforts, especially for savings and loan associations and savings banks. But, as economic conditions stabilized and bank margins improved, capital was replenished for most U.S. institutions since the early 1990s. Renewed confidence with sound oversight seemed to be re-established, but fresh strains emerged in the new millennium, prompting new statutory and regulatory responses. These latest developments will be discussed in context throughout this book.

Meanwhile, a longer term trend toward globalization linked financial markets from many countries more closely. Debt overload strains had affected many countries in the 1980s, with extensive rescheduling arrangements. As confidence revived, capital flowed more freely in the 1990s, and many emerging markets received large investments. Speculative booms followed in many countries. Disruptive crises and devaluations occurred in some nations, although an overall expansion in global finance seemed fairly well established. Increasingly, finance became internationalized, with serious challenges for supervision and transparency, which still operated almost exclusively at a national level.

Unfortunately, lax surveillance reappeared in U.S. mortgage finance, global securitization, and off-balance sheet activities. This brought an even bigger wave of bank losses in 2008–2009. Another round of bank failures in the U.S. and Europe combined with several trillion dollars of contaminated assets. Awkward uncertainties hit the largest U.S. and European banking and securities firms. Many of the biggest institutions needed multi-billion dollar bailouts, guarantees, and/or loan support. Over-leveraging, over-confidence, and gaps in supervision were to blame. Once again, regulatory agencies and financial markets were strained. But lessons from the Great Depression, the 1970s, 1980s, and the 1990s should be helpful as we emerge from the latest crisis.

This book explains the economic, historical, and legal background for banking and financial intermediaries. Law and policy-makers have tried to compromise conflicting interests, with a view toward improved competition and overall performance. These efforts sometimes neglect the bigger picture.

An extensive body of literature and law exists in each area summarized by this book. But hardly any legal writing properly integrates these developments for banking and financial intermediaries as a whole. This book meets that need and has been heavily revised in light of recent developments.

MICHAEL P. MALLOY
Distinguished Professor

University of the Pacific
McGeorge School of Law
Sacramento, California
March 2024

OUTLINE

PART B. BANK REGULATION

PART D. EMERGING ISSUES IN THE LAW OF FINANCIAL INTERMEDIARIES

TABLE OF CASES

References are to Pages

LIST OF TABLES AND CHARTS

References are to Pages

BANKING AND FINANCIAL INSTITUTIONS LAW

IN A NUTSHELL®

TENTH EDITION

PART A

THE LAW AND POLICY OF FINANCIAL INTERMEDIARIES

CHAPTER I

EVOLUTION OF BANKING AND FINANCIAL INSTITUTIONS LAW

A. INTRODUCTION

Modern industrial societies need banking and other financial institutions to trade and prosper. Money serves as our medium of exchange and standard of value, but financial deposits are convenient, liquid stores of value for individuals, families, businesses, and other organizations. Banks and financial institutions collect money and deposits from all elements of society, and invest these funds in loans, securities, and various other productive assets. Every healthy economic system requires that money, banks, and financing intermediaries provide this service efficiently and reliably. Production, saving, investment, and efficient industrial development are facilitated thereby. Such work is vital for the transactions flow of each nation and the world economy.

With the exception of monetary unions like the Euro Zone within the European Union, each country legislates its own currency, with unique regulations for the network of banking, credit, and financial transactions within its jurisdiction. These arrangements, hopefully, should ensure that money, banking, and finance operate smoothly. In many ways, such arrangements are often similar. But considerable differences exist among national laws with respect to: (1) the scope for private enterprise;

(2) permissible entry into banking and finance, and the latitude for chartering and branching; (3) competition among financial institutions, their number, size and variety; (4) the role of monetary controls and interest regulations; (5) public finance, revenues, taxes, and deficits; and (6) the macro-economic policies designed to coordinate fiscal, monetary, trade and capital flows, foreign exchange and other regulatory activities.

This book mainly emphasizes the law and policies affecting banking and financial institutions in the United States of America. But we must never forget that money, finance, and commerce are increasingly transnational in character. Financial markets, transactions, and credit-borrowing flows are world-wide, and the entire network has been experiencing an onslaught of technical change for some time now. Electronic communications, funds transfer, coding, access, cards, telephone, and computerized linkages are transforming finance and accounting. These changes, along with conflicting pressures from industry groups, moderate and conservative, together with liberal and socialist reformers, in various countries, have made the law of banking and financial institutions an exciting, if somewhat unsettled, field of activity. Our purpose is to summarize the American legal arrangements in detail, and to put them in the context of powerful international forces and technological trends.

B. EARLIER MONEY AND BANKING

In traditional societies, money consisted almost entirely of "specie" (usually gold or silver). The supply of specie was limited to the supply of metal available for coinage, which increased slowly each year by the amounts newly mined. A great virtue of this arrangement was relative stability in the specie money supply. So long as governments avoided debasement of the coinage, specie retained its value and served reliably as the medium of exchange.

Credit was granted by wealthier asset holders (landowners, merchants, temples, or artisans), who could afford to lend to borrowers. Stable money values provided a convenient measuring rod for debt transactions, but loans were often extended in kind—food, seed, animals, tools, materials, and so forth. Payment obligations were expressed commonly in money, although shares of crops, production, or other profits were often specified. Thus, credits flowed from the affluent to some of the more needy, or at least, to those considered capable of using credits responsibly and repaying their loans.

Early banking was provided by leading merchants, money changers, goldsmiths, or nobles, who took specie deposits from other merchants and individuals for safekeeping and convenience. These "stronger" houses provided care for specie deposits, frequently paid interest, and the "banker" could lend out the accumulated deposits (at higher interest) to borrowers. Generally, the banker would provide receipts or "notes" in place of actual specie, so that risk of physical loss in handling specie could be minimized. Soon thereafter bankers discovered the advantage of "fractional reserves," a profitable innovation. If bankers merely loaned out a portion of their deposits received, they would serve merely as financial intermediaries or trustees. But bankers go beyond this level of lending, and grant more loans (in return for promissory notes and mortgages) than the original amount of deposits. This is the "credit function" of banking.

How is this possible? So long as banks keep enough cash as a reserve fund, the confidence of original depositors can be retained, and their needs for occasional withdrawal will be satisfied. Bear in mind the banks are still solvent, *at least to the extent that "good" loans and security exist* for the additional issue of receipts, notes, checks, etc. Provided most borrowers are able to repay their loans and meet interest obligations, this expansion of bank note "money" (or even checking account "money") will be highly profitable for bankers. (The small proportion of defaulting loans can be covered by a slight increase in the interest risk premium charged to borrowers.) Meanwhile, the city, province or country served by the bankers benefits from enlarged access to credit, increased liquidity and investment potential, and expanded prosperity. In this way, through fractional reserve banking, the specie (gold and silver) money supply can be multiplied several-fold, or even more in the course of modern industrial development.

1. NATIONAL BANKS AND CURRENCY

Private banking enlarged the financial potential of city states, republics, kingdoms, and empires through much of history. Financial activity might flourish with military success or expanding trade and prosperity. But risks were inherent in private family (or partnership) banking. Depositors received no more assurance than the private fortunes and reputation of their bankers could guarantee, and banker's notes in circulation might fluctuate in value and suffer significant discounting. To achieve stronger, more reliable banking activity, many countries in the Mercantilist era (roughly from the 16th to the 18th Centuries) created national banks, such as the Bank of Amsterdam, Banque Royal, Bank of England, Bank of Sweden, Banque de France, Bank of Prussia (later the Reichsbank), along with the first and second Bank of the United States. (The second Bank was, of course, the subject of the seminal Supreme Court decision *McCulloch v. Maryland*, 17 U.S. (4 Wheat.) 316 (1819), upholding the authority of the federal government to create a central bank.) These institutions were early "central banks," and some of them survive today.

Early national banks were typically quasi-public corporations, with much broader access to deposits, and substantial government support. Shareholders were wealthy citizens, and might include the government, too. The national bank's notes usually became legal tender, or "currency," along with the country's coinage.[1] This added another dimension to the money supply, along with potential for excessive currency issue. Countries learned, however, that a currency would be more stable in value if its convertibility into specie were guaranteed. Thus, apart from unfortunate inflationary experiences—Chinese paper currency during the Yuan Dynasty (13th Century), John Law's Banque Royal in France (1716–1720), the French Revolution's assignats, the American "continentals" during the revolutionary war, or the Southern Confederate currency—governments generally recognized that such "paper" money should not be enlarged unreasonably beyond the specie or "liquid" capital reserves available to back the value of such currency.

2. SPREAD OF CORPORATE BANKING

In most countries, corporate banks were chartered to supplement national banks and private family (or partnership) banks. Gradually, corporate banks outgrew private banks, and took over the leading role in bank finance. This allowed more banking activity and competition, which flourished when checking accounts and bank drafts became almost as reliable as currency. Wealthier individuals would provide the initial corporate bank capital, and additional shares might be sold to the general public. Some risk of insolvency existed, though, for corporate banks that lacked the support and guarantee of deposits that

---

[1] Currency could be created directly by government "fiat" as well, with great potential for debasement or inflation if specie redemption or convertibility were not assured.

governments could provide. Although a large, successful bank corporation might offer more strength and reliability than the typical private family bank, the danger of mismanagement, a weak loan and investment portfolio, or the adverse financial impact of wars, depressions or financial panics meant that runs and failures might still occur. These risks increased with easy entry of small, under-capitalized corporate banks that often popped up in rural areas, or when bank management fell into questionable or incompetent hands.

A serious problem, therefore, in the evolution of modern banking law was to regulate banking practices and to reduce the risk of financial panics, disrupted business, and enlarged unemployment. As industrial specialization and inter-dependence increased, this need for banking and financial regulation led to stronger reforms, greater supervision and restriction, and, in some countries, even partial or complete "nationalization" of banking.

A great variety of policies have been employed to strengthen bank integrity, along with protectionist measures designed more narrowly to favor parochial interests. Central banks frequently received a monopoly of the power to issue notes; less favored institutions might have their notes taxed, limited, or prohibited altogether. Checking account deposits gradually evolved as a close substitute, however, for banknote issue, and by-passed these restrictions. Central banks normally became "lenders of last resort" to the corporate and private banks, and regulated interest rates and economic conditions through the rate (or discount rates) at which such loans were allowed.[2] Legal restrictions were usually placed on bank charters and new entry, sometimes drastically limiting bank competition. Capital requirements became common (especially as to initial capitalization), along with percentage reserve (or liquidity) requirements applied to deposits. Limits were sometimes placed on the interest payable on deposits to limit competition and/or to cushion established banks. In periods of serious financial crisis, emergency government loans, suspension of customer payments, or increased capitalization requirements could be employed. These techniques evolved in many countries during the last several centuries. Most, at one stage or another, are illustrated by banking law and regulation in the United States.

C. BANKING DEVELOPMENT IN THE UNITED STATES

United States banking history is dominated by federalism. National and state-chartered banks struggled for ascendancy from the beginning. It took until 1913 for a relatively weak Federal Reserve System to be enacted. And only the Great Depression and New Deal Reforms led to a stronger system of national supervision, federal deposit insurance, and

---

[2] Central bank loans to banks might be made directly, or by discounting the promissory notes and commercial paper received by the banks in their normal extension of credits to businesses and the public.

more systematic federal regulation of banking and financial markets.

1. FIRST AND SECOND BANK OF THE UNITED STATES

The first Bank of the United States (1791–1811) was a centerpiece of Hamiltonian finance. Its share capital was $10 million (20 percent held by the federal government), a substantial note issue followed, and it played an important role in public finance and tax collection. But the states chartered more than a hundred banks in the same period, and their aggregate deposits and notes issue became more important. Lobbying by agrarian and state bank interests prevented rechartering of the national bank in 1811.

But difficulties in raising federal loans for the War of 1812 (1812–1815), unreliable state banknotes, and shaky finance generally led to a second Bank of the United States (1816–1836). This new national bank had $35 million share capital (20 percent held by the federal government), its notes were declared legal tender, and convertibility into specie was required for all banknotes (national or state chartered) used for payments to the federal government. Soon this latter authority was employed to crack down on loose lending practices and excessive note issue by state banks, although at the cost of a substantial deflation-recession (1819–1822). Nicholas Biddle of Philadelphia then led the Bank of the United States (and some state systems) into a period of healthy expansion, with sounder banking. The Suffolk system in New England (1824–1858)[3] and the New York Safety Fund (1829–1837) also helped to strengthen banking in the states.[4]

But President Jackson and agrarian interests in the South and West opposed the second Bank of the United States, being suspicious of its Northeastern leaders and shareholders, and preferring to rely only on state banks. Jackson vetoed charter extension in 1832, and won re-election over Henry Clay (who supported the national bank). Soon thereafter, Jackson began transferring federal deposits to selected state "pet" banks. When national bank supporters failed to elect enough members of Congress to override a second veto, Biddle accepted defeat and liquidated the Bank of the United States in 1836. (It was reorganized as a Pennsylvania state bank, but failed in the subsequent depression.) In these Jackson years state banks multiplied nearly three-fold. Between 1830–1837 state banknote issue more than doubled, and their loans and discounts increased from less than $200 million to more than $500 million. Alarmed at this expansion, Jackson finally tightened up on federal land sales, requiring specie (instead of state banknotes) for payment. This triggered a collapse of the speculative land-boom,

---

[3] The Suffolk system in Boston featured prompt redemption of country bank notes, provided sufficient deposits were placed in leading Boston banks to back them up.

[4] The New York Safety Fund was a compulsory state insurance against bank failures, financed by small percentage assessments from all their banks.

excessive note issue caused many bank failures, and a general depression ensued (1837–1842).

2. FREE BANKING ERA

Between 1836 and 1863 the states served as the sole chartering authority for banking institutions. Even more significantly, standards for new charters relaxed considerably. In many states, including New York, access to bank charters became relatively automatic or freely available, provided that moderate initial capital requirements were satisfied by the incorporators. States varied in their regulatory policies, but a general lesson seemed to be that firm capital requirements, reasonable supervision, and/or enforcing specie convertibility would yield sound banking. Laxity in these respects typically resulted in bank failures. Among the "stronger" systems were New York's tightened reserve system (after 1843), the Suffolk system in New England (from 1824 until 1858), Indiana's government sponsored state bank (between 1834–1855), and Louisiana's 100 percent "reserve" system, one-third specie and two-thirds 90-day commercial paper (between 1842–1862). In stronger states, clearing operations among banks improved greatly in the 1850s. But many states allowed loose practices, and in those areas state banks had unreliable note issue, suffered frequent runs, and did not enjoy full public confidence.

3. NATIONAL BANK ACT AND THE DUAL BANKING SYSTEM

During the Civil War, with eleven Southern and agrarian states out of the Congress, it was possible to enact stronger federal banking legislation. The creation of the position of Comptroller of the Currency in 1863, with further amendments in the National Bank Act of 1864 (NBA,} encouraged federal chartering of privately owned banks with modest capitalization requirements, but imposed stronger reserve requirements and limitations on the note issue of federally chartered banks. These were officially called "national banking associations," or more commonly "national banks," but they are commercial enterprises, not quasi-central banks like the first and second Banks of the United States or "national banks" in other countries.[5]

Within two years Congress increased federal taxes on state bank notes to onerous levels (10 percent), and by late 1866 there were 1,644 "national" banks with $280 million in banknote circulation. State banknotes largely disappeared from circulation. This was less significant than it seemed, though, because

[5] It is not entirely clear that the Supreme Court in that era fully understood this distinction. In its decision in *Farmers' & Mechanics' National Bank v. Dearing*, 91 U.S. (1 Otto) 29, 33 (1875), upholding the constitutionality of the act to grant federal banking charters, the Supreme Court stated that the constitutionality of the NBA rested "on the same principle as the act creating the second bank of the United States," which had been upheld under the "necessary and proper" clause of the Constitution in *McCulloch* and in *Osborn v. Bank of the United States*, 22 U.S. (9 Wheat.) 738 (1824). The validity of the NBA has been unchallenged since then.

checking accounts were an easy substitute for banknotes. (Checks had become more important in the volume of transactions even in the 1850s, and by the late 1880s less than 10 percent of the total volume of business transactions was in currency, *i.e.*, greenbacks and national banknotes.)

State banking reached a low ebb after the Panic of 1873 and the subsequent depression, when many more state banks failed than national banks. In 1878 there were 2,056 national banks with $653 million deposits, and only 475 state banks with $143 million in deposits. But rivalry in chartering, less restrictive requirements, and the growing importance of checkbook money led to a more rapid revival of state banks.[6] The country seemed to like easier banking. For these reasons, unfortunately, the problems of fragility and periodic panic were never fully solved until the reforms of the 1930s.

Money and banking remained controversial until the enactment of the Federal Reserve Act of 1913. Western and agrarian states felt inadequately served, state bank interests complained of favoritism, and the limited national banknote issue was a constraint on access to liquidity in some areas.

---

[6] Congress liberalized access to national bank charters in the Currency Act of 1900, and as a result, 3,046 new national banks were created between 1900 and 1908, two-thirds with initial capitalization of less than $50,000 each. State chartering standards were eased too, and the ranks of state banks increased from 8,696 in 1900 to 18,478 in 1912.

Another factor explaining the proliferation of smaller banks was a prohibition on national bank branching in the National Bank Act of 1864.

Populist movements for enlarged greenback issue (fiat currency) and more silver coinage reflected this dissatisfaction as well. Yet overall economic growth and prosperity allowed the country to tolerate an imperfect system, partly because checkbook money proved adequate for most business purposes. The most serious problem was vulnerability to periodic panic and failures, especially among smaller banks, and this provoked recurrent concern about banking regulation. Finally, the Panic of 1907, though relatively brief, triggered serious effort toward more reliable banking.

4. FEDERAL RESERVE SYSTEM AND THE GREAT DEPRESSION

The Federal Reserve System, established in 1913, evolved out of a search for consensus among bankers, politicians, and some academic experts. It was a move toward "central bank" regulation in the European sense, though weaknesses were not evident until the Great Depression. The major features were: (i) An association of District Federal Reserve banks was established, regulated by a Board of Governors, appointed by the President. (ii) Every national bank was required to be a member, and state banks were allowed to become members. (iii) Member banks had to purchase district reserve bank stock equal to 6 percent of their capital and surplus. (iv) Member banks had to maintain reserves against their demand and time deposits (from 12–18 percent and 4 percent, respectively). (v) Member banks could get loans from their district reserve bank by discounting commercial paper.[7] (vi) District reserve banks would issue Federal Reserve notes ("currency") fully secured by commercial paper and gold reserves. (vii) District reserve banks could purchase and sell government obligations under regulations established by the Board of Governors. (viii) District reserve banks would operate a check clearing system for their member banks. (ix) District reserve banks would be managed by nine-member boards—three representing banks, three representing business, commerce, and agriculture, and three representing the public at large. This legal structure is the foundation for most subsequent monetary and banking policy developments and influenced later regulation of savings institutions by the Federal Home Loan Bank Board (FHLBB).

These reforms seemed to resolve the outstanding problems in money and banking. Federal Reserve bank notes could grow with expanding commercial paper and economic prosperity, and assure a more adequate, reliable monetary growth. Government borrowing capacity was firmly established to support emergency finance and wartime needs. At the same time, ample safeguards were provided in stronger reserves, Federal Reserve lending authority, and discount rate discipline. By standards of past

---

7 "Discounting" commercial paper (typically, notes) means selling notes to the bank at some point prior to the note's maturity date. The term "discount" is used because the bank deducts the interest it charges from the note's maturity value ("face value"), and thus "discounts" the note.

American history, the country had brought its banking laws up to date.

Unfortunately, leaders in the Federal Reserve system, Congress, and the President failed to act boldly, and with large enough emergency credits in the 1929–1932 crisis. With the wisdom of hindsight, economists now believe the Federal Reserve could have greatly restricted the scope and duration of the Great Depression, provided that leadership from the President and support from Congress had been available. Special legislation and emergency funding would have been required soon after the stock market crash in 1929.[8] But things were allowed to get out of hand, and the growing depression reduced revenues, and deficits weakened the will of politicians to act. There was a rapid and tragic decline in business and employment. Gross national product was cut in half, and unemployment reached a peak of 24 percent of the work force. Large financial losses for businesses and families put loans into default throughout much of the economy and brought insolvency to a large portion of the nation's banks. These banking problems were most acute in agricultural areas, where greatly reduced farm prices made loans hard to collect, and low land prices greatly weakened collateral values. Smaller rural banks failed in large numbers.

---

8 Also, the severity of the stock market crash could have been limited substantially by earlier restrictions on excess stock margin speculation and margin accounts.

5. NEW DEAL REFORMS

The incoming administration of Franklin D. Roosevelt responded immediately to the banking and financial crisis with a bank holiday, emergency loans for banks, and suspension of the gold standard. (Britain and many other countries had devalued earlier, and there were substantial gold outflows from the United States) Within several months, the Federal Reserve received authority to increase the currency issue, more authority to use government obligations as collateral for bank notes, but also powers to restrict undue credit expansion. New law prohibited the payment of interest on demand deposits, to help limit "destructive competition" among banks. Most importantly, the Federal Deposit Insurance Corporation was created to insure all accounts up to $2,500 (currently a "standard maximum deposit insurance amount" of $250,000, to be adjusted periodically for inflation) for depository institutions. The FDIC was financed by modest insurance premiums imposed on insured banks, and it was armed with auditing, examination, and receivership authority, along with other corrective powers to deal with troubled banks.

Meanwhile, new federal securities legislation imposed major responsibilities for disclosure of financial information with respect to publicly owned corporations; and investment banking (the underwriting of stock and bond issues) was legally separated from commercial banking. The Securities and Exchange Commission (SEC) was created in 1934 to enforce these disclosure requirements, and to regulate the stock exchanges and brokerage industry. In 1935, further legislation strengthened the Federal Reserve Board (taking its present form, with 14-year terms for Board members), and created the Federal Open Market Committee (FOMC), comprising the seven Board members and five representatives from district reserve banks. A more flexible, wider range for reserve requirements was established, with Board discretion to set reserve ratios according to economic conditions. The Board also received authority to limit interest rates on time deposits, later implemented under Regulation Q.

The Federal Reserve Board—or "the Fed," as it is popularly called—became a much stronger central bank as a result, and social insurance (FDIC protection) of smaller bank deposits greatly alleviated the dangers of bank failure, virtually eliminating runs on banks. The Fed encouraged monetary ease, with excess reserves and low interest rates through most of the 1930s. But this stimulus, by itself, only partly restored economic activity. Moderate government deficits were carried also in the New Deal years, but full employment was not achieved until World War II mobilization, when much larger deficits expanded industrial output to record levels.

6. WORLD WAR II FINANCE

The war brought concern for inflation, and the Federal Reserve began tightening reserve requirements and credit in the fall of 1940. But the Treasury ran increasingly huge deficits in the war years, and this forced the Fed to support low interest rates on massive government borrowing. Government debt expanded from $48 to $260 billion, and the money supply increased from $48 to $106 billion during the war years. Wage and price controls, along with some rationing, and a big savings bond program were used to contain and drain off excess inflationary pressure. On the whole, these policies were successful, and consumer prices went up only 25 percent between 1941 and 1945. When controls were lifted after the war, however, more inflation occurred, raising the cost of living another 33 percent by 1948. But strong fiscal restraint, budget surpluses between 1946 and 1948, and a rapid postwar conversion of industry (assisted by low interest rates) stopped inflation in the 1948–1949 recession. In the 1940s, banking policy had been subordinated to war finance and borrowing needs.

7. POSTWAR PROSPERITY AND POLICIES

Bankers and the Federal Reserve wanted to restore normal market conditions for money and credit markets reasonably soon in the postwar era. When inflationary pressure cooled, and it seemed likely that regular debt service could be handled satisfactorily, it was time to free the Fed from responsibility to support government borrowing at pegged rates. During the Korean War (1950–1953), the Fed began to tighten money and increase interest rates to help limit inflation, even though the Treasury sought resumption of low interest rates to support renewed borrowing. Early in 1951, the FOMC broke with Treasury policy, and sold part of its bond portfolio (for open market operations) at a discount to raise effective interest rates. This led to the famous "Accord of 1951," under which the Federal Reserve gradually achieved its independence as the dominant force in monetary policy. This led to firmer monetary policy, and it helped tighten the free reserves of banks. Interest rates moved up somewhat. This action combined with partial price controls, increased taxes, and modest surpluses to limit inflation during the Korean War.

During subsequent years, monetary management by the Federal Reserve has become an important element in macroeconomic policy. Along with government budgets, tax and fiscal management, and various forms of wage-price guidance and industrial encouragement, monetary policy has played an increasing role in efforts to coordinate overall economic performance. In general, Federal Reserve monetary policy since 1953 can be characterized as an effort to provide restraint against inflationary pressures, and a relaxation or easing of this restraint when significant recession and unemployment developed. This has required often controversial estimates, forecasts, and judgments about bank reserves, monetary growth, interest rates, price levels, excess capacity, unemployment, international trade, the balance of payments, and economic expansion.

Inevitably, these issues have become entangled with presidential politics. Hence, monetary policy for the Federal Reserve is closely linked to national economic policy.

Another significant development in postwar banking law was the increased importance of antitrust policy, and concern for adequate competition in financial markets. Because new entry into banking slowed greatly since the 1930s, while bank mergers, holding companies, consolidations, and branching became more widespread, Congress and the antitrust authorities imposed constraints. The Bank Holding Company Act of 1956 limited "chain banking," in which a bank holding company would expand its market by acquiring a string of bank subsidiaries. The Bank Merger Acts of 1960 and 1966 (along with the Supreme Court's decision in *United States v. Philadelphia Nat. Bank,* 374 U.S. 321 (1963)) limited larger bank mergers in the same cities or metropolitan areas. In 1970, Bank Holding Company Act amendments narrowly restricted diversification by banks into other industries. But then, in 1974, Supreme Court merger policy relaxed with *United States v. Marine Bancorporation*, 418 U.S. 602 (1974), which allowed leading banks to make major bank acquisitions in other cities within the same state. In 1980 a Presidential Committee urged that branching be liberalized, and that interstate banking should be allowed. Later in the 1980s many states began to allow regional interstate bank holding companies (often on a reciprocal basis), and more frequent bank failures led to some increased consolidation. During the 1990s, more branching and interpenetration of financial markets was allowed. In 1999 the Gramm-Leach-Bliley Act authorized "financial holding companies" to operate in banking, insurance, and securities markets. Thus, even more consolidation in banking and some conglomerate financial integration has begun to occur.

Greater competition for banks had come from saving institutions as well. Savings and loan associations traditionally collected passive, medium-term deposits with slightly higher interest rates than banks, and invested these funds mostly in long term real estate mortgages.[9] This specialized intermediation could be handled with minimum staff and paperwork, and often involved low profit margins for savings institutions in competitive markets. Banks concentrated more on collecting demand and short-term deposits and invested in shorter-term loans and highly liquid securities. By the late 1960s, deposits in all savings institutions (*i.e.*, savings and loan associations, savings banks, and credit unions) were approaching the scale of domestic commercial banking. In the 1970s, some of the larger savings institutions began to offer NOW accounts (*i.e.*, demand deposits that pay interest) and sought broadened lending opportunities.

This rivalry among financial intermediaries was accentuated in the late 1970s by new competition from money market funds. Money market funds were an outgrowth of mutual funds sponsored by the securities and brokerage industry. Because interest rates on savings deposits had been kept down artificially in the 1970s under Regulation Q, in order

---

9 The savings institutions industry began modestly in the 19th Century, but grew rapidly with post-World War II prosperity and housing investments.

to protect savings institutions and banks, this led to an increasing gap in the late 1970s between passbook rates and world market interest rates. Although banks and savings institutions were forced to create large denomination money market certificates for big depositors, they resisted any rapid lifting of Regulation Q ceilings for small depositors. Passbook rates in 1978–1981 were still 4¾–5½ percent—with ¼ percent more allowed for savings institutions—while money market certificates, money market funds, and world market interest rates ranged from 10–20 percent. Money market funds offered by major brokerage firms greatly reduced their initial deposits and allowed prompt withdrawal. Naturally, money market fund deposits grew rapidly, with an additional advantage of interstate operations and national advertising.

These increased competitive pressures led to the Depository Institutions Deregulation and Monetary Control Act of 1980 ("DIDMCA"). This compromise featured uniform reserve requirements for banks and savings institutions (but not money market funds) to be phased in over seven years, the gradual elimination of Regulation Q limits on interest rates over a six-year period, broader investment and service authority for federal savings and loan associations, and immediate authority to offer NOW accounts for most financial institutions. In addition, the DIDMCA strengthened Federal Reserve authority to regulate and supervise growth of the monetary aggregates.

In the fall of 1982, the Garn-St. Germain Act gave further impetus to the erosion of boundaries between banks and savings institutions. It added more federal savings institution powers, led to liberalized real estate investment authority, allowed mergers between weakened savings institutions and banks, and mandated new money market accounts equivalent to and competitive with money market mutual funds. But later, as many savings institutions got into trouble and failed in the later 1980s, extensive mergers were allowed, and banks began to acquire them in some areas.

Another important development during the postwar era was the spread of international banking in London, Switzerland, Germany, Japan, and various other countries, including many off-shore tax havens. Multinational business found it increasingly profitable to relocate many of their financial activities abroad to avoid domestic regulation and taxation, often involving "Eurodollar banking," deposits denominated in U.S. dollars, but held in accounts located outside the United States. Banks in Europe were eager to encourage this business, and the biggest U.S. banks followed their customers overseas through expanded branch networks. An increasing flow of deposits also was collected world-wide from international entrepreneurs, who generated higher profits by skillfully routing production, sales, and service transactions to minimize taxes. Much of this activity escaped effective regulation, but a growth of foreign bank branching (in one form or another) into the United States led to the International Banking Act of 1978.

This legislation imposed restrictions on foreign banks in the United States similar to those already affecting American domestic banks.

Further legal developments since the late 1960s brought important federal regulation to protect consumers, and to limit discrimination based upon sex, race, religion, national origin, or age in access to credit. Truth-in-Lending disclosure requirements were imposed in 1968 upon consumer loans and retail credit transactions, with rulemaking originally delegated to the Federal Reserve Board, and enforcement by federal financial regulatory agencies, the Federal Trade Commission, and private lawsuits. Additional consumer safeguards and limits on liability with respect to credit cards followed in 1970, with regulation of consumer credit reporting services in 1974. Congress outlawed discrimination in access to credit with respect to sex or marital status in 1974, and extended this policy in 1976 to other bases for discrimination, including race, receipt of public assistance, religion, national origin, or age. And in 1978, the Electronic Funds Transfer Act was enacted to protect consumers, and it defined rights, liabilities, and responsibilities with respect to bankcards and electronic funds transfer systems. More recently, improved privacy and internet safeguards are receiving more attention, with tighter regulations likely.

A new crisis loomed in the early 2000s. It centered on the subprime mortgage market in the United States—real estate mortgages at higher, usually variable interest rates due to the relatively poor quality of the borrower's credit ratings. During the five years preceding the crisis that exploded in 2008, the subprime mortgage market experienced very aggressive growth. However, once it became evident that these mortgage loans were not being paid according to their terms, the banks that had lent to the mortgagors—and the U.S. and foreign banks and investors who had bought interests in the pools of these mortgages (referred to as "securitization")—were caught in the 2008 collapse of the subprime mortgage market.[10] This eventually led to the enactment of the Dodd-Frank Wall Street Reform and Consumer Protection Act (Dodd-Frank Act) in 2010, with a range of reforms including: (1) abolition of the Office of Thrift Supervision and the transfer of its functions and responsibilities to the Office of the Comptroller of the Currency (who regulates national banks), the FDIC, and the Fed; (2) establishment of the Financial Stability Oversight Council (FSOC), a committee of financial services regulators, to identify systemic risks, promote market discipline, and respond to emerging threats to the U.S. financial system; (3) establishment of the Consumer Financial Protection Bureau (CFPB) within the Fed to create and enforce consumer protection principles with respect to financial services; (4) restriction of proprietary securities trading by banks; (5) new mortgage lending standards; (6) new standards with respect to securitization of pools of financial instruments; and, (7) expansion of securities

---

[10] For background on the subprime mortgage crisis and its legal implications, see Michael P. Malloy, Anatomy of a Meltdown (Aspen 2010).

disclosure requirements and the enhancement of the enforcement powers of the SEC and the Commodity Futures Trading Commission (CFTC).

D. CURRENT PROSPECTS AND CHALLENGES

Three major themes dominate recent concerns about the regulation of banking and financial institutions. The first is anti-inflation and macroeconomic policy. The second involves the potential for restructuring financial markets through cost savings, service improvements, new roles resulting from electronic funds transfer, and changing boundaries between financial institutions. The third is the rise of cryptocurrency, a digital or "virtual" currency using cryptography for security that could challenge the role of banks as financial intermediaries.

1. ECONOMIC STRAINS

Inflation used to be associated mainly with wartime disruption, scarcities, and related strains on finance. But in the late 1960s–1970s, significant peacetime inflation spread to many countries, including the United States. Inflation picked up momentum at significant annual rates of increase. Concern for inflationary distortions, lower saving and investment, reduced productivity, distributional inequities, and gradual demoralization caused most economists to urge that inflation be minimized, if at all possible. But a sustained reduction in inflation requires strong fiscal and monetary discipline for a considerable period of years. Other policies to improve saving, investment, productivity, and healthy competition would also be helpful.

In contemporary practice, cycles of inflation and deflation in the economy—both domestic and international—have been a continuing source of concern in the financial services sector. For example, the U.S. and transnational banking and financial network suffered a serious wave of losses and strains, some arising within the financial sector and some external to it. The collapse of the subprime mortgage market has continued to strain the stability of the market, despite the reforms of the Dodd-Frank Act and related reforms in other jurisdictions. This is a shared challenge for the United States, the European Union, China, India, Russia, Japan, United Kingdom, and other nations, and for tax havens scattered around the globe.

The international crisis caused by the coronavirus pandemic in the 2020s illustrates a situation in which financial services regulators must respond flexibly to a threat to economic and financial stability arising out of a health crisis, not a political one. In response to this crisis, the federal banking regulators eased various restrictions on banks to allow them some relief from the economic impact of the pandemic. In addition, in March 2020, the President signed into law the Coronavirus Aid, Relief, and Economic Security Act (CARES Act), which, among other things, created the Paycheck Protection Program (PPP), intended to facilitate lending to small businesses affected by the economic impact of the pandemic.

The recent invasion of Ukraine by Russian armed forces has had a significant impact on the stability of the financial services sector. It triggered, among other responses, the 2021 imposition of U.S. economic sanctions on the Government of Russia, its officials, and many Russian nationals. Building on this sanctions program, there has been a continuing series of executive orders and proclamations imposing additional sanctions in response to the extended invasion of Ukraine by Russia. These presidential actions were followed by a cascade of implementing regulatory measures that has continued to unfold, along with a stream of specific designations of Russian officials, affiliates, and property that have been subjected to prohibitions.

One common feature of all of these developments has been the reactive and limited or gradual nature of the responses to crisis, reflecting a fear of costly mistakes. For these reasons, the law of banking and financial institutions reflects considerable continuity, while these markets cope with new competition, technical innovation, and the financial strains resulting from uneven growth, monetary restraint, speculation, trade imbalances, and global markets.

2. ELECTRONIC FINANCE

Added complications come through cost reduction, service improvement and new competitive forces associated with electronic banking and finance.

Electronic funds transfer, securitization, mobile banking, and other innovations raise new technical issues—how should these innovative methods and processes be regulated and supervised. In the case of emerging developments, like "fintech" (the provision of banking and finance services by online, nonbanking entities, national and state regulatory systems have only recently begun to consider appropriate responses. There is a pressing need to develop consistent regulatory approaches to e-banking and to digital finance generally.

With the emergence of electronic banking and finance, traditional boundaries and roles in financial markets have eroded substantially. Understandably, when inflation rates increase, strains of disintermediation affect traditional financial institutions faced with competition from electronic provision of services.

3. CRYPTOCURRENCIES AND THE THREAT OF A NEW DISINTERMEDIATION

Since 2009, banking and finance has been confronted with a new electronic phenomenon—privately generated "virtual currency," not connected to the currency role of governments. As it has developed, cryptocurrency has raised a threat of new kind of disintermediation in which money and credit is sourced *outside* the banking and finance system supervised by central banks.

Bitcoin, perhaps the best-known cryptocurrency enterprise, started in 2009 based on a computer science research paper by the pseudonymous

"Satoshi Nakamoto," an individual or group of individuals that developed complex algorithms the solution of which earns players digital tokens called Bitcoins. As early users entered the network, they became a part of a decentralized infrastructure that hosts Bitcoin's open-source program. Computers joining the network immediately began capturing virtual coins. The network's protocol was designed to release a new block of Bitcoins every 10 minutes until all 21 million were released, with the blocks getting smaller as time went on. (While the network is programmed to release 21 million coins eventually, as of year-end 2013, slightly more than half of the anticipated maximum number of bitcoins was already out in the world. However, since the system is designed to release Bitcoins at a progressively slower rate, the complete mining of all bitcoins could take more than 100 years.)

If a user takes more than ten minutes to determine the correct code, the Bitcoin program adapts to make the puzzle easier. If the user solves the problems in less than ten minutes, the code becomes harder. Within this peer-to-peer network, earned Bitcoins can be passed among players and other participants digitally by computer or phone. Apparently from the very beginning, this decentralized network used Bitcoins as a form of currency in exchange for real-world goods and services from willing providers. A participant with the necessary free, open-source software could send or receive Bitcoins from other participants, all of whom remain anonymous, while the Bitcoin itself acts as a digital marker recording the series of trades.

Until the latter half of 2013, most Bitcoin origination was done on the individual computers of digital-money enthusiasts. However, as the value of a single Bitcoin skyrocketed, the competition for new coins quickly turned into "mining" as an industrial enterprise. Efficiencies were achieved through the use of "miners," specialists that vied to solve algorithms at competitive rates to generate large quantities of Bitcoins.

Cryptocurrency trading is tracked and recorded through the use of an independent digital register known as blockchain. A cryptocurrency is difficult to counterfeit because of this security feature. A defining feature of a cryptocurrency, and arguably its most endearing allure, is its organic nature; it is not issued by any central authority, rendering it theoretically immune to government interference or manipulation.

The disadvantage of this independence, of course, is that there is little that the regulatory system can do to avoid or correct a collapse or other significant dysfunction in cryptocurrency markets. Bitcoin itself has lately suffered significant deterioration of value, and other forms of cryptocurrency are vying to replace it as the preferred medium. If cryptocurrency continues to erode reliance on the banking system as the basic form of financial intermediation, its unregulated status could become a serious concern in economic policy.

But what would be an appropriate legal response, as a technical matter? How to characterize, as a legal matter, what is involved in cryptocurrency origination and trading remains a critical issue. For example, if a cryptocurrency really *is* a "virtual currency," then fiscal supervision by the Federal Reserve and other central banks might be the most appropriate approach to regulating this activity.

However, if cryptocurrency is in any significant sense "currency," then treatment under the U.S. securities regulation framework is categorically ruled out, since "currency" is excluded from the statutory definition of "security" for those purposes. In contrast, as currency—at least if involved in a contract for future delivery—cryptocurrency would be a "commodity" subject to supervision by the Commodity Futures Trading Commission (CFTC). On the other hand, if we consider the term "currency"—undefined in the federal securities and commodities laws—as referring only to conventional, government-sponsored currency, then we may need to consider whether the financial obligation represented by a Bitcoin and similar arrangements may actually be a form of "note." As a "note," a Bitcoin would be a "security" for certain purposes under the securities laws.

Furthermore, as cryptocurrency continues to gain acceptance by vendors as a form of payment, we must deal with the possibility that it should be subject to transactional rules of article 3 of the Uniform Commercial Code (UCC), and possibly other selected provisions of the Code. In this regard, in 2022 the Uniform Law Commission approved a package of amendments to the UCC to address matters relating to emerging technologies. Much of the package addresses matters relating to digital assets referred to as "controllable electronic records" and payment obligations that are "tethered" to them. These are addressed generally in a new Article 12 of the UCC and in new provisions in Article 9 addressing security interests in these assets, as well as conforming amendments to other UCC articles.

CHAPTER II

MONEY AND BANKING

A. MONEY, CENTRAL BANKING, AND THE FEDERAL RESERVE SYSTEM

Under the U.S. Constitution, Congress has the power to establish the currency, to regulate money and foreign exchange, to borrow funds, to collect taxes and regulate commerce, and to carry on expenditure programs within the broad authority of the federal government. Each year Congress appropriates spending authority to federal agencies and carefully defines the tax laws. But the President and the executive branch of government strongly influence these policies through detailed recommendations and the exercise of delegated authority to administer programs and regulations. The Office of Management and Budget (formerly the Budget Bureau) is the principal executive oversight agency for spending; the Treasury Department collects the revenues and manages debt financing. The OMB Director and Treasury Secretary are normally among the President's top economic policy makers, along with the Council of Economic Advisors.

Within this framework, however, considerable latitude has been granted to the Board of Governors of the Federal Reserve System (the Fed) and its Federal Open Market Committee (FOMC). Although extensive federal and state legislation regulates chartering, growth, and supervision of banks and other financial institutions, the Fed has great influence over bank reserves, monetary expansion, and interest rates.

Yet it would be inapt to say, as some suggest, that the Fed simply *controls* the money supply, as easily as one might turn a faucet of water. Actually, the supply and demand for money, bank deposits, and liquidity is more complicated, subtle, and partly the result of self-operating, market forces (both national and international). Government budgets, deficits, and public sector borrowing also have important effects on money markets and interest rates, especially when large deficits and borrowing requirements are involved. Nonetheless, the Fed has become increasingly significant as an independent force in shaping monetary policy, especially in recent years.

This dual structure of (i) centralized finance for government, with a strong Treasury Department (or Ministry of Finance) and an executive economic staff, and (ii) a more decentralized financial services industry for the rest of the economy, coordinated and disciplined by a quasi-independent "Central Bank" is typical of most modern countries. Even in smaller countries, this dual structure is the normal pattern, supported by relatively simple, informal bureaucracies. In the United States, however, with a larger, more complex economy than most and a complicated regulatory history, the network of agencies has become bigger and more complicated.[1]

---

[1] Under U.S. federal regulation, the Office of the Comptroller of the Currency (OCC) within the Treasury, the Federal Deposit Insurance Corporation (FDIC), the Federal

Coordination of their policies is not always easy, especially when national economic crises, *e.g.*, wars, depressions, inflationary momentum or stagflation, place awkward strains on accumulated compromises.

Remember that the United States evolved rapidly over more than 230 years from a small country of 3 million to a large industrial society of 332 million. Its institutional development of money, finance, and banking institutions is the accumulated legacy of that lively history. Bear in mind that national economic crises have tended to provoke emergency actions from government finance or supervisory regulation. These interventions are a counterweight to the natural momentum of government finance and decentralized banking. In U.S. financial history, serious economic strains have typically brought, sooner or later, significant adjustments, usually led by executive leadership, Treasury action or Fed policy. As a practical matter, this means that the structure of U.S. banking and bank regulation exhibits an odd "layering" of successive legislative or regulatory responses to successive crises that often persist long after a crisis has subsided.[2]

Reserve Board, and the Consumer Financial Protection Bureau (CFPB) within the Fed are the key bank regulatory institutions.

[2] The classic example of this historical phenomenon is the OCC, created as just one ad hoc response to the critical need to finance the Civil War (*i.e.*, by requiring the purchase of bonds as a condition for obtaining a national bank charter). Yet 160 years later, the OCC is the federal regulator of the largest, most internationally active U.S. commercial banks, and has nothing to do with "Currency," despite the title of the office.

1. FINANCIAL BEGINNINGS AND THE BANKS OF THE UNITED STATES

The British colonies in North America suffered a shortage of specie. Tools and capital goods imported from the mother country absorbed a heavy deficit in payments from the colonies with substantial net credits from English merchants and bankers. And while the balance of payments with the West Indies was favorable, leading to a steady inflow of Spanish dollars, the better coins were sent back to England. This left a scarce supply of specie in the colonies, featuring a considerable residue of worn and clipped dollars. For this reason, the colonists constantly sought additional forms of money to serve their needs. Leading commodities in each section were employed early as a medium of exchange, including furs, corn, livestock, tobacco, rice, and even Indian wampum (seashells). These were supplemented later by merchant bank notes and periodic note issues from colonial legislatures. When such paper was used with reasonable restraint, and not as a substitute for taxes to pay current expenses, results were satisfactory. But with excessive circulation, serious depreciation naturally followed. British policy, meanwhile, tried to restrict and inhibit colonial paper, fearing losses to their merchant creditors, and wanting to bring specie home to the mother country. This conflict left an important impression in colonial minds at Independence and a sympathy for paper money circulation.

The Continental Congress issued $242 million in paper money to finance the Revolutionary War, which depreciated rapidly during the conflict. The states separately issued another $209 million of paper, which depreciated at varying rates. Meanwhile, $8 million in foreign specie (mostly French funds) were borrowed, much of which remained abroad to cover drafts on supplies. Of this borrowing, Congress used merely $254,000 as the initial capitalization for the Bank of North America in Philadelphia (1781), along with $85,000 subscribed privately. This was the first corporate bank in the United States, and its note issue was kept responsibly limited and redeemable in specie. (It became a Pennsylvania chartered bank in 1787, and was bypassed consciously by Hamilton in 1791.) These emergency arrangements could not suffice for long.

When the American Republic won military and political independence in the early 1780s, its finances were a shambles. Congress tried to stabilize the currency by exchanging most of the depreciated "older" notes for "new" ones, but a sizeable discount below specie remained. The "national" debt was largely in arrears, tax receipts were negligible, and public land sales were the largest source of revenue. Clearly, for the nation to survive, money and finance had to be organized more soundly. This was the task achieved under Alexander Hamilton's leadership as first Secretary of the Treasury.

The Treasury Department was created in 1789, internal taxes were levied, the budget soon balanced, and the whole national debt (including state war loans) was funded in 1790 with long-term bonds (mostly at 6 percent). Regular borrowing authority remained, though, to supplement revenues, if necessary. In 1791 the first Bank of the United States was established, with $10 million capital (one-fifth from the federal government), and a substantially larger note issue potential. In 1792 the U.S. Mint was established on a bi-metallic basis (gold and silver), coining gold eagles ($10) at 247.5 grains, and silver dollars at 371.25 grains. In addition, the states chartered more banks to expand bank money even further. Bank notes issued by these state banks and the Bank of the United States soon became the larger part of the money supply, supplementing U.S. and foreign coins in circulation. On the whole, these measures were successful, and the credit of the new republic was established in the world market.

While opposition from state bank and agrarian interests prevented charter renewal for the first Bank of the United States in 1811, the War of 1812 promptly proved the need for a more reliable note issue and a strong method of federal government borrowing. Many state banks had become increasingly lax, and it was widely felt that specie redeemability should be enforced more systematically for bank notes. Accordingly, Congress created the second Bank of the United States in 1816. The new "national" bank was larger, with $35 million share capital (one-fifth from the federal government) and stronger powers. Congress also required all payments to the government to be made in specie, Treasury notes, or notes of the Bank of the United States. At first, Bank leadership was lenient, allowed extensive loans, and accepted too many state bank notes for deposit without proper specie redemption, which encouraged a land speculation boom and a subsequent recession in 1819. Meanwhile, the Supreme Court sustained the constitutionality of the Bank in *McCulloch v. Maryland*, 17 U.S. 316 (1819), and held that its banknotes were immune from state taxation. Then a new Bank president, Langdon Cheves (1819–1823), tightened up on lending practices, curtailed the note issue, collected state banknotes promptly, and floated a $2 million specie loan in Europe. These measures were not popular in agrarian states, but achieved the basic goals intended. Banknote issue for the country was tightened up, and made much more reliable.

The next Bank president, Nicholas Biddle (1823–1836), had more ambitious objectives. Under his leadership the Bank of the United States expanded its branch network aggressively, and allowed the branches to issue their own notes in the form of "branch drafts," even though Congress refused to grant branch note issue authority. In this way, Biddle's Bank offered strong competition to state banks. Meanwhile, the Bank systematically presented state banknotes promptly for specie redemption, thus preventing looseness or "over expansion" from his state bank rivals. Biddle became rather arrogant and boastful, unfortunately, and was labeled, not surprisingly, as Tsar Nicholas by his enemies. But the country enjoyed increasing prosperity in this period, with reasonably sound money, growing revenues from tariffs and public land sales, rapid immigration, and the spread of new settlements and population. While it would be wrong to say the Bank had evolved a modern Central Bank role as a money market regulator, the potential for such activity was established. If the second Bank of the United States had become a permanent institution, the economic history of the country might have been quite different, with a much earlier, stronger centralized influence on economic policy.

But Andrew Jackson's administration (1829–1837) destroyed the Bank of the United States, leaving decentralized, local banks as the dominant tradition in American banking history. (It took another full century before Franklin Roosevelt's New Deal (1933–1935) achieved a comparable strengthening of "central bank" influence for the Federal Reserve System.) Jacksonians distrusted Eastern bankers, feared centralized authority, and wanted more latitude for state banks and local business interests. Perhaps if Biddle had resigned and allowed Jackson to appoint another President of the Bank, its survival might have been managed, because the majority of Jackson's cabinet favored the Bank. But Biddle not only stayed on; he collaborated with Jackson's political opposition and his chief rival, Henry Clay. Upon Clay's nomination by the Whigs in December 1831, they planned to drive Jackson from the White House over the bank issue, and they applied early (four years ahead of schedule) for charter renewal for the Bank of the United States. Congress enacted the measure on July 3, 1832, but Jackson vetoed it.

The controversy became a key issue in the 1832 campaign, but to the surprise and distress of the pro-Bank forces, Clay was badly defeated. Relations between the Bank and Jackson were further embittered. Meanwhile, state banks were growing more rapidly, which encouraged land speculation, and Biddle attempted deflationary measures, still hoping to influence charter renewal. Jackson recommended an investigation of the Bank's solvency (actually in strong condition), which Congress refused. Then Jackson stopped further U.S. deposits in the Bank, and switched them into some 29 state "pet" banks. When the Whigs failed to elect enough members of Congress in 1834 to override Jackson's veto, Biddle accepted his fate, paid off the federal government's stock for $7.9 million, and reorganized the Bank as a Pennsylvania state-chartered bank. Thus ended the first era of "central bank" development in the United States.

What could have become a strong institution, like the Bank of England, died in its youth. True central banking in the United States came much later. The Federal Reserve System, created in 1913, only gradually assumed greater powers with New Deal reforms (1933–1935), and did not assume much independence until the Accord with Treasury in 1951. An important political lesson is illustrated, too. Central bank leaders and the Federal Reserve System must coordinate their activities, within reason, to the political realities and moods of their time. If conflict with powerful political leaders is pressed too far, a central bank's institutional independence and strength may be undermined. And yet, the disciplinary role of healthy central bank traditions, in enforcing sounder money, reducing inflationary pressure, and preventing loose practices, can be very helpful, if wisely sustained with realism and political prudence.

The Panic of 1837, and subsequent depression until 1842, illustrate the weakness of financial institutions without disciplines to enforce sound banking, and without a lender of last resort to limit a chain reaction of bank failures. Looser banking, excessive loans and state banknote issue had helped to sustain a speculative land boom in the 1830s. Liberal loans and investments from Europe added momentum. When Jackson's administration, alarmed at speculation and worried about government deposits in selected state banks, cracked down and enforced specie payments for public lands (instead of state banknotes), the bubble burst. A panic followed, with a rapidly spreading financial crisis. By May 1837, most of the country's banks (now entirely state-chartered) had suspended specie payments, and many failed. Foreign capital stopped flowing, many states defaulted on their debts for a while, and a few actually repudiated their obligations. Foreigners were distressed when the federal government offered no support to the states. But federal powers and responsibilities were felt to be limited in this period and it took years for the natural productivity of the country to rebuild prosperity.

2. DECENTRALIZED BANKING, 1837–1913

For the next generation (1837–1862) state-chartered banks were the sole form of banking activity in the United States of America. The nation muddled through the years before the Civil War with states' rights pre-eminent. During most of this period, the federal government used an Independent Treasury system to collect, store and disburse specie for federal finance. Banking was left entirely to the states, with increasingly liberal chartering policies (the free-banking era) in most areas. This "system" had serious weaknesses. Specie circulation tended to be constricted. State banknote issue was unreliable (except in those states which enforced tougher reserve requirements, specie redemption, and regular examination). But the country enjoyed reasonably good fortune. New lands were rapidly opening up, production was expanding, immigrants and foreign capital kept flowing, railroads proliferated, and the California gold boom added specie resources. Federal funding requirements were generally modest, and the Mexican War (1847–1848) was successfully brief, so that it could be conveniently financed—only $65 million—with short-term federal notes (later refinanced into long-term federal bonds). When the long boom ebbed, the vulnerability of banking facilities helped to exaggerate somewhat the Panic of 1857. But in this Panic the banks were left to fend for themselves, and after a period of widespread suspension in specie payments on bank notes, things slowly improved.

3. CIVIL WAR AND THE DUAL CHARTERING SYSTEM

The Civil War emergency greatly multiplied the financial needs of government. Federal expenditures grew from $67 million in 1861 to $1,297 million in

1865. The Union war effort was financed mainly with government borrowing and paper currency (Treasury notes or "greenbacks"), although tax revenues increased from $40 million in 1861 to $300 million in 1865. (Confederate finance was even more heavily dependent on paper currency, repudiated by the Union at the end of the war.) This vast expansion of the money supply (including roughly $400 million of federal greenbacks) produced a substantial inflation, though less than might have been expected. A large industrial expansion and surge of output was called forth by the war effort, especially in the Union states. (The federal debt mushroomed from only $65 million in 1860 to $2.8 billion at its peak in 1865, and was still $1.8 billion in 1898 before the Spanish American War. But the interest burden required to service the debt declined from one third of federal spending in 1869 to less than one tenth of the federal budget in 1898; this reflected expanded national income, along with reduced interest rates, as the debt was refinanced into longer-term obligations.)

The next major financial development was enactment of the banking legislation in March 1863. With 11 agrarian states out of the Congress, it was possible to take a substantial step toward federal coordination and strengthening of the banking system. Under this legislation banks were "encouraged" to recharter themselves as national banks, with the Comptroller of the Currency as the new agency for screening and supervision. Modest capitalization requirements were involved, although somewhat stronger reserves against deposits were mandated: (i) 25 percent for "reserve city" banks; (ii)

15 percent for "country" banks. However, reserve banks outside New York City could keep half their reserves in interest-bearing accounts in N.Y.C. banks; meanwhile, country banks could keep three-fifths of their reserves in interest bearing accounts in any reserve bank. Initially a small tax (½ percent annually) was placed on average banknote circulation for all banks. But when relatively few state banks converted to national bank charters, this annual tax was raised to 10 percent in 1866 for state banknotes. This onerous, prejudicial tax virtually ended state banknote circulation; it also forced the majority of state banks to switch into federal charters and become national banks. [The Supreme Court held this tax constitutional in *Veazie Bank v. Fenno*, 75 U.S. 533 (1869).] This "national banking" reform did not really create a "central bank." But it did strengthen banking reserves, facilitate assistance from larger city banks, and encourage a stronger banking center for the nation in New York City.

But gradually the tendencies toward decentralized, state charter banking resumed their influence. As shown in Chapter I, state banks grew in number from 475 in 1878, to 8,696 in 1900 and 17,440 in 1929. Meanwhile, national banks increased their numbers more slowly, from 2,056 in 1878, to 3,731 in 1900 and 7,530 in 1929. The share of deposits in state banks grew from 7 percent in 1868 to 18 percent in 1878, 43 percent in 1900, and reached 56 percent in 1929. Key factors were rapid development of checking accounts as a substitute for banknotes, which allowed state banks to compete effectively, together with more relaxed, liberal reserve requirements and easier chartering and entry for state banks. Eventually, national bank charter and reserve requirements were liberalized, too, so that national banks could compete more equally, and their numbers expanded very substantially. A final factor was the prohibition on branching for national banks in the National Bank Act of 1864 (NBA). Branching for national banks was only partly liberalized, right before the Great Depression, in the McFadden Act of 1927, which allowed branching for national banks to the same extent, in each state, as state banks. (Branching had begun, mainly in the 1920s, in some states; the states divided into three roughly equal camps—unit banking or no branches at all, limited branching [usually county-wide only], and statewide branching.) This restriction against branching had greatly encouraged new bank formation in cities and towns with growing population and increased prosperity. Thus, laws regulating market structure and allowing easy entry strongly sustained the decentralized banking tradition of the United States from the Civil War through the Great Depression, and even into the post-World War II prosperity. National banks represented only a limited incursion of federal chartering into an industry that had become greatly decentralized, with liberal state standards setting the dominant style for the industry until the New Deal reforms of 1933–1935.

Unfortunately, this decentralized banking system was vulnerable to financial panics. Three major panics and depressions occurred between 1865–1913. Each featured over-expanded credit, thin reserves, and vulnerability to a chain reaction of liquidation and bank failures. The Panic of 1873 and subsequent depression resulted from excessive credits after a long boom, weak bank reserves, collapse of many banks (including Jay Cooke's in N.Y.), and government help that was too small and late. Controversy about "excessive" greenbacks left outstanding from the Civil War crippled government policy, and it took years for renewed agricultural exports and revived industry to restore prosperity. A smaller panic and recession occurred in 1883–1884, but this decade was largely prosperous.

The next setback came in the early 1890s, as the terms of trade shifted against the United States, and a substantial gold outflow weakened confidence. Then the Panic of 1893 erupted, with insufficient bank reserves, substantial contraction of liquidity, and a serious recession. Many blamed renewed silver coinage after the Sherman Silver Purchase Act of 1890. But silver's impact on the money supply was modest, and over-expansion of bank-money and fragility of the banking system were the important problems. Although this depression affected the industrial economy, and caused populist pressure for easier money and "free silver" coinage, fear of strikes, radicalism and "unsound" money proved stronger in the 1896 election. By 1897 the economy revived, and another decade of renewed prosperity ensued, strengthened by expanded industry and new gold production.

The last setback was the Panic of 1907. It involved another excessive accumulation of bank credit, insufficient reserves, and a run on the banks. The Treasury provided somewhat more aid to the banks this time, and this financial crisis was not so serious or lasting. A healthier balance of payments facilitated recovery, and prosperity soon resumed. But the limitations on bank reserves and potential fragility had finally become evident to conservative and sound money interests, and the appeal of silver and populist inflationism had abated.

4. FEDERAL RESERVE SYSTEM, 1913–1932

a. Establishment of the Federal Reserve

The problem facing the National Monetary Commission of 1908–1912 (and drafters of the Federal Reserve Act) was how to create stronger, centralized national reserves and discipline in a tradition of decentralized, easy entry banking institutions. Such a compromise was not easy, nor in retrospect, should we be surprised that achievements proved to be limited. A crucial conflict emerged between (i) banker views, favoring a National Reserve Association of Banks (voluntary membership) under control of bankers, with broad note issue authority, lending and discount authority, and reserve regulation, and (ii) the populist wing of the Democratic party, which wanted limited banker influence, government (greenback) currency issue, and strong government supervision. Due to the Pujo Committee investigations of the "money trust" and malpractices leading to the Panic of 1907, and Democratic control of the Congress, the Monetary Commission's bill (favoring the banker view) could not be enacted. But President Wilson supported compromise legislation which led to the Federal Reserve Act of 1913. Although some bankers complained of "socialistic" potential for government control, and some agrarians wanted more credit and increased currency along with less influence from bankers, the compromise was enacted by large majorities in both Senate and House.

The result was as far as the United States could go toward central bank regulation at that stage in its history. The new Federal Reserve Board comprised seven members, including the Secretary of Treasury, Comptroller of the Currency, and five other presidential appointees serving 10 year terms (with at least two required to have banking or financial experience).[3] Federal Reserve District Banks would be established in every region with nine member boards, including three banker representatives; three representing business, commerce or agriculture; and three public representatives. Member banks would elect the first six directors and the Board would appoint the last three directors. All national banks became members, and state banks could become members. Member banks had to purchase District Bank stock equal to six percent of

[3] Many Fed chairs (originally, *ex officio* the Secretary of the Treasury, then an appointed "Governor," and since 1936 an appointed Chair) became important and long-serving leaders of economic and financial policy. For example, Marriner S. Eccles (1934–1948), William McChesney Martin Jr. (1951–1970), and Paul A. Volcker (1979–1987). For historical and biographical information about all Governors and Chairs of the Federal Reserve Board, 1913–present, see https://www.federalreserve.gov/aboutthefed/bios/board/boardmembership.htm.

their own capital and surplus accounts. This would capitalize the Reserve Banks. The Reserve Banks could issue "Federal reserve" notes secured 100 percent by commercial paper, and by 40 percent reserves in gold or gold certificates. Additional notes might be issued, but subject to a graduated tax that tended to limit such circulation. These federal reserve notes would be legal tender and serve as currency. This arrangement provided substantial gold backing for an enlarged currency issue, with some flexibility allowed the Reserve Banks to "meet the needs of trade." In addition, presumably, the Treasury could issue more of its own Treasury notes (or greenbacks) in emergency situations, or alter the gold backing percentage with Congressional approval.

The Federal Reserve Banks would carry on lending operations to member banks, rediscounting 90-day commercial paper or six-month agricultural obligations. The discount rates for such lending would be a discipline on member banks. In addition, reserve requirements were specified for demand deposits in all the member banks: 18 percent for reserve city banks, 15 percent for city banks, and 12 percent for country banks. On time deposits all banks had to maintain 5 percent reserves. Along with this statutory power, the Federal Reserve Board received financial supervision authority, and the right to enforce special reports from all member and reserve banks, to suspend and remove officers, and to suspend District banks. The Board could also allow District banks to make loans to each other. Thus, financial integrity and emergency lending support would be assured to all member banks, in all Districts of the country.

To help the Treasury in government debt financing, each District bank was permitted to buy and sell government obligations under rules and regulations of the Federal Reserve Board. This provided a sound basis for emergency borrowing by the federal government through the banking system. This authority enabled also what later came to be known as "open market operations," designed to influence the size of bank reserves and money market conditions. Sales of government securities can absorb bank reserves and "tighten" credit markets, while purchases of government securities may increase bank reserves and "ease" credit and money market conditions. Open market operations work more delicately and sensitively to affect bank reserves on a daily basis, provided that a large volume of government debt is outstanding and extensively traded. (In later years open market operations would become the most frequently employed instrument of monetary control.)

b. World War I and the Twenties

Federal Reserve operations before World War I were limited. Reserve requirements had been higher, on the average, for national banks than under the new Federal Reserve Act. Thus, "free" reserves were created at the outset for member banks. Because District banks did little lending to member banks, in these circumstances their discount rates had little impact. The principal result, in fact, of the new legislation was to encourage more agricultural lending, and to allow easier credit for industrial activity in the World War I boom. Britain, France, and other allies required greatly increased raw materials and munitions imports for their war efforts. Gold exports to America increased rapidly during the war, and the United States quickly became a substantial net creditor nation. This further expanded the gold base for bank reserves in the Federal Reserve System, and sustained easy credit conditions.

When the United States entered the war in April 1917, it faced major mobilization requirements. Taxes were increased substantially, but government borrowing at relatively low interest rates was the major source of war-time finance. Altogether $21.5 billion of new long-term bonds was issued, along with another $3.8 billion in short-term debt. (Federal debt in 1914 was merely $2.9 billion.) The money supply and credit expanded rapidly. Some rationing was used for scarce materials, but consumer prices went up about 60 percent between 1914–1919. Treasury policies on war finance and borrowing left little scope for Federal Reserve action, especially since substantial excess bank reserves and rapidly expanding gold imports enabled monetary ease and ample credit.

Post-war conditions allowed somewhat more active Federal Reserve policy, and the discount rate was raised sharply in 1920, reaching a peak of 7 per cent in June 1920. But demobilization and conversion from war industry had already caused a significant recession. This particular tight money policy aggravated the recession, and has been widely criticized by economists. But soon Federal Reserve policy eased, with lower discount rates, along with modest open market operations through purchases of government securities to increase bank reserves. In April 1923, under Governor Strong's leadership at the New York Reserve Bank, an Open Market Investment Committee was set up to coordinate open market operations. (This was the forerunner of the present FOMC.) Throughout most of the 1920s money market conditions remained relatively easy. This is especially important in light of the increasing stock market speculation of the later 1920s. While some economists warned of speculative excess, the government and Federal Reserve authorities could not agree on strong measures. Modest increases in the discount rate, and "moral suasion" to discourage speculation were the main responses.

Meanwhile, easy entry into banking, low capitalization requirements, and sagging farm prices allowed a considerable number of bank failures, mostly among small rural banks. Some 5,700 banks "failed" between 1921–1929, and the aggregate number of banks declined from 30,500 to 25,300 in this period. Federal Reserve Act reforms, in other words, had not entirely eliminated the problem of banking "fragility" in the country.

c. The Great Depression

The stock market crash of October 1929 and the Great Depression of the 1930s was a severe economic tragedy. It brought increased regulation of banking, financial institutions, and securities markets. Controversy followed over the causes of this derangement, which still divides conservative, moderate and Keynesian economists. But consensus exists on many aspects of the Depression. Most importantly, excess speculation, featuring over-valued stocks and highly leveraged margin accounts, was a prime difficulty. Once a rapid collapse in stock values occurred, it forced extensive losses upon many well-to-do and ordinary families, led to a spreading slump in sales, rapidly increasing unemployment, and eventually, a severe crisis of defaulting loans to banks and savings institutions. Unfortunately, neither the Federal Reserve, Congress, nor the President acted with sufficient aid or boldness to halt this slump quickly.

The Hoover administration urged that "public confidence" had to be restored, but not enough was done to limit the growing depression. Soon it became world-wide in scope, with aggravated difficulties brought on by European currency devaluations, and a substantial gold outflow. Relief efforts were controversial, and inhibited by budget deficits. Easier monetary policy from the Federal Reserve, including open market purchases of government securities (to increase bank reserves) and reduced discount rates had little impact. Alarmed at the gold drain and its threat to sufficient backing for the currency (federal reserve notes), emergency authority was enacted in February 1932 to use government obligations as currency backing. Finally, stronger open market operations were conducted in the Spring and Summer 1932 to increase credit, but by this time the economy, employment, and the use of credit by business had sagged drastically. A more constructive step, the establishment of the Reconstruction Finance Corporation (RFC), came late in January 1932, but it had only loaned $2.2 billion by March 1933.

The Great Depression was the country's worst financial panic, with most tragic consequences. Gross national product dropped from $103.4 to $55.8 billion between 1929–1933. The index of industrial production declined from 100 to 63. The money supply (currency and demand deposits) fell from $26.6 to $19.9 billion. Half the banks in the nation (mostly smaller banks) closed by the Summer 1933. Unemployment increased from 3.2 to 24.9 percent of the civilian labor force, and reached a total of 15 million workers. And prices declined substantially, especially for agricultural commodities (which hurt farmers badly, although some people still employed without loss in income may have benefitted).

5. NEW DEAL REFORMS AND THE FEDERAL RESERVE, 1933–1941

The "New Deal" policies initiated by the incoming administration of Franklin D. Roosevelt included banking, financial, and securities legislation intended to reform the U.S. financial system, and much of that legislation survives today. On the whole, it strengthened the financial system. But it should be understood as a series of emergency and other corrective measures designed to be helpful, rather than as a single master plan or ideological program. The dominant theme was pragmatism, and a feeling that government should act forcefully to restore prosperity, if possible, and to prevent another depression. (These "reforms" are summarized in Chapter I, and set forth in more detail with respect to money and banking in Chapters II and III, savings institutions in Chapter IV, and securities markets in Chapter V.)

When Roosevelt took office in March 1933, the most immediate problem was a nationwide banking crisis, *i.e.*, a massive run on the banks. Rapid gold withdrawals and outflows to other countries were undermining the gold base for the currency. Almost all the commercial banks had closed, expecting some form of relief by the new administration. The new Treasury Secretary, William Woodin, helped orchestrate the following emergency action: (i) temporary closure of all banks; (ii) financial aid on a much larger scale to the weaker banks through "soft" RFC loans and Federal Reserve advances; (iii) authorizing banks to issue 6 percent preferred stock in return for RFC capital loans; (iv) authorizing the Comptroller of the Currency to appoint conservators for closed banks with powers to reopen or liquidate them; and (v) strict prohibitions on any export of gold except under license by the Treasury Secretary. Emergency legislation gave the President broad powers to regulate transactions in specie, and by Executive Order the United States left the gold standard, meaning that reserve notes were no longer convertible to gold. The Federal Reserve issued $200 million in emergency reserve notes, substantial new loans were made to banks and the RFC purchased $1.3 billion in banks' stock to strengthen their capital structures. This latter injection of capital approached nearly half the equity or capital accounts in the banks surviving the depression. Thus, when large scale aid at last came to the banking system, it was sufficient to restore depleted bank capital and viability.

But more action quickly followed to ensure public confidence in money and banking. Most significant, for the long term, was the Banking Act of June 16, 1933. This law established the Federal Deposit Insurance Corporation. The FDIC expanded the old New York safety fund concept (1829–1837) and created a federal insurance guarantee system for bank deposits up to $2,500 (now a "standard maximum deposit insurance amount" of $250,000, periodically adjusted for inflation) on each account. Its initial capital was provided by the Treasury and the surplus in Federal Reserve District Banks, and was replenished by modest insurance premiums on the insured banks. Virtually all banks joined the new system (whether national or state-chartered), because most depositors wanted this protection for their bank deposits. Every normal commercial bank now maintains this insurance to stay in business. This provided much greater supervisory leverage for bank examination purposes. The FDIC staff, along with the Comptroller's staff for national banks, the Federal Reserve staff for state-chartered member banks, and the various state banking commissioners have subsequently developed a much better, comprehensive surveillance system for commercial banks than existed before the Depression. For over 70 years since the FDIC system was established, bank runs have been largely eliminated. Only a few hundred American banks had failed between 1940 and 1980, and the majority of these were salvaged in forced merger transactions in which all depositors were fully protected (even those not insured). Unfortunately, bank and thrift institution failures became more common in the 1980s and early 1990s; about 1,500 banks and 1,000 thrifts became insolvent in this period. Much greater FDIC (and Federal Savings and Loan Insurance Corporation) expenses were incurred as a result. In response, improved supervision, tougher capital requirements and risk-oriented deposit insurance premiums have been implemented to overhaul the deposit insurance system between 1989 and 1992.

Other provisions of the Banking Act of 1933 became more controversial: (i) Interest payments on demand deposits were outlawed to prevent "excessive" and cut-throat competition among banks that might weaken their financial strength. In the Depository Institutions Deregulation and Monetary Control Act (DIDMCA) of 1980, this provision was finally rescinded for NOW accounts with any financial institution. (ii) Investment banking was separated from commercial banking, and some of the biggest commercial banks in New York divested their investment banking operations, which were spun off into separate companies. This provision, often referred to as the "Glass-Steagall Wall," operated into the 1980s, but was gradually relaxed, and largely eliminated in 1999. Some doubted the need for it today, especially since major brokerage and investment banking houses (like Merrill-Lynch) developed money market accounts and CMAs rather like checking accounts, and compete more directly with banks. But this provision did help to maintain more detachment in commercial bank lending and trust account management, with little cost to anyone in society. (iii) Another provision, credit control authority, was designed to prevent speculative excesses. It has been used occasionally to limit credit and restrict inflation in emergencies, and most recently, in the Spring 1980. (iv) Another aspect of qualitative credit control was the power for the Federal Reserve Board to suspend a member bank if it made undue use of credit for speculative purposes. The broad purpose of these provisions in the Glass-Steagall compromise (the Banking Act of 1933) was to reduce risk for commercial banks, and allow regulators more power to prevent another depression. But these "risk-limiting" measures could be misused, especially if employed to limit healthy and desirable competition among financial institutions.

Other steps completed the abandonment of the gold standard. Congress declared "gold clauses" void in government and private obligations in June 1933. In mid-summer, the International Monetary Conference in London broke up with a failure to agree on measures to restore the gold standard. Although U.S. devaluation brought some immediate "stimulus" to the economy (and slightly increased commodity prices, greatly desired by farmers), this "gain" was reversed by the late summer, as it gradually became apparent that floating exchange rates were stabilizing. By January 1934 Congress stabilized the dollar's value in terms of gold at $35 per oz., a ratio that was to last until President Nixon's devaluation of August 15, 1971. Thus, the United States created a gold-exchange standard for international dealings but used an irredeemable paper dollar for domestic trade.

In the Banking Act of 1935 Congress strengthened the powers of the Federal Reserve Board to act as a central bank. The Board received authority to regulate the discount rates of District Reserve Banks. The Board could set reserve requirements for demand deposits within a broader range, *i.e.*, 13–26 percent for reserve city banks, 10–20 percent for city banks, and 7–14 percent for country banks. (This leeway was restricted recently by the DIDMCA of 1980, which restored a more uniform reserve requirements policy, *i.e.*, 12 percent for "transaction accounts" and 3 percent for time deposits, except for emergency periods when higher reserves could be required.) The Board's influence on open market operations was strengthened by restructuring the FOMC. Formerly an adjunct of the New York Federal Reserve Bank, the FOMC became an extension of the Federal Reserve Board (with the seven Board members on the FOMC, along with five District bank representatives). The Board also received authority to regulate interest on time deposits, which led to Regulation Q limits on interest rates for savings accounts. (This limitation on interest rates served to strengthen the Fed's disciplinary authority, but became controversial in the 1970s after Regulation Q limits restricted the competitiveness of passbook savings accounts in periods of high market interest rates, and caused substantial disintermediation from savings institutions and reduced the funds available for housing finance. The DIDMCA of 1980 scheduled a phased elimination of Reg. Q limits on interest rates by 1986.)

Finally, the Federal Reserve Board itself was restructured to increase its independence. Although the Board retained seven members, the Secretary of the Treasury and Comptroller of the Currency were eliminated. All seven simply became presidential appointees, but with terms lengthened from 10 to 14 years. This led over the years to an increasing independence from political control, a result favored by most bankers, though controversial at times among political leaders.

Monetary policy during the New Deal years was designed to facilitate recovery. The system had substantial free reserves and surplus liquidity, interest rates remained low, and the discount rate was kept down too. However, after July 1936, the Federal Reserve tightened reserve requirements substantially. It feared that accumulated deficits, excess reserves, and the gradual economic recovery could launch a surge of inflation. So, reserve requirements were stepped up to the new maximum levels of 14, 20, and 26 percent by May 1937. In this way, a large part of the *excess* reserves in the banking system were absorbed. Nonetheless, interest rates remained low and money markets reflected ease throughout the 1930s.

Fiscal policy was mostly stimulative, and considerable deficits were run throughout the 1930s. But in 1936–1938, expecting a stronger, more rapid recovery, the federal government increased taxes (including new social security levies), slowed the growth in spending, and tried seriously to bring the budget into balance. But a significant recession developed in 1937–1938, after which larger scale deficits resumed in 1939–1941. Unemployment increased substantially from 6.4 to 9.8 million between 1937 and 1938, and was still 8.8 million or 17.2 percent in 1939. Unemployment declined to 14.6 percent in 1940, 4.7 percent in 1942, and reached an all-time low of 1.2 percent in 1944. Clearly, the American economy only reached "full" employment during World War II, when much larger deficits were used in the national mobilization effort. This experience with the 1937–1938 recession was significant for postwar Keynesian economics, for it led to the view that fiscal policy would be more important as stimulus for the economy than easy money market conditions. Thus, government deficits might be more important than low interest rates to achieve full employment.

6. WORLD WAR II AND POSTWAR ADJUSTMENTS, 1941–1951

World War II brought forth the largest military and industrial mobilization effort in the nation's history. Between 1941 and 1946 the war cost $330 billion in direct expenditures. Taxes increased from $6.6 to $46.5 billion between 1941 to 1945, while annual spending (civilian, military, and foreign aid) grew from $13.8 to $100.4 billion in these years. The cumulative federal deficits were $210 billion. Fortunately, these deficits and patriotic enthusiasm virtually ended unemployment, and brought many new millions of women into the work force. At the peak of mobilization in 1944–1945 the war absorbed half the national output. In World War I, by contrast, only one-fourth of the nation's production was diverted into the war. And yet, World War II was financed to a greater extent by taxes, with more extensive rationing and wage-price controls, and more comprehensive economic planning.

Economic policy was dominated by the war effort. The larger portion of military outlays was financed by government borrowing. The federal debt expanded from $49 billion in 1941 to $279 billion in 1946. This growing burden led the government to insist upon low interest rates to keep the carrying charges bearable, and to limit "excess" profits for financiers, when many families were sacrificing lives and crippling injuries. In the early part of the war, substantial slack, unemployment and excess capacity absorbed these deficits nicely. Later, the war called forth production and employment (with many more women) that went beyond previous national capacity. Inflation developed, especially in critical war materials, but controls and limited rationing kept increases in the cost of living to 25 percent between 1941 and 1945. On the whole, World War II economic policy was successful.

Banking and monetary policy during the war was tailored to the support of government borrowing.

Altogether $230 billion of new government debt was created to finance the war, nearly twice the 1941 GNP of $125 billion. Although real economic growth was substantial during the war, the total debt of $279 billion in 1946 substantially exceeded that year's GNP of $210 billion. Even with low interest rates enforced by Treasury Department policy, this debt interest burden reached 3½ percent of the GNP. Higher interest rates would have greatly increased the government's carrying charges. This debt burden explains why the Treasury wanted to impose "pegged" low rates on government borrowing upon the Federal Reserve and money markets.

Postwar financial policy brought changes. The country promptly demanded demobilization, and an end to war-time controls. A strong surge of price inflation followed, caused by the buildup of savings and purchasing power during the war. The cost of living increased 33 percent between 1945 and 1948. Many feared a major postwar depression, but the adjustment process proved relatively smooth. While the 1948–1949 recession slowed the economy, inflation was halted. Unemployment only reached 5.9 percent in 1949, and declined to 2.9 percent by 1953. Strong prosperity with fuller employment proved a great blessing to the nation.

But some disagreements arose as to the postwar level of government spending, taxes, national defense, foreign aid, inflationary pressure, and the dangers of unemployment and recession. Clearly, military forces had to be reduced greatly from their war-time peak of nine million. But tensions with the

Soviet Union and the vulnerability of Western Europe, Japan, and other parts of the world led to a stronger peacetime defense effort. The Cold War began, with defense and foreign aid accounting for 6–8 percent of GNP between 1947 and 1950, and increasing to 9–10 percent between 1951 and 1969. Veteran's benefits and interest on the national debt accounted initially for another 4–5 percent of GNP. Civilian and non-war related expenditures of the federal government were reduced, compared to the later New Deal years. Federal civilian outlays were only 2½ percent of the GNP in the Truman years. By contrast such expenditures had been 6 percent of the GNP in 1939. A large part of the difference was explained by unemployment relief programs in the mid-late 1930s, which had accounted for 3 percent of GNP in 1939. After World War II such relief expenditures were relatively modest, because the economy was stronger and unemployment was reduced.

The Korean War provoked open conflict between the Treasury and the Federal Reserve over interest rates for increased federal debt. The Korean War emergency and stronger support for European rearmament (NATO) forced increased spending. Federal outlays went from $40 billion in 1949–1950 to $60 billion in 1951. Defense expenditures grew from $13 billion in 1949 to $45–50 billion annually between 1951 and 1965 (on average). While taxes were increased promptly, and economic growth provided more revenue, the Treasury feared that substantial new debt had to be floated, and wanted low interest rates pegged (as in World War II and its immediate aftermath). But the Federal Reserve refused to go along this time. Instead, the Federal Reserve began (in September 1950) to sell short-term government obligations in open market operations at slightly higher interest rates (1.30 instead of 1.25 percent) to sop up credit. Later that fall and winter the Federal Reserve board members made it clear that they would no longer support low interest re-financing of the government's debt (then at 2½ percent for long-term obligations).

Gradually, banking and monetary policy in the post-war era settled down to a more stable, predictable pattern. Once the size of government and defense outlays had been established, with appropriate tax revenues to support them, more "normal" money market conditions could be restored. With stronger economic growth, fuller employment, and relatively low inflation, the Federal Reserve Board sought an end to "pegged" low interest rates for government debt.

This led to the famous "Accord of 1951" between the Treasury Department and the Federal Reserve Board. Public disagreement embarrassed the Administration, and congressional committees threatened to launch investigations into the subject. On March 4, 1951, the Treasury and the Board jointly announced, "full accord with respect to debt management and monetary policies—[and] to minimize monetization of the public debt." Its immediate impact was to relax support of lower interest rates by the Federal Reserve, though it did not, as some bankers preferred, bring a strong switch in policy to higher interest rates. Fortunately, tax increases reduced the scale of budget deficits, so that less pressure was placed on debt markets and interest rates. Moderate increases in interest rates followed, with Treasury accommodation to the asserted independence of monetary policy. The long run impact has been to establish more firmly a general presumption, though not an absolute rule, in favor of Federal Reserve independence in monetary policy management.

7. MONETARY AND ECONOMIC POLICY, 1951–PRESENT

During the early postwar era, America's economy enjoyed expanded growth and prosperity. Money and banking policy reflected continuity, for the most part, and made its contribution to healthy economic conditions. Fiscal policy and modest government deficits came to be relied upon as the main response to recessions, slack, and unemployment. The Federal Reserve leaned against the breeze, to some degree, tightening upon interest rates slightly in boom periods, and easing money market conditions when softness appeared in the economy. This policy worked reasonably well, so long as inflation remained low, and the overall growth trend was strongly upward in the 1950s and 1960s.

But in the late 1960s and 1970s the economy suffered greater inflation, which was soon followed by more unemployment and slack, *i.e.*, what became known as "stagflation." Macro-economic coordination became more erratic, and the role for monetary policy became controversial in these later years. Inflationary momentum and expectations built up gradually, with intermittent surges of substantial deficit spending. More strain was placed on monetary policy in these circumstances, and restraint from the Federal Reserve became much stricter in late 1979 and most of the early 1980s. In this later period the Federal Reserve was the focus of increasing argument, although inflation slowed markedly in late 1981 and 1982 with substantially enlarged slack and unemployment. But government deficits increased, too, which brought upward pressure on interest rates through large public sector borrowing. This also sustained inflationary expectations to some degree, and weakened prospects for economic recovery. Disagreements emerged among politicians and conflicting schools of economic thought about tax burdens and government spending. It took 15 years to eliminate excess deficits, *i.e.*, until the later 1990s. Better balanced budgets and sound monetary policy were needed together.

a. Truman-Eisenhower, 1951–1960

Economic and monetary policy in the Truman-Eisenhower years featured nearly balanced budgets, except in recession periods, when deficits were run to offset slack and unemployment. The Korean War and NATO defense efforts brought military spending up to 9–10 percent of GNP, but taxes (including income tax bracket creep) kept revenues pretty much in line with expenditures. Moderate deficits were allowed in recessions, i.e., 1954, 1957, and 1960. But the deficits in these peak years never exceeded 2 percent of GNP and averaged less than 1 percent overall. Inflation remained low, for the most part, except for wage-price pressures from powerful unions and in some concentrated industries, especially in 1957–1959. In this situation the strain on monetary policy was limited.

b. Kennedy-Johnson, 1961–1968

While the Kennedy Administration implemented a limited policy of wage and price guidelines, its fiscal policy remained relatively conservative, and budget deficits were slightly lower (on average) than the Eisenhower years. In fact, a moderate tax cut in 1963 roughly approximated an adjustment for accumulated bracket creep. And economic growth improved, with low inflation between 1961 and 1966. This put little strain on monetary policy, at least until the second half of 1966. In 1966 the economy was approaching full employment in most sectors, and the Vietnam War mobilization added further deficit pressure. At this stage, the Federal Reserve tightened monetary policy considerably. Growth slowed in 1967, and in 1968 the Vietnam War surtax came into effect, which balanced the federal budget.

c. Nixon-Ford, 1969–1976

The Federal Reserve tightened up more restrictively in 1969 and tried to break the inflationary spiral. A sustained boom in stock prices ended with a substantial retreat, and a moderate recession began later that year. Then in the Summer of 1970, Penn Central filed for bankruptcy, and nervousness spread in financial markets. The Fed eased fears by announcing that its discount window would open wider to accommodate squeezed borrowers. Reserve requirements were relaxed slightly, but interest rates remained reasonably firm.

Meanwhile, the balance of payments deficit had grown, and an accumulated buildup of dollar holdings abroad (as reserve currency) began to be cashed in for gold or harder currencies. In August 1971, a run on the dollar began, and a rapid decline in U.S. gold reserves ensued. On August 15, 1971, wage and price controls were imposed, and convertibility of the dollar for gold ended, forcing the dollar to float against other currencies. This eased the capital outflow problem, and currencies could, presumably, find their own values. Budget stimulus was added to the mix, and the Federal Reserve accommodated with easier monetary policy and lower interest rates. Short-term results of this new economic policy were successful, but bad harvests in Europe and Russia, the trebling of oil prices by the OPEC cartel, and scarcities in other raw materials markets caused 12 percent inflation in the United States, spreading quickly to the majority of industrial nations and many less developed countries. A major recession developed in 1974–1975, with unemployment reaching a postwar peak of 9 percent.

d. Carter, 1977–1980

After Nixon's resignation and Ford's brief interim presidency, Carter won the 1976 election with a moderate campaign, emphasizing his success as a farmer, and claiming to be a "social liberal" and a "fiscal conservative." His economic policies reflected this compromise approach, and he slowly reduced the federal deficit between 1977 and 1979. However, in 1979–1980 a second round of OPEC oil price increases added further inflationary pressure. The economy and its troubles, along with the Iranian hostage crisis that had begun in November 1979. led to a 51–44 percent sweep for Reagan in the 1980 presidential election.

e. Reagan, 1981–1988

The Reagan administration wanted to reduce the share of government spending in GNP, cut the tax load, and increase defense outlays. These policies met with mixed results, as domestic politics and world events blunted many of these efforts. Reagan's successor, the first President Bush, confronted much of the fallout from these continuing problems.

f. Bush, 1989–1992

A new economic problem was the need to recapitalize FSLIC—the FDIC counterpart for S & Ls and savings banks.[4] By Winter 1988–1989 a costly bailout of FSLIC and a massive cleanup operation was required. This led to the Financial Institutions Reform, Recovery, and Enforcement Act of 1989 (FIRREA), which absorbed the FSLIC into the FDIC. Meanwhile, the FHLBB was brought into the

---

[4] For details, see Chapter IV-D, Regulating Thrifts in Transition.

Treasury Department (like the OCC) as the Office of Thrift Supervision (OTS), and FIRREA created the Resolution Trust Corporation (RTC) as a receivership agency for failed thrifts. The FSLIC bailout was expensive, but most of the cost was handled off-budget through Treasury borrowing (at least for the first 5 years), as an unanticipated, non-recurring expense.

Attention then shifted to foreign affairs. A dramatic liberalization began in Eastern Europe and U.S.S.R. that brought down their Communist governments, with a transformation to more democratic, market-oriented regimes between 1989 and the end of 1991. Meanwhile, Iraq's invasion of Kuwait in August 1990, and the U.S.-led rescue and six-week war between January–February 1991, led to a remarkable joint effort by many nations toward collective security. In these years, the European Community also moved toward greater unification through 1992 and beyond, which helped inspire and reinforce East bloc developments. Meanwhile, the Uruguay Round of negotiations over the General Agreement on Tariffs and Trade (GATT) started at Punta del Este, Uruguay, in 1986, and made some limited progress toward freer trade. But conflicts over agricultural subsidies, liberalization of GATT treatment of financial, investment, and other services forced delays until 1993. In a parallel effort, the U.S. broadened trade talks on a regional basis and worked toward a North American Free Trade Area (NAFTA), involving the U.S., Mexico, and Canada, and a wider Enterprise for the Americas

Initiative (EAI) to bring other Western Hemisphere nations into closer economic relations.

As the economy slowed further into recession in late 1991, government revenues slowed, and federal budget deficits rose to $375 and $350 billion for 1992 and 1993, respectively. This slowdown hurt the prospects for Bush in the 1992 election. In addition, Germany and Japan had tightened their credit markets in 1991, which contributed to a global slowdown among many industrial nations, along with serious economic disruptions and reduced output in the former U.S.S.R.

g. Clinton, 1993–2000

When Clinton won the 1992 presidential election, many saw a mandate for stronger economic and trade policies. On trade policy, Clinton implemented the free trade initiatives of the Bush administration. NAFTA was signed by Clinton in 1993, with modest Side Agreements for import surges, environmental problems, and labor standards. Shortly thereafter Clinton accepted the Uruguay Round GATT 1994 Agreement (largely as negotiated by the Bush administration) with a new World Trade Organization (WTO). Multinational corporations were relieved, and more capital flowed from nations that are members of the Organisation for Economic Co-operation and Development (OECD) to emerging nation markets. However, Clinton's complex plan for broader health care coverage collapsed in the Fall 1994, and mid-term elections gave majorities to Republicans in both the Senate and the House.

Clinton was able to win reelection in the 1996 elections, but Republicans held the Congress. Thereafter, presidential scandals led to a big struggle over impeachment in 1997–1998. Clinton ultimately survived, but public attention on the economy was distracted for a while. Yet U.S. trade and current account deficits were growing again, with sizeable net deficits accumulating.

In this context, Europe's movement toward a European Monetary Union (EMU) and a single currency, the "Euro," was significant. The Euro, for a larger trading area, could challenge the dollar's place as the world's leading reserve currency. Nevertheless, a U.S. stock market boom surged into a "bubble" stage of speculative exuberance. In the 2000 presidential election, the Republicans and the George W. Bush campaign emphasized tax cuts, while the Democrats and then Vice President Gore offered somewhat larger spending. The election was close, with disputed returns in Florida and a recount controversy resolved by the U.S. Supreme Court. George W. Bush won a narrow victory in the Electoral College.

h. Bush, 2001–2008

A major stock market downslide followed the 1994–2000 boom, especially in "tech" stocks and the over-the-counter NASD Automated Quotation System (NASDAQ). At issue was how quickly the U.S. and global economy could recover more broadly. Then, on September 11, 2001, Al Qaeda terrorists high-jacked U.S. airliners for suicide bomber attacks.

The World Trade Center in New York City was destroyed by two planes, and a third crashed into the Pentagon in Washington, D.C. This disruptive event aggravated economic uncertainty, and the Federal Reserve eased credit further. Meanwhile, the Bush administration launched retaliatory strikes against Al Qaeda terrorists in Afghanistan, and gave extensive support to Northern Alliance rebels against the Taliban, which controlled the Afghan Government. Within a few months the Taliban that hosted Al Qaeda terrorists in Afghanistan was overthrown, with wide international support for U.S. efforts.

During the Fall and Winter 2002–2003 the Bush administration next decided to overthrow Saddam Hussein's regime in Iraq. Sanctions against Saddam's programs for development of prohibited weapons of mass destruction (WMD) seemed to be collapsing. With increased Iraqi oil revenues Saddam could soon get nuclear weapons, and he threatened to undermine moderate Arab regimes and get more influence over Persian Gulf oil supplies. Although most Arab Gulf states allowed U.S. forces to deploy for intervention in Iraq, European allies (except for the United Kingdom) were reluctant to join the operation. Another round of WMD inspections was suggested, but the Bush Administration felt it essential to begin military operations promptly. France and Germany strongly opposed the action, and the United States and the United Kingdom could not obtain a Security Council majority in support.

From an economic standpoint, the Iraq intervention accentuated fiscal stimulus in the United States as war outlays increased. This encouraged broader economic recovery. But increased "outsourcing" of manufacturing and service jobs to low-wage countries also reduced the employment gains from recovery. This was a structural implication of wider globalization, in which the United States had been leading the way since the late 1980s. Energy markets were stressed with Mid-East conflicts, and also by broad economic growth in China, India, other parts of Asia, Latin America, and much of Europe. The Federal Reserve began to tighten credit and interest rates increased somewhat in the Summer of 2004.

In November 2004, the United States faced another contentious presidential election. Bush managed a narrow electoral victory, but during 2005 and following the Iraq war worsened, with escalating casualties and growing public concern. In the Fall 2006 Congressional elections the political tide turned. Democrats gained in many states and carried majorities in the U.S. Senate and House of Representatives.

But then, gradually, new economic difficulties emerged in 2007–2008 from the banking sector. A growing problem were subprime home mortgages and securitized loans. Some large U.S. and European financial institutions disclosed big losses, often related to their direct or indirect investments in the U.S. mortgage boom. Anxieties spread over credit default obligations. Risks multiplied as to counterparty liabilities. "Toxic" securities and loan problems contaminated many balance sheets. Housing prices slumped in many areas. A surprising number of big U.S. commercial banks, investment banks, and other financial and insurance conglomerates (like Citigroup and AIG) were threatened. With unexpected speed a U.S. financial crisis morphed during 2008 into a broad international recession and slump. Bailouts of Bear Stearns, Citigroup and Merrill Lynch, and the September failure of Lehman Bros. (the fourth largest U.S. investment bank), sent shock waves through world markets and eroded confidence. By mid-September 2008 it was evident that the United States, much of Europe, and parts of Asia were heading into a global business slump. This was potentially the worst financial crisis and global recession since the 1930s.

i. Obama, 2009–2016

Not surprisingly, the backlash from a troubled economy proved to be significant in the 2008 presidential election. Obama won the election decisively, but daunting challenges faced the new leadership. On the security front, international terrorists and nuclear weapons proliferation remained dangerous threats. Problems in the Mid-East, the Arab-Israeli conflict, and insecurities in Iraq, Afghanistan, Syria, North Africa, and Pakistan were problematic. Russia had tensions with some of its neighbors, with open conflict in the Crimea and Eastern Ukraine. In Latin America "Chavistas" were trying to organize anti-U.S. opposition and trouble for the global economy. The United States suffered major trade, investment, and current account imbalances with spreading recessions and losses for financial institutions. Increased health costs, growing longevity, pension burdens, and social security were awkward problems. Energy scarcities and other resource constraints, together with inflation, limited progress. Environmental overcrowding and climate change menaced many areas. All of these problems created economic strains on banking and financial institutions and their regulators.

In response to the U.S.-world financial crisis that followed the collapse of the subprime mortgage market, in the last year of the Bush presidency Congress had enacted an initial, modest stimulus package, followed later by the Troubled Asset Relief Program (TARP) of $700 billion in Fall 2008. A larger Obama stimulus package of $790 billion came in mid-February 2009. None of this addressed the structural problems of ineffective bank regulation that underlay the collapse.

The single biggest regulatory challenge facing the Obama Administration was the implementation and enforcement of the Dodd-Frank Wall Street Reform and Consumer Protection Act of 2010 (Dodd-Frank Act), enacted as a direct response to the financial crisis precipitated by the collapse of the U.S. mortgage market. The act required regulatory implementation of almost 400 separate statutory mandates by a wide assortment of departments and administrative agencies, including Treasury, the

SEC, CFTC, the bank regulators, and the newly created Consumer Financial Protection Bureau (CFPB), an independent agency within the Federal Reserve. Unfortunately, full implementation of the act was not achieved during the Obama Administration. (Approximately 30 percent of the regulatory mandates in the act remains unfulfilled.)

The two basic objectives of the Dodd-Frank Act were to establish new supervision and controls over large and "systemically significant" financial institutions, and not just banks, and to create genuine consumer protection mechanisms at the federal level. Administrative implementation of the act is still incomplete as of this writing, and it remains to be seen whether these two basic but diametrical goals can be maintained in balance.

Most of the statutory mandates that were implemented by the regulators missed their statutory deadlines or otherwise took an unusually long time to be finalized. Of course, given the complex issues addressed by the Dodd-Frank Act, some delay in implementation might be understandable. But while the act itself allowed one or two years for implementation of many important measures, six years after its enactment the Dodd-Frank Act's reforms had still not been completed by the Obama Administration.

j. Trump, 2017–2020

Following the election of Donald Trump in November 2016, rhetoric about "excessive regulation" became the basic policy of the new administration with respect to financial services regulation. However, his initiative for legislative revision or repeal of the Dodd-Frank Act in whole or in part went nowhere. More selective legislative proposals targeting issues like excessive regulatory burdens on small or mid-size financial institutions gained wider support in Congress in early 2018. This led to the enactment in May 2018 of the Economic Growth, Regulatory Relief, and Consumer Protection Act (Economic Growth Act). The act primarily affects small and regional depository institutions, rather than large financial services firms or the financial sector generally. Among other things, Title I of the Economic Growth Act purports to improve consumer access to mortgage credit by removing regulatory requirements applicable to lenders. (However, there is no explicit condition that requires expanded lending in exchange for eased regulatory requirements.) Title II eases capital requirements and exempts relatively small banks from restrictions on proprietary trading in securities. Title IV eases regulatory burdens for relatively smaller bank holding companies (BHCs).

As to administrative action, by the end of January 2017, the president had signed an executive order directing federal agencies to eliminate two regulations for each new regulation issued and to limit costs for the current fiscal year to zero. This "two-for-one sale" was followed in February 2017 by another executive order requiring agencies to convene a regulatory reform task force to assist in the implementation of the January order. However, as a practical matter, there was little in terms of concrete effects from this presidential initiative.

k. Biden, 2021–

Biden's election in 2020 might be expected to reverse this tendency to minimize supervision of banking and financial services firms. However, two major international crises—each arising towards the end of the Trump presidency—have to some extent preoccupied the attention of the Biden Administration. The first is the continuing escalation of Russian aggression against Ukraine. (See Chapter I.D.1 at 31.) The second is the persistent struggle to contain the coronavirus pandemic and deal with its economic impact. (See Chapter 1.D.1 at 30–31.)

l. Lessons for Regulatory Policy

It should be evident from this brief review that monetary policy and Federal Reserve decisions, although taken "independently," cannot be understood apart from overall economic policy and trends, and the broader world market. Some lessons can be drawn from this experience. First, monetary and fiscal policy should be closely coordinated. Thus, for example, national economic performance tends to suffer when budget deficits and monetary restraint conflict with each other as investment, growth, and employment are weakened. Second, it is desirable to mesh monetary and fiscal stimulus together to encourage economic growth and full employment. Third, there are limits to the degree of stimulus that an economy can absorb without inflationary pressure and the danger of building up sustained inflationary momentum.

That is all very well, but what about banking law and regulation? We need to keep in mind two basic objectives of bank regulatory policy, each reflected in the Federal Deposit Insurance Act: safety and soundness of the banking system, and public confidence in that system. Recent developments may be at odds with those objectives. A caste system is emerging in bank regulatory policy. Supervision of safety and soundness is being bifurcated, with one policy for small and regional banks and another for large and internationally active banks. This could go well beyond typical de minimis exceptions. Financial services markets do not separate out so neatly, and there is more interaction among participants of all sizes than emerging public policy would suggest. This bifurcation could allow critical instability to develop in a regional bank and spread throughout the financial services market with greater alacrity than a circumscribed supervisory system could intercept.

That is one of the dangers regulators faced in dealing with the 2023 failure of Silicon Valley Bank (SVB) in California. That regional bank was overly concentrated in its sources of deposits—e.g., tech start-ups and related firms—and it invested an unusually large proportion of the deposited funds it received into long-term Treasury bonds and mortgage bonds with modest but steady returns at a time when interest rates on such investments were low. Over-concentration in its balance sheet—both on the asset side (the long-term bonds) and the liability side (the deposits of tech firms)—did not promote a safe and sound banking operation. The softening of the tech sector triggered a decline in deposits, and the recent rise in interest rates on bonds resulted in discounted current value for long-term low-interest debt securities. As it became apparent that SVB would be vulnerable to a withdrawal trend on the deposit side of its business, this itself triggered a sharp rise in demands for deposit withdrawals, which the bank could not handle. This is a classic example of a "bank run." The reverberations of this "regional collapse" are being felt by banks of all sizes, both within the United States and around the world.

Furthermore, the most significant danger emerging from enactment of the Economic Growth Act may well be the underlying political story that its enactment suggests. This story is that the vigilance spurred by the Dodd-Frank Act is now disfavored, and that regulators should act accordingly. Thus, the real danger to safety and soundness in the banking system today may actually come from administrative implementation of supervisory rules—or the lack thereof.

B. GUIDELINES AND CONSTRAINTS

The legal authority for money and banking policy is the accumulated legacy of legislation (supported by constitutional powers) in effect today. As this historical review demonstrates, such a complex, pragmatic accumulation of law-making and regulatory practice does not reflect any single viewpoint or interpretation. Its thrust, rather, is a framework of authority, powers, and general responsibilities. This framework has been regularly adjusted, often enlarged, and tailored to evolving national policies and current economic objectives. And, to some degree, overall standards or goals have been provided by Congress. But for the most part, money and banking policy has been allowed considerable latitude for discretion, partly because Congress, bankers, and economists have not achieved complete agreement on these matters, and because important questions remain to be specified in contingent circumstances—involving economic growth, employment, capacity utilization, prices, exchange rates, and varied money market conditions.

1. INSTRUMENTS OF MONETARY AND BANKING POLICY

The monetary authorities (Federal Reserve System and the Treasury) do not "control" the money supply, the demand for liquidity, or market interest rates in any direct or comprehensive sense. Instead, the Federal Reserve strongly influences bank reserves and lending potential, and affects interest rates, mainly through the *supply* of bank liquidity (under domestic regulatory jurisdiction), and also through the discount rate for loans to the banking system. The Treasury and the Federal Reserve together affect the *demand* for liquidity and interest rates through management of government debt (federal liabilities), deficits, and borrowing policies, which can have a very substantial impact on money markets. Meanwhile, Congress and the Executive branch influence money markets and the entire economy with spending programs, taxes and their allocation, and government deficits, borrowing requirements or surpluses.

The most important instruments of monetary "control" or policy have been open-market operations, reserve requirements, and the discount rate. Credit regulations have been employed as well. And, though not always considered a part of monetary policy in the narrow sense, government debt and deficit policies have had, at times, a powerful, even overriding, impact upon money and credit markets.

a. Open-Market Operations

FOMC directives to the account manager at the New York Federal Reserve Bank (called the "Desk") regulate the Fed's purchases and sales of government securities. This authority has existed for the FOMC since 1935, but open market operations were carried out informally by the New York Federal Reserve Bank since the early 1920's. The discretion of the Desk is limited to achieving target objectives established by the FOMC, such as easing or tightening money market conditions.

b. Reserve Requirements

Legal reserve requirements have been specified in the Federal Reserve Act of 1913 in terms of a range of alternative reserve ratios, rather than a single fixed percentage. Originally, the reserve requirements of federal law applied only to national banks and all state-chartered member banks. This provides a powerful, but relatively crude method of ensuring that banks have some liquidity available. Adjusting reserve requirements works slowly and indirectly as a device for adjusting conditions in the economy, as shown by the experience of many recessions, and the Great Depression.

Most recently, the DIDMCA of 1980 phased in "standardized" reserve requirements of 12 percent for "transactions" deposits (including NOW accounts), and up to 3 percent for non-personal time deposits, subject to substantial emergency increase authority. These requirements apply to *all* depository institutions, not just national banks and state-chartered member banks.

c. Discount Rates

The "discount window" is the main direct lending facility provided by the Federal Reserve to support stability and provide liquidity to the banking system. Acting as the U.S. central bank pursuant to the Federal Reserve Act of 1913, it lends banks money for up to 90 days. The discount rates charged by the Fed as "lender of last resort" for emergency credits, or for more routine credits for seasonal borrowing or very short-term credits, do have some significance. However, for a number of reasons, the discount rate has proved less important over the years than open market operations in the United States.

First, U.S. banks never became very dependent on borrowing from the Federal Reserve. In the Fed's first 16 years—including World War I and the 1920's—banks did not seem to need the discount window very heavily, though the rate was used consciously as a discipline in the 1920's.

Second, during the New Deal years monetary policy was generally "easy," with surplus reserves and little need for discounting by the Fed. This continued during 1941–51, as the Fed supported cheap war debt borrowing, and "relative ease" also prevailed.

Third, by the time the need for monetary restraint resumed in the 1950's, a large private market in government securities had already developed, which allowed open market operations to be a more effective economic instrument for the Fed than the less direct, more occasional leverage of the discount rate. Likewise, a private market for excess reserves among banks, *i.e.*, so-called "federal funds," had become a more routine source of borrowing for additional bank reserves. Thus, open market operations were more directly influential on this channel for expanding (or reducing) bank reserves, given the more significant and more flexible federal funds rate. The discount rate remains important as a "signal" to the market that the Fed is trying to tighten or loosen the availability of credit, and this signaling will typically have an impact on the attitudes of participants in the broader open market.

d. Direct Controls

Typically, then, the Fed affects or sways the open market by its *participation* in the market, or by its hortatory signaling to the market through its discount rates. Nevertheless, direct credit controls and allocations, or limits on the uses of credit, or the interest rates available are another dimension of monetary policy. However, in capitalist countries with free market traditions such controls are normally avoided, except in wartime or other serious national emergencies.

Exchange controls involving international flows of currency, financing, or payments in any form can be considered another dimension of money and credit restriction.[5] In addition, war-time controls on foreign exchange and credit transactions were initially authorized by Congress as part of the Trading With Enemy Act (TWEA) in 1917. This authority for "qualitative" restrictions on credit was broadened by Congress in 1933, as part of the first wave of New Deal emergency banking legislation. (Collateral legislation, previously explained, limited interest rates on demand deposits, and prohibited interest on checking accounts.) Further exchange and credit control authority was enacted in 1941, and the Federal Reserve restricted consumer credit significantly during World War II and the Korean War.

---

5 Socialist and developing countries, however, have been more aggressive in using credit and exchange controls to direct and limit the flows of saving, lending, investment and trade in accordance with national policy priorities. Strong preferences are often imposed for approved investment activity, while credits or financing for consumption—especially for "luxuries," automobiles, or some types of real estate—may be discouraged, or even prohibited. In capitalist countries like the United States, such encouragements take a milder, and often more complicated form of tax subsidies and incentives.

The "national emergency" authority of the President under the TWEA was substantially narrowed in 1977, with emergency authority outside of actual wartime subject to a new International Emergency Economic Authority Act (IEEPA).) Presidents have increasingly relied on general emergency statutes like IEEPA in a wide range of situations, some involving international hostilities and others involving economic problems like the balance of payments crisis in 1971.[6]

2. GOVERNMENT DEBT POLICIES, DEFICITS, AND WORLD MARKETS

The management of government debt, its financing, and the size of deficits relative to national income, savings and investment have great impact on money markets. Government borrowing competes with private credit demand, and may raise interest rates significantly—unless the Treasury, Federal Reserve and banks increase the money supply enough to offset this additional pressure. If the money and credit supply increases substantially, this may affect aggregate demand and enlarge the inflation rate appreciably, unless there is general slack and unemployment in the economy.

3. CAPITAL REGULATION AND SUPERVISION

With the exception of some thrift institutions that are organized as mutual enterprises, owned and

---

[6] *See, e.g., United States v. Yoshida International, Inc.*, 526 F.2d 560 (C.C.P.A. 1975) (upholding trade controls as authorized by president's power under TWEA).

operated by their "members," the overwhelming majority of financial services firms are corporate entities. As such, their operations are funded—at least initially—by purchases of securities by their investors. Regulation of the capital of these firms may therefore represent another means of government supervision of their operations. There is in fact a long historical pedigree for the use of capital rules in support of regulation and supervision of financial institutions.

a. Minimum Capital Requirements

Requiring a specified minimum amount of capital as a condition to entry into business may seem an obvious way to ensure that the business will be operated in a safe and sensible manner. The first generation of general incorporation statutes required those seeking to organize a corporation to invest a specified minimum dollar amount in the equity capital of the proposed company. Specialized statutes for the incorporation ("chartering") of banks, including the NBA, conformed to this pattern. By the middle of the Twentieth Century, the pattern was markedly changing for general incorporation statutes; they required less minimum capital as a condition for incorporation. Eventually the requirement was removed entirely from modern corporation statutes like the Delaware General Corporation Law.

However, the requirement persisted in banking statutes, often with only infrequent amendments updating the minimum dollar amount required. The end result was an NBA that, until the end of 2000, required banks organized in the largest cities in the country to have capital of not less than $200,000, an amount that probably would not have covered the cost of their building leases. (Such requirements were reinforced by OCC regulations that typically required a minimum capital of $1 million.)

In December 2000, the NBA was amended to repeal the provision as to minimum capital, but the requirement continued in effect under OCC regulations. The current version of those regulations requires "sufficient initial capital, net of any organizational expenses . . . to support the institution's projected volume and type of business." This version reflects quite clearly the reason why minimum capital requirements have remained a prominent feature of *bank* incorporation despite the abandonment of the requirement in general corporate law. The level of capital is viewed as an important safety-and-soundness criterion—how much capital is necessary to support the banking business?

Given the business model of banking, however, this requirement makes little sense. Banks and other financial institutions are the most thinly capitalized enterprises in the world, and they are intended to be so. Simply put, the business of banking runs on *debt*—the deposits accepted by the bank and intermediated into loans and other investments—not on the equity capital of its investors. So, the emphasis on minimum capital requirements, beyond the coverage of start-up costs, may seem misplaced if not outright misleading.

b. Capital Adequacy

The most recent development in capital supervision appears to take into account the particulars of the typical banking business model. This involves the ongoing or continuous supervision of capital adequacy of existing institutions, usually measured as a ratio of their capital to assets. By the late 1970s the regulators had increased their attention to capital adequacy; if a bank's inadequate capital ratio constituted an unsafe and unsound practice, its regulator would use broad statutory authority to define and remedy capital inadequacy.

This authority was questioned in *First National Bank of Bellaire v. Comptroller of the Currency*, 697 F.2d 674 (5th Cir. 1983), but it was quickly confirmed by congressional action. The International Lending Supervision Act ("ILSA"), enacted in 1983, explicitly provided that the failure of a bank to maintain prescribed capital adequacy levels may be deemed to constitute an unsafe and unsound practice. ILSA went so far as to require each federal agency to "cause banking institutions to achieve and maintain adequate capital by establishing minimum levels of capital for such banking institutions." What constitutes "adequate capital" was within the discretion of each agency, and ILSA explicitly gave them authority to establish capital adequacy levels as they deemed "necessary or appropriate in light of the particular circumstances of the banking institution." A bank's failure to maintain capital adequacy may also lead to the issuance of a directive requiring it to submit and comply with a capital plan to reform capital levels. Pursuant to their statutory authority, the federal bank regulators have developed specific, detailed capital adequacy policies. And through the Bank for International Settlements (BIS) in Basel, Switzerland, they have cooperated with many of the principal U.S. trading partners to create international capital adequacy standards (the "Basel Accord"[7]) that have been adopted by over 100 nations. These standards have been progressively refined to take into account, in an explicit way, the relative degrees of risk among the various types of assets of financial institutions, and to define more precisely the elements of "capital." Currently, the United States and its BIS partners are trying to make the capital adequacy even more attuned to the differences in particular asset categories. Thus, in calculating a bank's capital/assets ratio, certain assets (like cash on hand) are viewed as practically risk-free for these purposes, and are excluded from the calculation (*i.e.*, "risk-weighted" at zero percent of their value on the bank's balance sheet), while the amount of other assets like industrial loans would be included at full value in determining the "assets" denominator of the ratio (*i.e.*, "risk-weighted" at 100 percent of its value).

The devil is in the details, of course. As new iterations of the Basel Accord have become more

---

[7] The particulars of the Basel Accord are discussed in greater detail in Chapter III, pages 110–118, *infra*.

sophisticated, disputes have surfaced over the precise treatment of particular types of assets, and the way in which the capital adequacy system should be supervised. Thus, at the beginning of the Twenty-First Century, the Basel Accord allowed large, sophisticated internationally active banks to customize the details of their own capital/assets ratio internally (*i.e.*, the so called "internal ratings based," or "IRB," approach). With the emergence of the international financial crisis brought on by the meltdown of the U.S. mortgage market, however, the BIS participants have become very skeptical about allowing even large banks to set their own capital standards. This area of supervisory practice continues to evolve, but it seems clear that, in one form or another, capital adequacy rules will remain a prominent feature of modern financial institutions regulation and supervision.

PART B

BANK REGULATION

CHAPTER III

BANKING MARKET REGULATION

Commercial banking is extensively regulated for potential entrants, chartered bank corporations, and bank holding companies. Banks are subject to financial supervision and regular examination, with substantial corrective authority for dangerous practices. Reserve requirements are enforced for banks, and their capital adequacy is an important concern of the regulatory authorities. The growth of banks, along with their branching, diversification and merger activity is regulated.

Significant limitations also apply to other bank activities, including lending limits, insider lending, investments and certain types of deposit liabilities. Interest rate ceilings were placed on some deposits, and interest on demand deposits had been prohibited (between 1933–1980). There are disclosure requirements and privacy safeguards for borrowers and depositors. Although about 4,200 banks and 640 savings associations (*i.e.*, savings banks, savings & loan associations, and similar institutions) exist in the United States,[1] with substantial competition over many aspects of their activity, this rivalry had been softened and made less severe by protectionist regulation. To understand these dimensions of

---

[1] In addition, there are approximately 5,204 credit unions, offering partial competition with banks and savings associations. *See Park National Bank v. Park Community Credit Union, Inc.* 2020 WL 13016746 at *4 (W.D.Ken. 2020) (demonstrating structural differences between bank and credit union and their differing market emphases).

banking law, we shift our focus from the entire banking system, the central bank and national economic policy, and consider the role of individual banks and particular banking markets.

A. PRINCIPAL REGULATORS

Three federal banking agencies, the Office of the Comptroller of Currency ("OCC"), the Federal Reserve Board, and the Federal Deposit Insurance Corporation ("FDIC"), along with the state banking departments or commissioners, are the major regulatory agencies for bank market regulation. At the federal level, the OCC is the oldest agency, having served since 1863 as the chartering authority for national banks, and their primary agency for the supervision and examination process. The Federal Reserve Board, created in 1913, has supervision and examination authority for state chartered banks that are members of the Federal Reserve System. It has become increasingly important not just as a central bank but as a bank regulatory agency under many recent enactments (covering mergers, bank holding companies, truth-in-lending, fair credit reporting, and certain aspects of interstate and multinational banking.) [2] In 1933, the FDIC became a secondary supervising agency for national banks, and the primary federal agency for almost all state banks

[2] Since the enactment of the Dodd-Frank Act in 2010, the Fed's authority for consumer protection matters, such as the Truth in Lending Act and the Fair Credit Reporting Act, has been transferred to the Consumer Financial Protection Bureau (CFPB), discussed *infra*.

(those seeking FDIC insurance protection for their depositors.) In addition, the Federal Financial Institutions Examination Council (FFIEC) received regulatory or supervisory authority for certain aspects of banking and other financial institutions.[3] The state banking departments are the chartering authority for all state banks, and remain responsible for their supervision and examination.

Finally, pursuant to the Dodd-Frank Wall Street Reform and Consumer Protection Act of 2010 (Dodd-Frank Act), two new regulatory agencies were added to the structure of U.S. bank regulation. The act established the Financial Stability Oversight Council (FSOC), a committee of financial services regulators.[4]

---

[3] The FFIEC now comprises the Comptroller of the Currency, the FDIC Chair, one governor of the Board of Governors of the Federal Reserve Board designated by the Board Chair, the Director of the CFPB, the Chair of the National Credit Union Administration Board, and the Chair of FFIEC's State Liaison Committee. (The advisory State Liaison Committee is composed of five representatives of state supervisory agencies, and in accordance with the Financial Services Regulatory Relief Act of 2006, the Committee's Chair, as a representative state regulator, has been a FFIEC voting member since October 2006.)

[4] The FSOC consists of ten voting members (the Secretary of the Treasury, who serves as FSOC chair, the Chair of the Federal Reserve Board, the Comptroller of the Currency, the CFPB Director, the Chair of the Securities and Exchange Commission, the FDIC Chair, the Chair of the Commodity Futures Trading Commission, the Director of the Federal Housing Finance Agency, the Chair of the National Credit Union Administration Board, and an independent member appointed by the President, by and with the advice and consent of the Senate, who has insurance expertise), as well as five nonvoting members (the Director of the Office of Financial Research, the Director of the Federal Insurance Office, a state insurance commissioner designated by a selection process determined by the state

The FSOC is charged with the task of identifying systemic risks, promoting market discipline, and responding to emerging threats to the U.S. financial system.

The act also established the Consumer Financial Protection Bureau (CFPB), an independent agency within the Federal Reserve, to create and enforce effective consumer protection principles with respect to financial services. As of July 21, 2011, the CFPB took over responsibility for consumer financial protection provision from (1) the Board of Governors (and any federal reserve bank), (2) the FDIC, (3) the Federal Trade Commission, (4) the National Credit Union Administration, (5) the OCC, (6) the now defunct Office of Thrift Supervision, and (7) the Department of Housing and Urban Development. In particular, as of the transfer date the CFPB assumed responsibility for consumer compliance supervision of very large depository institutions and their affiliates and for promulgating regulations under various federal consumer financial laws, as well as for new authorities tasked to the CFPB under the act.

The Economic Growth, Regulatory Relief, and Consumer Protection Act of 2018, among other things, limits the scope of CFPB authority with respect to relatively small or mid-size financial institutions. So, for example, an insured depository

---

insurance commissioners, a state banking supervisor, designated by a selection process determined by the state banking supervisors, and a state securities commissioner (or an officer performing like functions) designated by a selection process determined by state securities commissioners).

institution or insured credit union that, together with its affiliates, has less than $10 billion in total consolidated assets will in many instances not be subject to many requirements of the Truth in Lending Act regulations. The act's rationale for easing consumer financial protection is that consumer access to financial services will expand if regulatory burdens are removed from lenders. However, there is no explicit condition in the act that requires expanded service by these smaller financial institutions in order to benefit from eased regulatory requirements.

B. CHARTERING AND ENTRY REQUIREMENTS

Entry into banking was easier when the federal government did not exercise disciplinary and restraining influence, *i.e.*, during the periods 1781–1791, 1811–1816 and 1837–1863. In those years state charters were the exclusive method for creating banking corporations. In particular, the period leading up to the Civil War, the "free banking era," established the predominant pattern for ease of entry that lasted until the Great Depression of 1929–1933. Thus, from the 1830s through the 1920s, if entrepreneurs could meet minimum capitalization standards to set up a bank, they routinely would obtain a bank charter in the great majority of states. By 1921, the peak year for bank population, there were 30,000 United States banks.

However, since the Great Depression, when more than 10,000 banks failed, entry into banking has become more difficult. Standards for new charters were raised substantially, and entrepreneurs have been less eager to enter banking. More demanding criteria were established, including tougher requirements for capitalization and management, the "convenience and needs" of the community involved, along with competitive circumstances. These additional factors have been interpreted frequently to require a showing that the geographic market of the proposed bank is not "over-banked," *i.e.*, that there is room for another bank to operate without impeding the safe operation of banks already in the market. In other words, new entrants often have to demonstrate not only financial resources and managerial competence but also that the market in question (a city or rural area) could accommodate another banking institution. This means, in practice, that a substantial limitation on new entry may be asserted by the existing banks in an area as protestants against additional rivals. Whether this resistance will be effective in a given case depends on how these factors are evaluated, in the discretion of the federal or state chartering authority making the decision.

Applicants for a bank charter must file a formal "application" with extensive supporting data. The organizers must outline their plan of operations, describe earning prospects, provide details on management capabilities (involving bank executives with appropriate experience, under contract or part of the organizing group), show adequate capitalization and soundness, and offer reasonable service to their community. In addition, the OCC and state bank departments require information on market circumstances, *i.e.*, size and growth potential, and competition from existing banks and related financial institutions. Notice of the application must be published, which allows other interested parties (normally competing institutions already in the market) to file protests and relevant data. This provides an ample basis for determining whether a proposed charter might meet the convenience and needs of its community, taking into account competitive circumstances. Occasionally, administrative hearings are organized to take additional evidence.

Obviously, the economic attractiveness of a banking enterprise, growth and income trends of an area, and the strength and branching networks of existing competitors will determine whether organizers materialize in the first place. Little new chartering activity occurred in the 1930s or during World War II. It picked up a bit right after the war, but not significantly until 1962–1965, when the OCC's attitude became more liberal under Comptroller Saxon, and as a longer term trend of improved prosperity became evident. This surge of liberality by the OCC induced a more relaxed attitude in many state banking departments. Gradually, a shift in thinking and emphasis developed, allowing soundly financed groups to enter banking markets more freely, and this was reflected in policy statements of the OCC. For example, in October 1980, the Comptroller stated:

> This shift in emphasis reflects the OCC's experience that a strong organizing group with solid financial backing and a well-conceived and developed operating plan generally is able to establish and operate a successful bank even in the most economically distressed areas or most highly competitive markets.

By 1996, OCC regulations discussing chartering policy stated:

> The marketplace is normally the best regulator of economic activity, and competition within the marketplace promotes efficiency and better customer service. Accordingly, it is the OCC's policy to approve proposals to establish national banks, including minority-owned institutions, that have a reasonable chance of success and that will be operated in a safe and sound manner. It is not the OCC's policy to ensure that a proposal to establish a national bank is without risk to the organizers or to protect existing institutions from healthy competition from a new national bank.

12 C.F.R. § 5.20(f)(1) (1997), This "marketplace" rationale has receded in the wake of the market meltdown of 2008. The language quoted above no longer appears in the OCC chartering regulation, which instead states as its basic policy that "in determining whether to approve an application to establish a national bank or Federal savings association, the OCC is guided by [among other] principles . . . [m]aintaining a safe and sound banking system." 12 C.F.R. § 5.20(f)(1)(i).

The marketplace rationale also developed in many state banking departments, partly in an effort to keep the state banking system competitive with national banks that might become more numerous. In any event, there was considerably greater bank chartering activity from the early 1960s until the late 1980s than during the preceding period 1933–1960. Beginning in the 1990s, however, with increased branching and interstate banking allowed, new charter entries declined greatly, a trend that has continued to the present.

Charter applicants may obtain the appropriate forms and current guidelines for national charters from the OCC in Washington, D.C., or the District Office responsible for the area where the proposed bank will be located, and for state charters from the state banking department or commissioner. Applicants may be able to obtain confidential treatment for portions of their submission data when requested. State charter applicants need to submit a separate application to the FDIC for deposit insurance, and currently that is also required for national bank charter applicants. FDIC insurance applications cover the same ground, *i.e.*, financial history and condition, capital adequacy, earnings prospects, management, and character, together with convenience and needs of the community. Capital and financial requirements for the FDIC may be somewhat stricter than what state law or state authorities demand. (Federal Reserve membership requirements are comparable to those for national banks, and tend to be more demanding than state charters or FDIC insurance. Hence, brand new state banks normally do not seek to become Federal Reserve members at the outset.)

Traditionally, national banks were required to be organized with no less than a statutorily required amount of capital, keyed to the size of the community in which the bank would be located. Federal statutes allowed minimum capital to be as low as $50,000 for towns of 6000 or less, and $200,000 in cities with 50,000 or more population. (Individual states may even be slightly more liberal.) All this reflected the statutory history of "free banking" and actual practice up to the Great Depression. These federal requirements became completely impractical in light of current economic conditions, and by regulation the OCC required at least $1 million of initial capital for a national charter. The outdated statutory requirements were repealed in 2001. Minimum capital requirements for formation are now found only in the OCC regulations, not the statute.

For Fed membership, the Federal Reserve requires the same minimum capital as the OCC does for national bank chartering. The FDIC also now requires at least $1 million of capital for a new insured bank or savings institution. But these threshold capital requirements should not be understood as sufficient for a growing bank. In fact, "capital adequacy" tends to be looked at now in terms of continued financial soundness, and as a ratio or percentage of total assets (or liabilities).

The typical bank in the United States normally had a capital account (shareholders' equity and retained earnings) equal to 6–7 percent of total assets. But the largest banks in the late 1970s–early 1980s had proportionately less capital, often equal to only 4–5 percent of total assets. Banks involved in a bailout absorption of a troubled bank may even have had part of their "capital" in long term debt (or notes owed to the FDIC or Federal Reserve). But most banks would be considered to have unsound management practices if their equity capital went much below these normal ranges. A "weak" capital position, in this more subjective, less definite sense, would raise questions, and perhaps invite a special examination or investigation as a possible "problem bank," particularly if other danger signs materialized, such as a significant growth of substandard loans, declining deposits, or unprofitable operations. For example, the 1981 Capital Adequacy Guidelines, issued by the Federal Reserve Board and the OCC, set *minimum* standards of capital adequacy, *i.e.*, 5 percent for regional banks and 6 percent, generally speaking, for community banks, with desirable ranges above 6.5 and 7 percent, respectively. Below 5.5 and 6.0 percent, respectively, banks were then presumed to be undercapitalized and required continuous monitoring. Major international banks tended to have somewhat lower capitalization, but the Federal Reserve and Comptroller encouraged these banks to improve their capital positions.

In 1984–1985 federal banking regulators promulgated new capital standards, *i.e.*, 5.5 percent for "primary capital" and 6 percent for total capital, for all banks, regardless of size. (Statutory authority for minimum capital adequacy had been strengthened with the International Lending Supervision Act of 1983.) Then in 1987 central banks and regulators for 12 major banking nations (U.S., Canada, Japan, U.K., W. Germany, Switzerland, France, Italy, Netherlands, Belgium, Luxembourg, and Sweden), meeting at the Bank for International Settlements in Basel, Switzerland, agreed jointly to harmonize and strengthen bank capital requirements to 7.25 percent of total "risk assets" by 1990, and to 8 percent of total "risk assets" by 1992.

But "risk assets" were defined in the new Basel Accord in a special way: (i) cash and guaranteed obligations of central banks and governments (*e.g.*, U.S. T-bills and bonds) were weighted at zero risk, along with FDIC and FSLIC securities issued to recapitalize troubled institutions; (ii) securities issued by development banks or quasi-government corporations might carry 20 to 50 percent risk weight, depending on national policies; (iii) residential mortgage loans carried 50 percent risk weight, provided that realistic appraisals support collateral values; and (iv) normal risk applied to most commercial lending, commercial real estate loans, and even standby guarantees (except those related to particular transactions, *e.g.*, performance or bid bonds, warranties, or letters of credit related to particular transactions, which might carry 50 percent risk). In this way, 60–80 percent of typical bank balance sheet assets would carry normal risk, and thus require overall capital of 6–7 percent (within the "traditional" range for modern banking).

On the other hand, "capital" was defined somewhat more liberally in the Basel Accord. "Core capital" (Tier 1) included common stock equity and retained earnings, *plus* noncumulative preferred stock (but not, in most circumstances, "good will"). Only half the required capital had to be Tier 1. "Supplementary capital" (Tier 2) could include hybrid (debt/equity) securities, subordinated capital debt, general loan loss reserves or provisioning for contingent (possible) losses, or "undisclosed reserves" (hidden retained earnings or assets not marked up to current market values). But by the end of 1992 no more than half the Tier 2 capital could be in subordinated debt, and no more than 1.25 percent of total risk assets should be in general loan loss reserves (in other than exceptional and temporary circumstances). In this way, most U.S. banks could qualify as adequately capitalized, although the largest banks, which can more readily market hybrid securities and subordinated debt, might carry a substantial part of their "capital" in supplementary form, *i.e.*, as "debt" serving the function of capital and taking equity-like risks.[5] So long as purchasers of such bank securities

---

[5] A few leading U.S. banks averaged only 3.5–4 percent capital on assets in 1981–1982, which they claimed was reasonable for multinational risk diversification. Many believed this to be insufficient capital coverage, however, especially for country risk exposure. But regulators found it hard to complain publicly in the early 1980s in the midst of rescheduling for international debts. An awkward rescheduling situation, requiring collaboration among many countries and international banks, would be more difficult if worries spread over capital adequacy in major multinational banks. Leading banks in some other major banking countries had even lower capital ratios, which reflected more explicit government or central bank support (or some degree of

understood this capital risk, and received an appropriate premium in the marketplace, no fundamental change was involved (except a restructuring of the capital accounts and risks within larger banks).

Because of heavy losses experienced by the FSLIC in the mid-late 1980s (when many institutions were undercapitalized, and some were allowed to operate although insolvent), banking regulators became more concerned with capital adequacy. The FIRREA of 1989 tightened up on loose accounting and capital standards (see Chapter IV-D *Regulating Thrifts in Transition*) for thrift institutions. Most experts agreed that somewhat earlier corrective intervention for capital "weak" institutions was generally desirable, *i.e.*, a major lesson from the S & L debacle. When Congress voted $70 billion of additional borrowing to recapitalize the FDIC (which had also suffered bigger losses 1988–1992) in the FDIC Improvement Act of 1991 ("FDICIA"), it tried to impose more stringent minimum capital standards, and restrict regulatory discretion in the supervision process.

A key feature of the 1991 FDICIA was a new "critical capital level" ratio of equity/total assets

---

nationalized banking). Hence, the Federal Reserve and the OCC worked to encourage improved capitalization. Between December 1981, and June 1987, the average "primary capital" ratio for the 12 largest U.S. multinational banks was strengthened from 3.66 to 6.86 percent, through the issue of $4 billion common stock, $9.96 billion preferred stock, and almost $20 billion of convertible securities and provisional loan loss reserves allowed to serve as "primary capital."

equal to 2 percent. Regulators continued to set the normal "minimums", *i.e.*, the "leverage" capital requirement (3 percent equity/total assets) and "risk-based" capital requirement (8 percent capital/risk-assets, including both Tier 1 and Tier 2 capital elements), and corrective action was authorized for institutions falling significantly below these minimums (*e.g.*, changes in management, removal of officers and directors, restrictions on growth, suspension of dividends, and/or a plan to increase capital). But when an institution fell below the "critical capital level," regulators should take control (by appointing a conservator) or seize and close the institution (by appointing a receiver), *unless* other action would better protect the deposit insurance fund. If an institution stayed below the "critical capital level" for more than a year, closure and receivership should follow in most cases, *unless* the regulators certified the institution was viable and making progress in a capital restoration plan. Meanwhile, regulators were mandated under the 1991 legislation to adjust risk-based capital standards within 18 months to take account of risks associated with fluctuations in interest rates, concentration of loans, and non-traditional activities.

In the 1990s, however, the capital requirements of the Basel Accord were criticized by some of the largest banks as being too restrictive. Accordingly, "Basel II" improvements were worked out to allow somewhat relaxed capital minimums. Where big banks can mitigate their risks with collateralization, hedging, securitization, and derivative securities, somewhat lower capital may be sufficient. But substantial oversight would still be needed by bank regulators. U.S. banking regulators expected to implement this alternate framework in 2008–2009, with only the largest 12–25 U.S. multinational banks initially falling into the new, relaxed requirements category, known as the "advanced approach." The EU banking authorities wanted to move in this direction, too.

U.S. regulators had expected to ask for comment on proposed rules implementing Basel II during the Summer 2005, but new quantitative studies demonstrated that banks adopting the new rules would on balance hold significantly less capital than previously assumed. The data also raised questions about the ability of second-tier banks relegated to a revised Basel I—the so-called "Basel IA"—to compete with banks that were permitted to adopt the Basel II methodology. This would give Basel II banks significant competitive advantages over Basel IA banks, leaving the latter vulnerable to acquisition by the former. As a result, the regulators put their plans on hold in May 2005 to allow more time to analyze the quantitative results.

By December 2007, the OCC, Federal Reserve Board, FDIC, and OTS had jointly published final rules implementing Basel II for the largest, internationally active U.S. banks. The final rules were effective April 1, 2008. The new standards were to begin being phased in over a three-year period commencing January 1, 2009. In July 2008, the agencies proposed a new more risk-sensitive capital framework—the Basel IA—for banks and thrifts that did not qualify for Basel II. The deadline for comments on the proposed Basel IA rules was October 27, 2008, by which time the financial services industry was in complete disarray as a result of the financial crisis that began in September 2008. Understandably, the Basel approach and its revisions were criticized by some commentators for their failure to account adequately for various risks, particularly off-balance-sheet exposures, and the treatment of trading book assets. A new approach would necessarily be required in response to the continuing crisis.

Before Basel II was even fully implemented, a new "Basel III" approach emerged, involving revisions to the market risk framework, guidelines on incremental risk in an institution's trading book, new rules for securitization exposures in a bank's trading book, and revised capital charges for equity exposures. Given the significance of securitization in the collapse, enhancements to the framework included revised risk weights for re-securitizations held in a bank's trading book. In August 2012, the OCC, the Fed, and the FDIC (the OTS having been absorbed into the OCC in the wake of the crisis) proposed to revise their risk-based and leverage capital requirements, consistent with the new Basel III. The proposed revisions included implementation of a new common equity tier 1 minimum capital requirement, a higher minimum tier 1 capital requirement, and, for banking organizations subject to the advanced approach capital rules, a supplementary leverage ratio that incorporates a broader set of asset risk exposures in the denominator of the ratio. In addition, consistent with Basel III, the agencies proposed to apply limits on a banking organization's capital distributions and certain discretionary bonus payments if the banking organization does not hold a specified amount of common equity tier 1 capital in addition to the amount necessary to meet its minimum risk-based capital requirements.

According to an October 2011 report by the Basel Committee at the Bank for International Settlements, the United States—as compared with other nations that have endorsed the Basel III approach—was lagging behind in adopting the regulatory requirements under the existing Basel II and the new Basel III. A second report, issued in April 2012, gave the United States a "red flag" for its failure to implement revisions. Nevertheless, the U.S. regulators continued to inch ahead. With recovery from the 2008 crisis continuing at a very slow pace, the regulators have been very cautious in implementing any new regulatory burdens with respect to capital.

C. BANK INSURANCE AND SUPERVISION

A fundamental goal of modern United States banking law is to prevent another Great Depression, with its massive runs on banks and heavy costs to society. Clearly, the looseness of previous banking practices—with too many weak and undercapitalized banks, and inadequate lender of last resort assistance to limit a spreading panic—are considered major reasons for excessive frequency of bank failures in the past. The United States economy suffered too many panics and depressions in its earlier history, a burden now considered unacceptable when most people are employed in highly interdependent industry, services and trade sectors, and family farms no longer provide a widespread cushion of livelihoods to absorb heavy unemployment.

Four policies supported a more secure and panic-resistant banking system. (1) Our system of federal deposit insurance for bank accounts and savings and loan association accounts (FDIC), and credit union accounts (NCUSIF). The FDIC is the most important, which set the pattern on insurance and risk pooling for other institutions. (2) Greatly expanded credit backing from the Federal Reserve and FDIC, along with congressional commitments to further aid in emergencies.[6] (3) Consensus among policy-makers reflected in the Employment Act of 1946 and subsequent measures, that government fiscal and monetary policy should be managed to support the

---

[6] In the wake of the market collapse in September 2008 and the continuing financial crisis since then, there has been much political discussion about discouraging public belief and perception that the government will always intervene to "bail out" financial institutions perceived to be "too big to fail." The Dodd-Frank Act in 2010 sought to blunt these perceptions by creating FDIC authority to supervise the resolution of failure of large, systemically significant financial institutions through a process of "orderly liquidation" of such institutions, distinct from the bankruptcy laws and parallel to FDIC receivership of banks and savings associations. This new authority is as yet untested, and it is not inconceivable that, in the face of another massive market failure in the future, the Congress might authorize emergency financial assistance to such institutions.

level of production, employment, and business activity, and help maintain the soundness of our financial credit system. (4) Stronger examination and supervision for commercial banks and related financial institutions, which enforces a higher level of responsible bank management, and tries to correct situations before too much damage can be done to depositors, business confidence and activity, and their communities. In this latter effort, the FDIC, the Federal Reserve, state banking departments, and comparable authorities for savings institutions should be able to change leadership, halt serious malpractices, and force absorption mergers in a great many situations involving troubled banks or financial institutions.

These policies have been successful in reducing the number of runs on banks and failures. In the 1920s an average of 600 banks suspended operations each year. Between 1930 and 1933, another 10,000 banks were closed. But after emergency measures in the Spring 1933, including the new FDIC and emergency bank lending on a large scale, the rate of bank closings was lowered dramatically. Some 470 banks closed between 1934 and 1940, which still reflected residual weakness from the depression crisis. (Of these 470 bank failures, 112 were uninsured.) In the next forty years, 1941–1980, only 242 banks failed (only 24 uninsured). From the 1920s to the years 1941–1980, the incidence of bank failures was cut roughly one hundred-fold, a truly impressive achievement.

Unfortunately, bank failures increased greatly during the 1980s (with 1,500 between 1981 and 1992), The deposits involved in bank failures totaled at least $200 billion during that period. In addition, some 1,000 savings institutions failed between 1981 and 1992, with ultimate costs of resolution perhaps $250–300 billion. including interest. (See Chapter IV-D. *Regulating Thrifts in Transition.*) If the Continental-Illinois Bank failure-bailout in 1984 is included, more than $230 billion in deposits were involved in failures during this period.

Why did bank failures (and the deposits involved) increase so drastically? Three explanations make sense: First, the 1970s inflation was greatly reduced by strong restraint, deflation, and financial stresses in the 1980s for many businesses in much of the world. Ironically, this weakened loan asset quality for most U.S. multinational banks, together with some regional and community banks (especially for Latin American lending, the grain belt, oil patch, and many real estate markets). Second, more banks became aggressive, sought higher earnings, and accepted greater risks. Third, bank regulators may have relaxed oversight somewhat at the end of the 1970s and into the 1980s. In any event, these events serve as a useful warning and lesson: we need continued vigilance, talent, and independent responsibility for the Federal Reserve, FDIC, OCC, and other regulators and their staff.[7]

---

7 Unfortunately, another failure wave occurred in 2007–2009. See pp. 126–128 *infra*.

The size of bank accounts protected by FDIC-FSLIC insurance has been increased substantially to allow for increased prosperity and inflation. The original coverage was $2,500 per account, but today accounts are insured up to a "standard maximum deposit insurance amount" of $250,000 ("SMDIA"), periodically adjusted for inflation. All deposits in an insured depository institution that are maintained in the same "right and capacity" (*i.e.*, by or for the benefit of a particular depositor or depositors) are aggregated and insured as one insured amount up to the current SMDIA.

By the same token, deposits maintained in different rights and capacities, are insured as separate insured amounts up to the current SMDIA. So, for example, If Mr. *A* has an account in his name in the amount of $250,000, and a joint savings account with Mrs. *A* in the amount of $360.25 at the same bank, each of these accounts is insured up to the current SMDIA. Deposit accounts held by Ms. *B* at two different banks would be insured separately, per bank, up to the current SMDIA, even if the two banks were owned by the same bank holding company. However, if Ms. *B*'s deposit accounts—maintained in the same right and capacity—are at different branches or offices of the same insured depository institution, then they are aggregated and insured as one insured amount, up to the current SMDIA.

In all the 568 insured bank failures between 1934–1980, the FDIC paid off its insured accounts virtually 100 percent; non-insured accounts (exceeding insurance coverage limits) are normally protected when absorption merger partners assume the deposits of a failing bank, and non-insured accounts (exceeding coverage limits) still received partial recoveries even in those bank failures involving closure and liquidation. Nearly 4 million depositors have received $6.2 billion in all of these payoffs. But the FDIC recovered the bulk of these disbursements from assets left in the liquidating banks, or from the assumptions of deposit liabilities by successor banks. Between 1934 and 1980, the FDIC lost only $301 million in all of these bank failures. In contrast, interest earnings for the FDIC on its reserve funds for 1980 alone were $868 million.

Most earlier bank failures involved smaller and less strongly capitalized banks. Overall, 97 percent of the failed banks between 1934 and 1980 (or at least those allowed to fail by the banking agencies) had less than $50 million in deposits. This reflects their greater vulnerability, and a conscious policy to "save" larger banks with merger bailout transactions (often with FDIC assistance). Allowing larger banks to fail would greatly increase FDIC payout expenses and bring more disruptive effects on business confidence and activity in the communities affected. Nonetheless, between 1970 and 1980 ten banks with more than $100 million deposits failed, and three banks with more than $500 million. From 1981 to 1992 bank failures became even more frequent, including Continental Illinois, the seventh largest

U.S. commercial bank in 1983–1984 (with $42 billion in assets).[8]

This reflected a new development, *i.e.*, greater risk for banks with more aggressive "liability management," seeking higher rates of return in a business environment with greater fluctuations in interest rates. Continued success for the FDIC (and the Federal Reserve) depends on preventing large bank failures. This requires that troubled banks with large deposits be merged into other big banks, and, in any event, that the incidence of bad practices and failures be kept to a minimum among bigger banking institutions.

Sadly, another big surge of bank and securities firm failures occurred in 2007–2009. Initially, this financial crisis began with a housing boom that got out of hand. Securitized bundles of mortgages and other debts were "over-valued," *i.e.*, pricing of these bundles neglected risks that were not properly foreseen. Meanwhile, unsupervised credit default obligations and swaps were being issued in growing volume (many took the form of complex derivative securities). A financial boom surged into 2007, when big financial losses began to surface. Counterparty obligations often became insecure. Large volumes of debt obligations and/or insurance coverage became unmarketable and tainted. Over-confidence and over-leveraging hit markets that were not adequately supervised. Some of the biggest problems were in the

---

[8] Technically, Continental Illinois Bank was not allowed to fail. It was a direct assistance "bailout" by the FDIC and other Federal authorities.

largest U.S. and E.U. investment banks and commercial banks, *i.e.*, those "too big to fail." Big bailouts, guarantees, mergers, and recapitalizations were needed.[9] As business slumped, exports slowed, and unemployment grew. What began as financial euphoria and financial stress morphed into a global financial and trade recession. Many experts saw this crisis of 2007–2009 as the worst slump and financial trade disruption since the 1930s. Policy makers in the United States, European Union, and elsewhere hoped to provide enough stimulus relief, but without significant inflation over the long run. If leading economies recovered quickly, less disruption would follow. But an extended slump could bring "stagflation," *i.e.*, a slump combined with considerable inflation (like much of the 1970s).

An interesting and important lesson came from U.S. banking supervision in 2007–2009. Because of inadequate surveillance for housing market euphoria, and insufficient supervision for many derivatives, credit default obligations and swaps, big losses (and a potential for much larger losses) developed in 2008. To prevent a broad financial collapse and another Great Depression—involving the largest financial enterprises—a massive U.S. bailout, guarantee, and recapitalization effort was launched in 2008–2009. More than $12 trillion in support was mobilized by the Federal Reserve, Treasury, and FDIC. Only a massive effort, with

[9] The $100,000 deposit insurance limit was increased substantially as an emergency guarantee measure in 2008–2009, and is now the "standard maximum deposit insurance amount" of $250,000, periodically adjusted for inflation.

tough "stress testing" for capital adequacy thereafter, could overcome widespread panic. By the Summer 2009 focus shifted to the best ways to strengthen oversight, supervision, and regulation. Derivatives would require more supervision, and the Federal Reserve, Treasury, and FDIC needed to exercise more active surveillance, especially against institutions "too big to fail." The Commodity Futures Trading Commission (CFTC) seemed likely to play a role, too (at least with respect to derivatives).

The end result of the efforts by Congress and the Administration to improve oversight of financial services was the July 2010 enactment of the Dodd-Frank Act, a massive piece of reform legislation. The act, which would take years to implement fully, was intended to improve supervision and prevent any future "too-big-to-fail" financial crisis; to create a new structure for supervision and control of large and "systemically significant" non-banking financial institutions; and to create an effective consumer protection regime at the federal level.

The principal features of the Dodd-Frank Act are as follows. The act transferred the functions and responsibilities of the OTS to the OCC, except for authority over savings and loan holding companies and affiliate transactions, which it transferred to the Federal Reserve. The transfer was effective July 21, 2011, and the OTS and its director were to be abolished 90 days after that effective date.

The act established the FSOC, with responsibility to identify systemic risks, to promote market discipline, and to respond to emerging threats to the

U.S. financial system. The Dodd-Frank Act made the Federal Reserve responsible for supervising any non-banking financial institutions identified by the FSOC as systemically significant. (This is in addition to the traditional authority of the Federal Reserve over bank holding companies.) The act also created FDIC authority to supervise the resolution of any financial crisis—or "orderly liquidation"—with respect to any systemically significant financial company. (This is distinct from FDIC authority over insured depository institutions.)

The Dodd-Frank Act established the Consumer Financial Protection Bureau (CFPB) within the Federal Reserve to create and enforce effective consumer protection principles with respect to financial services. The act also repudiated the broad preemption of state consumer protection law that resulted from the Supreme Court's 2007 decision in *Watters v. Wachovia Bank, N.A.*, 550 U.S. 1 (2007). However, the act still allows for substantial federal preemption over many areas of financial services regulation.

The Dodd-Frank Act restricts, but does not eliminate, proprietary securities trading by banks. For these purposes, "proprietary trading" is defined to mean:

> engaging as a principal for the trading account of the banking entity or nonbank financial company supervised by the [Fed] in any transaction to purchase or sell, or otherwise acquire or dispose of, any security, any derivative, any contract of sale of a commodity

> for future delivery, any option on any such security, derivative, or contract, or any other security or financial instrument that the appropriate Federal banking agencies, the Securities and Exchange Commission, and the Commodity Futures Trading Commission may, by rule . . . determine.

12 U.S.C. § 1851(h)(4). Establishing implementing regulations was a long and painful process for the regulators, but in December 2013, final rules were agreed upon among them. These rules prohibit proprietary trading, but with substantial exceptions. Among other things, banks are permitted to make "risk-mitigating hedges," to offset market risks. Second, banks may still trade on behalf of customers. Third, banks may continue as market makers in government-issued debt securities, including municipal bonds and foreign government bonds (through their foreign affiliates).

Trading on behalf of customers appears to be a significant loophole. The rule allows trading when "[t]he amount and type of the securities in [a bank's] trading desk's underwriting position are designed not to exceed the *reasonably expected* near term demand of clients, customers, or counterparties, [and *r*]*easonable efforts* are made to sell or otherwise reduce the underwriting position within a *reasonable period*, taking into account the liquidity, maturity, and depth of the market for the relevant type of security." 12 C.F.R. § 44.4(a)(2)(ii)(A)–(B) (emphasis added). This may be almost unenforceable. Take one practical example. Traders who make bets for the bank's own gain often work alongside traders who serve customers. As a result, it may be extremely difficult for examiners to decipher which trades are for clients and which are not. Even if we assume that you could segregate the proprietary traders from the customer traders, a bank could still build up significant inventory in any security on the judgment that this was in anticipation of "reasonably expected" customer demand. How would examiners test that? How near-term is "near term demand"?

The Dodd-Frank Act imposes new mortgage lending standards, including new requirements for real estate appraiser independence in consumer credit transactions secured by the consumer's principal dwelling. As early as October 2010, the Federal Reserve had already issued an interim final rule implementing appraiser independence standards.

The Dodd-Frank Act imposes new standards with respect to securitization of pools of financial instruments—one of the drivers of the 2008 collapse of the capital markets in the United States—for all market participants, not just banks. Among other things, the new standards require some degree of "risk retention," *i.e.*, requiring a loan originator or securitizer to retain some exposure to the credit risk of the underlying assets.

The Dodd-Frank Act enhances the enforcement powers of the SEC, including whistleblower protection provisions. The act also requires hedge fund and private equity fund advisers to register with the SEC and subjects them to SEC inspection and examination. Likewise, the act imposes disclosure requirements on credit rating agencies (CRAs), and requires their registration with and supervision by the SEC. (It also expands the availability of private rights of action against CRAs.)

The Dodd-Frank Act provides for comprehensive regulation of swaps and security-based swaps by the Commodity Futures Trading Commission (CFTC) and the SEC, in consultation with the Federal Reserve. The SEC and the CFTC have joint responsibility for swap products, to be allocated between the two agencies based on whether the product underlying the swap transaction is a "security" or not. Institutions deemed to be swap dealers—typically, large banks that make markets in swaps by creating and selling them—as well as "major swap participants" are required to register with either the SEC or CFTC, depending on the nature of their products.

D. BANK SUPERVISION AND PREVENTING FAILURE

The tradition of bank examination and supervision in the United States goes back to the 19th Century. More successful bank supervision and examination efforts followed in the wake of New Deal reforms and the creation of the FDIC in 1933. Comprehensive reporting responsibilities have been established, including regular "call reports" or reports of financial condition and income (on a quarterly basis, although some schedules of information are filed annually for smaller banks and savings associations, and quarterly for very large banks and savings associations), and regular examinations (annually for most banks and savings associations, and every 18 months for relatively small, well-capitalized and well-managed banks and savings associations). Special reports and examinations are imposed by the banking authorities for "problem banks," and almost continuous monitoring for banks facing imminent or likely failure. Because of this supervision regime, made increasingly easy, in some respects, by electronic data processing and computer techniques, most bank failures can be detected early enough to allow a possible absorption merger, and often in time to allow corrective remedies that eliminate the financial vulnerability of troubled banks.

Under the interagency Uniform Financial Institutions Rating System (first formalized in 1978) six elements are emphasized: (i) Capital adequacy; (ii) Asset quality; (iii) Management ability; (iv) Earnings performance; (v) Liquidity, and (vi) Sensitivity to market risk (hence the acronym "CAMELS"). Banks are rated in terms of each element on a scale of 1 through 5. The highest rating of 1 applies to a bank considered sound in almost every respect. A rating of 2 reflects fundamental soundness that may have modest, correctable weaknesses. The three lower categories involve descending levels of "problem banks." A rating of 3 shows a combination of weaknesses, moderately severe to unsatisfactory, and only nominally resistant to adverse business conditions. A rating of 4 represents an immoderate volume of asset weakness (usually a "soft" loan portfolio, with too large a proportion of "substandard", "doubtful" or "loss" loans), or a less than satisfactory combination of other elements, with a potential for failure (though not pronounced). A rating of 5 involves an immediate or near-term likelihood of failure, with urgent action and constant supervisory attention essential. In terms of previously articulated standards, a rating of 3 reflects a "problem bank", a rating of 4 a "serious problem" bank, and a rating of 5 a "likely failure" with probable FDIC deposit payoff (unless an assumption of deposits could be worked out with acquisition partners).

Banks rated 3 normally provoke some special surveillance and may invite corrective initiatives. Banks rated 4 require stricter supervision, and more urgent remedies if they are feasible. Banks with a 5 rating might be saved in some circumstances with drastic remedies, but failure is likely, and the regulators ordinarily canvass merger or assumption partners at the same time emergency corrective actions are reviewed.

Realize that legal "insolvency" is not required for corrective action, or even a forced merger transaction, if the regulatory authorities (and any court involved) find that a bank is likely to fail. (Liquidity insolvency arises when a bank cannot meet current obligations, including deposit withdrawals, with liquid assets and cash. Balance sheet insolvency arises when liabilities exceed assets, or net capital sinks below zero.) Even though regulatory agencies must justify a need for drastic intervention, *i.e.*, a forced merger or a closure and receivership, reviewing courts face great difficulty in opposing their recommendations when a bank is facing imminent failure. A run on the bank is likely in these circumstances, if not already in progress, with a drastic decline in deposits, the danger of liquidity insolvency, a further decline in net capital, and probable balance sheet insolvency. Thus, the modern tradition of bank regulation normally involves intervention before legal insolvency, with corrective remedies, forced merger or even closure and receivership, in order to prevent the larger losses to depositors associated with a "completed" run and actual insolvency.

Typical problems in troubled banks arise from taking undue risks in lending or borrowing activity; lax supervision of department managers by top officers and/or directors; unduly concentrated lending portfolios without enough diversification; losses from changing interest rates; bad luck in foreign exchange or international operations (caused by insufficient care to minimize risks); overly aggressive growth and profit maximizing strategies that involve excessive risk; self-dealing transactions or loans to friends, relations, or businesses owned by bank insiders; embezzlement, theft or fraudulent misappropriation of funds; even losses on bad checks, wire transfers, endorsements or guarantees. The strength of banks is power over spending, investments and business growth potential. Their vulnerability stems from losses or misuse of funds, whether through external forces, serious errors, negligence, selfish and irresponsible greed, or dishonest diversion of bank funds to illegitimate or unsound purposes.

Corrective options available to the regulatory authorities include: (i) expanding the capital available, through bringing in additional investors, levies on existing shareholders, or, conceivably, capital loans or assistance from the FDIC or Federal Reserve; (ii) changes in management practices, including tougher loan standards, avoiding areas of loan investment that have been unsuccessful or risky, reduced borrowing risks, along with cutbacks on growth, personnel, branching or other overhead expenses; (iii) suspension or removal of key management personnel, officers and directors, even when they might be substantial stockholders in the bank. Such actions may be difficult to impose upon a stubborn management, especially when the latter might lose community standing or economic advantages, or fear stockholder suits for "recognized" mismanagement. Loan portfolios may not be improved quickly, particularly when "doubtful" loan investments are involved—that may need extended rescheduling to improve prospects of eventual repayment. Errors in management policies may be identified with considerable precision afterwards, but turning them around may take some time. For these reasons, generally speaking, the FDIC avoids loan assistance to an existing bad management, and normally confines its capital loans to new management or an absorbing bank in a bailout merger situation. Federal Reserve discount borrowing, and even emergency loans are the more normal source of financial aid for a troubled bank management's effort to save itself. But Federal Reserve lending will cease to be available when community confidence has eroded, and the regulators believe a run on the bank is impending or has begun. Even if a management might still turn things around by changing its policies, when depositor confidence has been undermined, the best solution may be a new management and an absorption merger (or a closure and liquidation).

Legal authority for preventing bank failure is strongly established among the regulatory agencies, although good teamwork is needed for rapid combined effort. The most important leverage came in 1933 from FDIC authority to terminate insurance coverage, the threat of which could force substantial concessions from a bank management in serious trouble. Most modern banks could not sustain depositor confidence without FDIC membership, and its sudden loss probably would precipitate a run of panicked depositors. (Removal from Federal Reserve membership would have comparable effects now, and normally leads to loss of FDIC insurance coverage.) Charter revocation by the OCC or state authorities had been available earlier, but was hard to employ with enough speed or discretion in troubled bank cases. Much stronger justification and court action was needed earlier for charter revocation, whereas FDIC insurance coverage is an administrative determination that can be made more informally and discreetly. Preliminary action by the FDIC frequently took the form of a proposed order to show cause why insurance should be terminated, sent confidentially to the troubled bank's management, which normally provoked negotiations to correct malpractices. The bank's management would fear public disclosure and embarrassment, a possible run, or suits by minority shareholders for breach of fiduciary duty for having caused the bank's difficulties. This gave the FDIC and other supervising agencies powerful leverage.

Financial assistance could be provided, as a possible sweetener for corrective action, but the Federal Reserve is the main source of credit (as explained previously). The FDIC, having limited reserves for assistance compared to the Federal Reserve Banks, largely confines itself to assisting absorption mergers with loan guarantees and capital loans to the bank or banks that assume a failing bank's deposits.

The Financial Institutions Supervisory Act of 1966 strengthened federal regulatory authority by adding intermediate and less drastic remedies, *i.e.*, the issuance of cease and desist orders and the suspension or removal of officers, directors, or other key figures in a bank organization. This allowed more explicit intervention to correct unsound bank practices before a bank's situation had become too serious. The Financial Institutions Regulatory and Rate Control Act of 1978 (FIRA) extended these powers to bank holding companies, their non-bank subsidiaries, and Edge Act corporations, and it provided more supervision for inter-bank stock ownership holdings. Cease and desist order authority was broadened to cover individuals along with banks, and civil money penalties were added to the corrective remedy authority.

Cease and desist order proceedings may now involve a temporary stay or injunctive effect upon bank conduct and management until a formal hearing. To set aside such "freeze" action, a bank's management must go into federal district court and get a judge to intervene on its behalf. The regulatory authorities have broad authority and discretion to stop activities likely to cause insolvency, dissipation of assets or earnings, weaken a bank, or seriously prejudice the interest of depositors.[10] This reflects the logic of preventing bank failure and runs, *i.e.*, the need for speed, discretion, and powerful sanctions against a bank management's possible flight with the bank's liquid assets, and the imperatives for maintaining community and depositor confidence.

Bank management may fear *ex parte* action and sudden constraints on its behavior. But a soundly managed bank with adequate capital, quality assets, healthy earnings and reasonable liquidity has no cause for alarm. The banks that worry about corrective intervention are those with soft assets, or weakened capital or earnings, or illiquidity. For

---

[10] The FIRREA of 1989 and the FDIC Improvement Act of 1991 further strengthened the authority, corrective remedies, restitution for fraud, civil and criminal penalties available to bank regulators in protecting the safety and soundness of insured banks and other depository institutions, The Dodd-Frank Act of 2010 DFA established new supervision and controls over large and "systemically significant" financial institutions, including non-bank financial institutions, and created broader and more coordinated consumer financial protection mechanisms at the federal level.

weaker banks, public policy since the Great Depression has placed a priority upon protecting depositors, preventing runs and failure, and sustaining public confidence in the banking system in the communities involved. Bank management, therefore, is held to a special standard of quasi-trusteeship or fiduciary responsibility that goes beyond normal business leadership, because it is the peculiar role of banks (and similar deposit institutions) to receive and maintain deposits of the people and businesses in their area. Special profit opportunities and prestige are associated with playing the role of banker. Accordingly, the law and regulatory practice governing United States banks properly imposes a high standard of care in discharging this trust safely and prudently.

Successful collaboration among the OCC, FDIC, Federal Reserve, and the state banking departments or commissioners has developed over the last 80 years. Overlapping jurisdiction of two chartering authorities (OCC or the states), a separate insurance agency (FDIC), and the central bank and lender of last resort (the Federal Reserve) may seem complex, and it could have become cumbersome and unworkable. Fortunately, these agencies have worked well together. In fact, their overlapping mesh has been an advantage in limiting the risks of corrupt or irresponsible bank regulation. Because two or three different regulatory agencies may have access to the call reports, bank examination data, and other related information, it is more difficult for the staff or leadership in these agencies to be bribed or influenced by bank management, or their political friends. Improved integrity can be a by-product of multiple responsibility for bank supervision. This should be kept in mind when considering proposals to consolidate or "simplify" regulatory authority.

For the most part, bank supervision in the United States has been successful since the Great Depression. Hopefully, this record will continue. Concerns have been voiced, however, in recent years. Some critics have complained of relaxed bank and thrift supervision in the early–mid-1980s, especially with regard to weakened capitalization, aggressive growth, and risky lending policies for many institutions. Since 1,500 banks and 1,000 thrifts failed between 1981 and 1992, many believe weaker supervision played a role, but other factors contributed as well. As interest rate ceilings on deposits were removed, increased rivalry brought pressure on margins. Eroded boundaries and interpenetration of markets added risks. Interest rate rises in the late 1970s, and volatility on into the 1980s, brought more risks for many financial institutions. Still another influence was a slowed industrial economy, with less manufacturing at home, which encouraged lending in other areas. Because of profits for financial dealmakers (including some banks), it became fashionable for many corporations to carry greater debt, leading to over-leveraging and strains thereafter for both borrowers and creditors. Tax policies fostered commercial real estate investment and sheltering, particularly after the Economic Recovery Tax Act of 1981 (ERTA), but then cut back heavily on real estate investment incentives in the Tax Reform Act of 1986 (TRA), as loopholes were sharply reduced. These rules have been frequently refined and amended in subsequent tax legislation.

An overriding problem in the 1980s was the impact of deflationary pressures that followed the excessive inflation trend of the 1970s. Sustained tight money policies, and elevated interest rates, were needed to erode inflationary expectations in the 1980s. Unfortunately, this increased borrowing costs throughout much of the economy. Many corporations, farmers, and real estate projects took on more debt service than they could really afford, which weakened loan asset quality for banks and thrifts in many areas.

From another direction, complaints from some free market enthusiasts question the need for FDIC insurance, wondering whether sound banks are actually subsidizing the more adventurous institutions. According to this reasoning, there is a potential vulnerability to banking because the FDIC and Federal Reserve are taking away the "normal and natural" risk of bank failure. Thus, higher risk and dangerous loan practices may be encouraged, leading to reduced capitalization (or declining net capital as a percentage of total assets and liabilities). A logical response to this criticism is that bank regulators need not allow such malpractices to spread. However, the idea of completely eliminating FDIC insurance, or relying solely upon private insurance, lost ground badly after widespread bank failures in the later 1980s and early 1990s.

Instead, a strong consensus developed for risk related insurance premium charges by the FDIC for deposit insurance protection. In principle, it makes sense to charge "sound" banks less for FDIC insurance than "unsound" banks. Whether or not the bank regulators can make such distinctions publicly, however, without damaging the reputations and deposit business of banks involved is a practical question. Nevertheless, in 1989 FIRREA mandated serious study of risk-related deposit insurance premiums, and the FDIC Improvement Act of 1991 now requires the agency to implement them. Risk-based assessments can be related to capital levels, the mix of bank assets, activities, foreign deposits, and the structure of rates and maturities for assets and deposits. In addition, the FDIC is required to bring bank insurance reserves back up to 1.25 percent of aggregate insured deposits (over a 15-year period).

Another important controversy surrounds the phenomenon that some of the largest banks seem "too big to fail." Strictly speaking, however, this is not exactly bank regulatory policy. When larger banks become insolvent, their leadership and top managers are typically removed, and their shareholders are largely (if not totally) wiped out in a FDIC assisted recapitalization for a rejuvenated bank (like Continental Illinois in 1984), or in the more common "purchase and assumption" (P & A) deal.[11] Only if the

[11] In a P & A transaction, a failing bank has its deposit obligations assumed and its "clean assets" purchased by a larger, healthy, and properly capitalized bank (or banks). The assuming bank normally pays a modest "goodwill" premium to the FDIC,

assumed bank is *not quite* insolvent would the failing bank shareholders receive something after all other creditors are paid (including subordinated debt or holders of hybrid securities that serve a capital function). If the assumed failing bank was more or less insolvent (*i.e.*, with negative capitalization), then all its capital ownership would be wiped out, and the FDIC suffers net losses in the process of collecting on the bad assets.

In the normal P & A transaction (or the rare FDIC assisted recapitalization of a very large institution), *all* depositors are typically protected—the uninsured depositors (currently over $250,000) as well as the insured depositors. Why? This result minimizes the disruptive effects on local, regional, or national commerce (depending on the institution's size), and bank runs are prevented. By contrast, allowing *uninsured* depositors to suffer substantial losses would make commercial banking relationships more nervous, insecure, and weaken substantially the attractiveness of U.S. banks in competition for world deposits and international borrowing. Private depositors would find it hard to monitor bank managements efficiently because relevant information is closely held and hard to acquire.[12] But this means that the largest banks or institutions *do*

---

appropriate to the customers and branches involved. The "unclean" assets, *i.e.*, bad or questionable loans, normally remain with the FDIC, which collects on them as receiver to the extent possible (salvage value).

[12] Some scholars suggest the desirability of partial losses or "haircuts" for uninsured deposits, but there has been little support in Congress, banking, or industry generally.

need a P & A or recapitalization when they fail or become insolvent, in order to minimize disruptive impacts on commerce and losses to uninsured depositors. On the other hand, small institutions usually have no sizeable volume of uninsured deposits, so that a simple closure and payoff is often feasible and appropriate for the FDIC (although some discrimination against smaller institutions results). Thus, small banks should be prudent.

Heavy losses were in fact suffered by the FSLIC (and the FDIC) in the late 1980s, mainly due to a failure to enforce timely corrective actions and/or "resolutions" (*i.e.*, P & As, closure and payoff, or the rare assisted recapitalization for a very large institution). Because of this experience, Congress in the FDIC Improvement Act of 1991 tried to prevent any reoccurrences: (1) Stronger capitalization, earlier intervention, and "critical capital level" requirements are designed to minimize excessive forbearance; and (2) Least cost resolution is now required, which means *earlier* P & As or closures and payoffs (*before* significant insolvencies). Losses to *uninsured* depositors are allowed (if this is the least cost solution). However, under narrow circumstances of "systemic risk," *i.e.*, involving the largest institutions, banking regulators can protect *all* uninsured depositors, provided, however, that special assessments against total assets held by banks (*including overseas deposits*) are levied to pay these extra costs. In this way, presumably, Congress tried to restrict "too big to fail" relief to the very largest banks, and for that infrequent relief *special assessments* against total banking system assets (including overseas deposits) should share the premium insurance burden.

Finally, the overall success of modern U.S. bank supervision raises an important question in another direction. Could bank-like supervision and examination routines be extended more generally to cover insurance companies, securities firms, mutual funds, and pension fund fiduciaries?[13] Certainly electronic data processing and computer techniques have enlarged the potential for accountability quite substantially. The Securities and Exchange Commission already enforces extensive disclosure of financial data for publicly held companies. Other financial information, together with production, shipments, sales, and profits data for corporate performance is regularly collected. It is published in summary tabulations, with confidential treatment for most individual company reports. More information is collected and tabulated by the Internal Revenue Service from confidential tax returns, with limited summaries published as statistical data. An enormous amount of additional data is regularly generated by business in the normal course of operations, much of which might be standardized with more uniform accounting, records, and reporting disciplines.

It should be understood, however, that broader accountability for corporate enterprises outside the

---

[13] Actually, substantially improved capital requirements have been developed in recent years by the National Association of Insurance Commissioners (NAIC). See Chapter VI, *infra*. But more could be done with supervision.

financial institutions sector might be more difficult, with much greater divergencies in capitalization, investment planning, production and sales operations, research and development, management strategies, overhead, financing, insurance, and even tax avoidance among firms in so many different industries. More uniformity might be imposed than exists now, but greatly varied patterns remain unavoidable. Aside from the public utilities sector, which already tries to achieve some uniformity in their accounts, such as for railroads, power companies, etc., we see only modest government accounting efforts along these lines. More might be attempted over the years. This could happen with a Presidential administration that favored a more active supervisory role for international investments, and/or stronger accountability for corporate pensions, profit-sharing, and employee stock ownership plans (ESOPs). Problems in 2007–2009 suggested a need for stronger surveillance, but it was not until the enactment of the Dodd-Frank Act in 2010 that problems of corporate governance were significantly addressed.[14] In this regard, the act gave particular attention to executive compensation practices. It requires publicly traded companies (*i.e.*, those registered pursuant to the Securities Exchange Act of 1934) to permit their shareholders to have a nonbinding vote, at least once every three years, on executive compensation. The act also requires any person soliciting proxies in favor of a merger or other

---

[14] The principal features of the Dodd-Frank Act applicable to financial institutions are discussed at pages 126–130, *supra*.

acquisition to disclose any "golden parachute"[15] compensation agreement or understanding in favor of departing executives in connection with the merger or acquisition.

E. SPECIFIC LIMITATIONS ON BANKING ACTIVITIES

In addition to general banking market supervision, there are important special limitations placed on bank operations. Four major goals are reflected in these specific limitations: (i) Sound banking, reliable financial institutions, and reduced risk of irresponsibility; (ii) Competition, efficiency, and decentralization within financial and capital markets; (iii) Fairness for depositors, borrowers, and other customers of banks and financial institutions; and (iv) Adequate flows of credit to business, industry, housing and consumer markets.

1. LENDING LIMITS

The main purpose of lending limits is to enforce diversification of loan account risks, and to prevent banks from putting too many depositor eggs into any one basket of loan investments. For national banks, the most general limitation is 12 U.S.C.A. § 84, which

---

[15] The term "golden parachute" is characterized by the act as "any type of compensation (whether present, deferred, or contingent) that is based on or otherwise relates to the acquisition, merger, consolidation, sale, or other disposition of all or substantially all of the assets of the issuer and the aggregate total of all such compensation that may (and the conditions upon which it may) be paid or become payable to or on behalf of such executive officer." 15 U.S.C. § 78n–1(b)(1).

provided for many years that total obligations or loans extended on behalf of any person, co-partnership, association, or corporation shall not exceed an amount equal to 10 percent of the bank's unimpaired capital stock and surplus. Relating maximum permissible loans for any one person to a percentage of total capital and surplus is actually artificial line-drawing in two distinct ways. First, if you ask, "Why 10 percent," the only real answer is "Why not?" If we are using the lending limit to ensure diversification of lending risks, any reasonable benchmark would do. Second, there is no direct relationship between a bank's capital and its loans. Because loans are usually funded not from the bank's capital, but from its *deposits*, which are liabilities of the bank, the bank actually *creates* new assets—the loans—out of its deposit liabilities.

Since the capital stock and surplus accounts of a bank normally represent about 6–7 percent of total assets, this meant that an amount equal to no more than .6 or .7 percent of a national bank's assets could be invested in any single loan account relationship. However, the Depository Institutions Act of 1982 significantly increased this lending limit to 15 percent of capital and surplus for unsecured loans, and an additional 10 percent for loans fully secured by readily marketable collateral. This means now that a national bank may loan, roughly, an amount equal to as much as 1.5–1.8 percent of its total assets to any of its biggest customers, provided that at least 40 percent of these loans are secured by readily marketable collateral. But diversification discipline is still maintained, and courts have enforced strict

Section 84 liability upon officers and directors for knowing violation of this rule without need for proof of negligence. Thus, bank management is held accountable for compliance with the lending limits.

Until 2010, the "loans and extensions of credit" covered by these lending limitations did not necessarily include a bank's credit exposure as a result of derivative transactions, security repurchase agreements, reverse repurchase agreements, or securities lending or borrowing transactions between the bank and its customers. This loophole greatly increased the credit risks for banks during the overheated trading that preceded the market failures of 2007–2009. Section 84 was amended in July 2010 to change the definition of "loans and extensions of credit" to include these securities-related transactions. As a result, a bank's total credit risk to each customer is more effectively limited by section 84.

This general limit of Section 84 is subject to some further exceptions, based upon the reliability, strength of collateral, and liquidity of the loan obligations involved. But for most ordinary loan accounts, Section 84 limits the extent to which loans can be made to any particular customer. These lending limits force smaller and medium-sized banks to partner with other banks in "participation loans" for large loans that exceed their lending limit, and even the bigger banks are forced into multi-bank loan participations for their largest corporate or international customers.

Another restriction on national banks applied to real estate loans. Generally, 12 U.S.C.A. § 371 required that the bank's total first mortgage loans on real estate should not exceed an amount equal to the total of capital stock and surplus, or time and savings deposits, whichever might be larger. This explicit restriction was replaced in the Depositary Institutions Act of 1982 by general regulatory authority of the Comptroller of the Currency. These regulations were relaxed to allow more competition by banks against savings institutions with respect to real estate mortgage lending.

State chartered banks (including those which are members of the Federal Reserve) must comply with comparable state lending limits laws, but the specific limits and details vary from state to state.

2. BANK AFFILIATE TRANSACTIONS

Transactions between affiliated banks and related companies may bring possible advantages of mutual support, cost saving and convenience, but they also involve dangers of financial abuse and threats to the integrity of banking. Such transactions were regulated by the Banking Act of 1933 for member banks, with amended regulation extended to all FDIC insured banks in 1966. These "firewall" restrictions have been alleviated in part, and strengthened in other respects, by the Banking Affiliates Act of 1982 (a portion of the Depositary Institutions Act of 1982), and further strengthened by the Dodd-Frank Act with statutory changes that did not become effective until July 2012.

As amended, this legislation, 12 U.S.C.A. §§ 371c and 371c–1 imposes two major disciplines, *i.e.*, quantitative limitations and collateral requirements. In general, banks are not allowed to loan an amount equal to more than 10 percent of their capital stock and surplus to any single affiliate, and not more than an amount equal to 20 percent of their capital stock and surplus to the aggregate of all affiliates. The required collateral used to be stocks, bonds, debentures, or other commercial paper eligible for purchase by the Federal Reserve. Now a broader list of debt instruments is allowed, including receivables, leases, real and personal property, but with appropriate increases in value for collateral. Thus, the required collateral value for receivables is 120 percent of the loan, and for real and personal property 130 percent of the loan. This liberalization facilitates bank loans to mortgage, finance, leasing, and factoring company affiliates, by allowing more realistic collateral to be employed. However, low quality assets such as substandard, doubtful or loss loan obligations are not acceptable collateral.

As a further safeguard, the 1982 amendments required that all bank transactions with affiliates be on terms and conditions that are consistent with safe and sound banking practices. This allows a second line of defense against adverse transactions with affiliates, consistent with prior regulatory policies. More recently, for bank holding companies that became seriously troubled, federal banking regulators implemented tougher requirements and guarantees among holding company "family members" (parent companies and affiliates), *i.e.*, the so-called "source of strength" doctrine. See 12 C.F.R. § 225.4(a)(1). This can be interpreted as an obligation to use their combined capital to assist a troubled unit, and thus to save the FDIC from undue losses as far as possible. The FDIC has gone further in some assistance cases, where cross-guarantee obligations were imposed on BHCs and affiliates as a precondition for receiving "open bank assistance", *i.e.*, an assisted recapitalization.

This problem of inter-affiliate responsibilities and mutual vulnerability is also known as the "firewalls controversy." When bank holding companies are connected to corporate interests outside of banking, additional difficulties arise. Frequently banks were abused or endangered by holding company leaders who issued excess loans or loan guarantees in favor of corporate affiliates from the holding company group. The C. Arnholt Smith real estate enterprises were a classic example of this in the failure of U.S. National Bank of San Diego in 1973, one of the largest bank failures before the later 1980s. Another recent example of holding company abuses was the collapse of Bank of Commerce and Credit International (BCCI). These experiences suggest that as financial holding companies become more extensive and international, greater "firewalls" supervision by the Federal Reserve and other central banks will be required. This seems to be a clear lesson of the 2007–2009 financial crisis, but it was not until the enactment of the Dodd-Frank Act in 2010 that these problems were significantly addressed.[16] Among other things, the act included credit exposures such as securities borrowing or lending transactions and derivative transactions as inter-affiliate transactions that would be covered by these statutory rules.

3. INSIDER LENDING

Insider lending and "sweetheart" loans are subject to special restrictions and reporting requirements, which were strengthened by the Financial Institutions Regulatory and Interest Rate Control Act of 1978 (FIRA) and expanded by the Dodd-Frank Act to include credit exposures such as securities borrowing or lending transactions and derivative transactions among the kinds of "extensions of credit" covered by these statutory restrictions and requirements. Federal Reserve Board regulations implement these requirements. Insider lending transactions have been a common reflection of mismanagement, and often the source of bank failures. Consequently, no bank (whether national or FDIC insured), can make loans to executive officers, directors, affiliates, or to stockholders owning more than 10 percent of voting stock, unless such loans are on substantially equal terms to those granted outsiders. Board of directors approval also is required within the bank for such loans when the amounts are significant.

Originally, there were specific limitations on the amounts allowed for certain loans categories, *e.g.*,

---

[16] The principal features of the Dodd-Frank Act applicable to financial institutions are discussed at pages 128–130, *supra*.

home mortgage loans, education loans, and in other loans. Because of inflation, however, these specific limits became unrealistic, and the Depositary Institutions Act of 1982 repealed them, and simply replaced the loan limitations with a grant of regulatory authority to set appropriate limits.

Federal law also prohibits any preferential lending by Federal Reserve member banks to officers, directors, attorneys, or employees. 12 U.S.C.A. § 376. This provision had been added to the Federal Reserve Act in 1918.

4. BORROWING LIMITS

Originally, every national bank was prohibited from borrowing funds, becoming indebted, or becoming in any way liable beyond the level of its paid-in capital stock, together with the total of all its deposits and banknote circulation. This provision was designed to minimize the risk of excessive borrowing, and to enforce balance sheet solvency upon national banks. It was codified as 12 U.S.C.A. § 82. Further exceptions were added for liabilities to the Federal Reserve Banks, the Federal Deposit Insurance Corporation, and Reconstruction Finance Corporation, allowing "lender of last resort" borrowing beyond this level. A further liberalization followed in 1959, which permitted additional borrowing up to the level of 50 percent of a national bank's unimpaired surplus.

However, the Depositary Institutions Act of 1982 repealed 12 U.S.C.A. § 82. In an explanatory bulletin, the Comptroller of the Currency stated: "This deregulatory action places more responsibility on bank chief executives for sound asset and liability management. As the variety and volume of non-deposit liabilities increase, the job of maintaining net interest margins and adequate liquidity will become more difficult and complex. As always, bank asset and liability management policies and practices will be closely scrutinized by national bank examiners." However, these policies and practices have not always been as "closely scrutinized" as perhaps they should be. Historically, inadequate scrutiny has frequently been a contributing factor in a banking crisis, as it was in the case of the 2008 subprime mortgage crisis.

Obviously, the interest rates payable to depositors (a liability of banks) are a cost of funds somewhat equivalent to "borrowing" in the narrower sense of earlier banking law. Between 1933 and 1980, excessive deposit interest payments were prevented under Regulation Q. But between 1983 and 1990 some institutions, particularly the more aggressive S & Ls, were paying more for deposits than was prudent (especially those dependent on deposit brokers). Accordingly, the FDIC Improvement Act of 1991 has restricted above-market interest payments through deposit brokers, by greatly limiting this practice for undercapitalized institutions.

5. BRIBERY, FRAUD, AND EXTORTION

Criminal penalties are imposed on any person who corruptly gives, offers, or promises anything of value to any person, with the intent to influence or reward an officer, director, employee, agent, or attorney of a *financial institution* in connection with any business or transaction of such institution. (18 U.S.C.A. § 215(a)(1).) Likewise, it is a crime for an officer, director, employee, agent, or attorney of a financial institution to corruptly solicit or demand, or accept or agree to accept, anything of value with the intent of being influenced or rewarded as to any business or transaction of the institution. (18 U.S.C.A. § 215(a)(2).) The offer of such inducements is likewise unlawful with respect to Federal Reserve banks. (18 U.S.C.A. § 214.) In addition, criminal penalties apply to any officer, director, or employee of a financial institution who makes or grants a loan or gratuity to any examiner or assistant examiner with authority to examine such an institution or its affiliates.[17] (18 U.S.C.A. § 212(a).)

FIRREA of 1989 greatly increased the maximum penalties for false bank reports, entries, and unauthorized transactions by bank officers, directors, agents, or employees (18 U.S.C.A. § 1005) from $5,000 and/or 5 years imprisonment to $1,000,000 and/or 20 years imprisonment. FIRREA also created a new bank fraud crime (18 U.S.C.A. § 1344) with penalties of up to $1,000,000 and/or 20 years imprisonment. Subsequent amendments in 1990 increased maximum sentences to 30 years for both crimes.

---

17 For these purposes, the term *financial institution* "does not include a credit union, a Federal Reserve Bank, a Federal home loan bank, or a depository institution holding company." 18 U.S.C.A. § 212(c)(3).

Extortionate credit transactions are prohibited (18 U.S.C.A. § 892), with extortion defined as involving the threat of "violence or other criminal means to cause harm to the person, reputation, or property of any person." (18 U.S.C.A. § 891(6).) Knowing participation in any such transaction, or the collection of such debts, justifies imprisonment of up to 20 years, and/or substantial fines.

Whoever knowingly makes false statements or reports to obtain loans, extensions of loans, discounts, or release of security is criminally liable for imprisonment of up to 30 years, or up to $1,000,000 in fines. (18 U.S.C.A. § 1014.)

For the most part, the offenses discussed above all involve "public fraud"—deception or corruption of public officials or public processes. Banks and bank officials and employees are also subject to generally applicable rules and prohibitions against fraud and misrepresentation. A prominent example of this sort of problem is the LIBOR scandal that was brought to light in 2012.

In international banking, the LIBOR—the London Interbank Offered Rate—was a benchmark figure (like the "prime rate" in U.S. banking) that reflected the average interest rate being charged to the best, most credit-worthy customers. It was calculated on the basis of interest rate data submitted periodically by major banks in London to the British Bankers Association. It could be used in a loan or other extension of credit to indicate the market rate to be used in an agreement, where the parties wanted to adopt a rate that was adjusted over time to market conditions. So, for example, if a bank made a five-year loan to a good, but not necessarily the best, customer, it might negotiate for a contract term that required the interest rate charged to be adjusted each year to a rate equal to "LIBOR plus two percentage points."

In the LIBOR scandal, the LIBOR was manipulated by major lending banks to produce false benchmark rates for the pricing of loans and other extensions of credit. News reports uncovered the fact that banks were inflating or deflating rates actually charged in order to profit from subsequent transactions based on the benchmark, or to create the false impression that they were more creditworthy than they actually were. Since LIBOR was a key pricing mechanism for trillions of dollars' worth of trading in derivatives worldwide, the scandal that erupted from this news was considerable. The immediate result was a series of criminal and regulatory investigations both in the United Kingdom and in the United States, since the manipulation of LIBOR was also a manipulation of prices for derivatives publicly traded in U.S. markets. (This also affected pricing of any mortgages, student loans, financial derivatives, and other financial products that relied directly or indirectly on the LIBOR as a benchmark rate.)

By June 2012 there were already multiple criminal settlements by Barclays Bank—alleged to be a major participant in the manipulation—and a push for direct regulation of the LIBOR. As a result of U.K. legislation, the LIBOR became subject to government oversight, and it is now a crime knowingly or deliberately to make false or misleading statements relating to benchmarking. LIBOR and similar industry-set rates began to be disfavored, and many nations, including the United States, participated in negotiations to discontinue the use of such rates as benchmark reference rates and to replace them with alternative reference rates, predominantly overnight, nearly risk-free reference rates.

In October 2022, Congress enacted the Adjustable Interest Rate (LIBOR) Act,[18] which established a uniform process, on a nationwide basis, for replacing LIBOR in existing contracts that do not provide for the use of a clearly defined or practicable replacement benchmark rate, without affecting the ability of parties to use any appropriate benchmark rate in new contracts. The act has been implemented in Federal Reserve regulations, and other agency regulations.

6. SECURITIES MARKETING AND COMMERCIAL BANKING

The stock market Crash of 1929 led to a legal separation in 1933 of commercial banking from investment banking, securities marketing, and stock and bond trading. In previous years, some large New York banks had securities affiliates that were major underwriters of new securities issues and helped market stocks and bonds on a large scale. Similar

---

[18] Pub. L. No. 117–103 (March 15, 2022), 136 Stat 49, 825–834 (codified at 12 U.S.C. §§ 5801 note, 5801–5807, 15 U.S.C. § 77ppp(b), 20 U.S.C. § 1087–1).

links among regional banks and securities firms were permitted, but were less significant outside the Wall Street money market center. Most commercial banks only got involved in securities through holding part of their liquid assets this way (mostly high-grade bonds or preferred "blue chip" stocks), and in the management of trust account securities for many customers. But with the Crash and its tragic losses, a factor in restoring confidence in "commercial" banks was to insulate them from the securities business.

The whole experience left people suspicious of securities, brokers, and underwriters. Some commercial banks, including leaders on Wall Street, were accused of "dumping" less successful issues of securities, and even portions of their own securities with declining prices, into the trust accounts of unfortunate customers. Such transactions reflected conflicting interests, and often involved banks' breach of their fiduciary duties as trustees. In this context, it is understandable that the emergency banking legislation of 1933 should separate commercial banking from the securities business and underwriting activity.

Sections 16, 20, 21 and 32 of the Banking Act of 1933 (popularly known as the Glass-Steagall Act, for its principal sponsors) became known as the Glass-Steagall wall, because they prevented banks from underwriting, selling, or distributing securities, while securities firms and brokerage organizations were prohibited from receiving deposits like commercial banks. (*See* 12 U.S.C.A. §§ 24, 78, 377,

378(a), and §§ 221 and 335.) Thus, commercial banks and investment banks were prevented generally from entering each other's territory.

Throughout the 1980s, however, the Glass Steagall Wall was criticized as outmoded. Traditional bank loan business to bigger corporations was declining. Big companies increasingly issued commercial paper (notes) to the public, rather than getting loans from banks. This led larger banks into securities marketing loopholes, so that their loan business could be recovered. Banks were allowed to underwrite and deal in government obligations (federal, state, and local subdivisions), provided the full faith and credit of the issuer supported them. Many types of state and local revenue bonds could be underwritten by banks. On the other hand, banks were excluded from marketing mutual funds until the mid-1980s, under *Investment Co. Institute v. Camp,* 401 U.S. 617 (1971). For many years only a limited opportunity for combined trust accounts, and closed end investment company sponsorship was allowed to commercial banks, along with investment advisor roles for bank affiliates. But since the mid-1980s increasingly extensive securities transactions for individual customers were allowed to banks by banking regulators.

Money market mutual funds (MMMFs) grew rapidly in the late 1970s, at a time when savings institutions and commercial banks sought to keep Regulation Q limits on passbook deposit rates low. But large denomination certificates of deposit were issued by banks and large savings institutions at higher rates to corporate and institutional investors. Specialized mutual funds began to invest in highly liquid portfolios of such jumbo CD deposit accounts, along with Eurocurrency bank deposits and some corporate commercial paper. Limited check writing privileges were added by MMMFs to encourage money market accounts, and initial deposit requirements were reduced to broaden their appeal for the public. Ultimately, cash management accounts (CMAs) evolved from these MMMFs, which are close to commercial bank checking accounts in many respects.

The Depositary Institutions Act of 1982 allowed banks and savings institutions (but not credit unions) to respond with new money market accounts at comparable interest rates. Under regulations implementing the 1982 legislation, "money market deposit accounts" insured by the FDIC (or FSLIC) may be established by banks (and savings institutions) with the following characteristics: (i) initial deposits of $2500; (ii) average balance requirements of $2500; (iii) no minimum maturity or holding period; (iv) at least seven days' notice for withdrawals; (v) no interest rate ceilings on deposits that meet initial and average balance requirements; and (vii) availability to all depositors. Without the external rivalry from the securities brokerage industry and MMMFs, it is doubtful that banks (and savings institutions) would have increased interest paid to depositors, and their cost of funds from depositor accounts, to the same extent.

Another big break by banks into securities marketing occurred in 1982–1984 with Bank of America's acquisition of Charles Schwab & Co., the leading discount brokerage operation. When regulators and the courts approved, it opened the door for many large banks to offer similar services (by contractual relationship or otherwise). Bank lobbyists sought further securities powers, with emphasis on the underwriting of commercial paper, mortgage-backed securities, and revenue bonds, along with the marketing of mutual funds. Some large banks demanded full repeal of Glass-Steagall, but much of the securities industry challenged the need for that much change.

Although Congress refused for 15 years to repeal completely the Glass-Steagall Wall (despite lobbying pressure from many large banks, and the Reagan, Bush, and Clinton administrations), major erosion occurred between 1987 and 1996 with respect to the larger BHCs. In a series of regulatory decisions by the Federal Reserve Board and the OCC, many large banks were allowed to underwrite commercial paper, securitized mortgage-backed instruments, and even many corporate bonds and stocks, along with lending to support private placements of securities. However, most of this underwriting was carried on in affiliates where the new activities were not a large part of their business (so as to not violate a prohibition against being "principally engaged" in underwriting corporate securities). Moreover, overseas underwriting by big U.S. banks was already exempt, and had become a large loophole since the 1970s. Some of the biggest U.S. banks (*e.g.*, Citicorp,

Morgan, and Banker's Trust) had already become serious players in U.S. domestic underwriting by 1989, and they were even stronger abroad. Some large regional banks also sought underwriting access, but most smaller banks could never play an appreciable role in underwriting. Congress again refused to enact general underwriting authority for most BHCs in 1991, although the Bush administration proposed to authorize financial conglomerate holding companies that would participate in banking, insurance, and securities.

Some favored broad holding companies (along the lines of German-style "universal banking"), but resistance was still substantial. Many insisted that stronger "firewalls" supervision—like Section 23(A) and (B) of the Federal Reserve Act, would be needed as a safeguard measure in the event that broad financial service holding companies would be authorized by Congress.[19] Those opposing Glass-Steagall repeal believed that firewalls were inherently difficult to maintain and supervise, especially for troubled institutions that could borrow heavily from their subsidiaries, and leave disproportionate losses for the FDIC, SIPC, PBGC, and/or insurance guaranty insolvency funds.

Finally, the Gramm-Leach-Bliley Financial Services Modernization Act of 1999 resolved the

---

[19] In 1996 the Fed raised the limit on bank securities activities to 25 percent of revenue in their securities affiliates from 10 percent previously allowed. Only 23 U.S. and 15 foreign BHCs used such "Section 20 affiliates" by mid-1996. By 2003, 630 FHCs had been established; 57 of these FHCs were dealing or underwriting in securities.

conflict by allowing new Financial Holding Companies (FHCs). But FHCs are confined mainly to banking, securities, or insurance activities. A limited exemption for other commercial activities was allowed mainly as a transition rule to ease hardships. The central theme of Gramm-Leach-Bliley is to continue separate regulation for FHCs of banks by banking regulators, of most securities by the SEC, and of insurance by the state insurance departments and commissioners. However, the loophole already established for bank affiliate subsidiaries (Section 20 affiliates) was widened to 45 percent of parent bank assets, or $50 billion, whichever is smaller. In this way banks with Section 20 affiliates are given broader leeway and are not compelled to transform themselves into Financial Holding Companies (FHCs).

Unfortunately, major financial losses occurred in 2007–2009 that impacted some of the world's large investment and commercial banks, along with securitized lending, collateralized debt obligations, and many types of derivatives. Excessive leveraging and insufficient supervision have been problems. Some experts proposed that Glass-Steagall separations should be re-established, but an eventual political compromise in the enactment of the Dodd-Frank Act[20] limited the response to the restriction, not the elimination, of proprietary securities trading by banks.

---

[20] For discussion of the restriction—known as the "Volcker Rule," for former Federal Reserve Chairman Paul Volcker, who pushed for the restriction—see pages 127–129, *supra*.

7. TRUST ACCOUNTS AND DEPARTMENTS

Trust accounts have been important for bank deposits and as a vehicle for securities investment since the late 19th Century. State banks and trust companies (often consolidated into a bank, but with many independent trust companies) took the lead. National banks joined in this activity after the Federal Reserve Act of 1913 authorized them under Federal Reserve Board regulations first promulgated in 1915. Early regulations required separation of each trust account and its securities. But since the later 1920s common or "pooled" trust accounts also had become widely used for smaller trusts and fiduciary accounts, provided that settlors, testators, and others with appropriate powers have specified this treatment and signed the correct forms.

For many years, the Federal Reserve supervised national bank trust account activity under Regulation F, but in 1962 Congress transferred this authority to the Comptroller of the Currency (OCC). The current law and OCC regulations allow national banks as much latitude for fiduciary activities as enjoyed by state banks and trust companies. Bank trustees must keep their fiduciary records separate from all other records, with full information for each account (including any pending litigation). Annual audits of the trust department are required. Investments must be in accord with the instrument establishing the fiduciary relationship and state law. Self-dealing by the bank, its directors, officers, or employees generally is prohibited, except as it might be allowed under state law. Trust account investments must be kept separate from other banks assets, and responsible trust officers must be adequately bonded. The bank may charge reasonable compensation for services as allowed by local law.

Under this fiduciary authority commercial banks hold a considerable part of the assets they manage. Thus, commercial bank organizations are among the sizeable institutional investors in the securities markets. Bank trust departments compete with pension funds, insurance companies, mutual funds and other investment companies as institutional investors and securities traders. (In fact, many banks act as trustees for pension funds, along with other fiduciary accounts.) In this role, however, commercial banks are not underwriting or marketing securities as are the brokerage firms. The Glass-Steagall Act was drawn carefully to separate bank trust department activities from the securities marketing and investment banking business. (For more on this distinction, see the preceding section on Securities Marketing and Commercial Banking, and Chapter V, Securities Market Regulation, especially Investment Companies and Mutual Funds.)

8. REGULATION OF INTEREST ON DEPOSIT ACCOUNTS

Control of interest rates on deposit accounts entered banking law in the 1930s. Its goal was to limit "excessive" competition among banks, and was implemented by the Federal Reserve Board's Regulation Q. But between 1933 and 1965 Regulation Q ceilings were set either above or closely aligned with market rates of interest. Therefore, little "disintermediation" pressure was evident, *i.e.*, there was no appreciable outflow of savings and time deposits into other forms of investment activity.

Disintermediation problems developed in the later 1960s, 1973–1974, and most significantly, between 1978 and 1982. In these three periods, and especially the last, the gap between higher market rates of interest and the lower deposit rates on most forms of smaller bank accounts (and thrift institutions deposits since 1966, when Regulation Q was extended to them) was so large, that major shifts in consumer deposit activity occurred, benefiting particularly the new money market mutual funds.

Rates under Regulation Q had been gradually raised during the later 1950s, 1960s and 1970s, but not enough recently to keep pace with market interest rates. Thus, protection against "excessive" bank and savings institution interest rates to depositors became, in more recent years, an unsuccessful attempt to hold down the cost of funds for these institutions, and thereby "slow" the rising tide of increased interest rates.

This Regulation Q policy was abandoned in the DIDMCA of 1980, with the phased elimination of interest rate ceilings by March 31, 1986. This gradual phase-out was accelerated by the Depositary Institutions Act of October 15, 1982, which mandated higher interest rate "money market accounts," and speeded up the expiration of differentials favoring thrift institutions to January 1, 1984. Thus, money market accounts have narrowed the interest rate gap between MMMFs, on the one hand, and bank or savings institutions accounts on the other. (However, a gap remains in many areas.)

9. PROHIBITION OF INTEREST ON DEMAND DEPOSITS

Banks generally set interest rates on deposit accounts to meet competition and attract funds. This sometimes worked out so that interest would be paid on larger checking accounts, and interest normally was paid on all savings and time deposits. But in the crisis of banking in the Great Depression, many bankers felt interest on checking accounts had been excessive and led to cutthroat competition. Accordingly, the Banking Act of 1933 outlawed interest on demand deposits (checking accounts). This prohibition lasted until 1980, when the DIDMCA allowed nationwide NOW (negotiable order of withdrawal) accounts that paid interest on these demand deposits.

NOW accounts were initiated by mutual savings banks in the early 1970s within Massachusetts and New Hampshire. This started to break the ice on interest rates, and NOW accounts spread to all of New England in 1976, New York in 1978, and New Jersey in 1979. (Rising interest rates and the growth of money market funds also supported this trend.) The DIDMCA extended NOW accounts nationally the following year, and effectively ended the prohibition of interest on demand deposits.

In 1982 the Depositary Institutions Deregulation Committee (DIDC) authorized Super-NOW accounts with more generous interest rates. This brought banking practices back to the pre-1933 era, so that interest might be paid, according to local market competition, on the larger checking and NOW accounts. For smaller checking accounts service charges generally exceed any interest payable, and these customers have to pay for the cost of check writing and maintaining accounts.

10. TRUTH-IN-LENDING

In 1968 Congress required standard form disclosures for almost all types of consumer credit lending, so that citizens could be better informed and, supposedly, could bargain more effectively for fair treatment in credit finance. The Federal Reserve Board developed Regulation Z to specify the details of disclosure. Enforcement by the Federal Trade Commission was provided through administrative remedies, along with private rights of action (with attorney's fees). The Dodd-Frank Act transferred authority to administer federal consumer protection laws, including the Truth in Lending Act (TILA), to the newly created Consumer Financial Protection Bureau (CFPB). In December 2011, the CFPB published interim rules implementing its Regulation Z authority, but without imposing any new substantive obligations on persons subject to the previous Federal Reserve version. A series of further proposals and interim measures followed, until final TILA regulations were published in November 2012 and January 2013.

Although loan shark operators, high pressure sellers, and low-grade finance companies were the principal targets of this consumer protection regulation, it applies also to commercial banks, savings institutions, credit unions, consumer finance companies, and all other sellers of goods and services who extend credit to consumers. Transactions exceeding $25,000 are unregulated, except for purchases of homes, which are now covered by TILA. (The Real Estate Settlement Procedures Act [RESPA] of 1974 applies parallel disclosure requirements to real estate purchases.)

Required disclosures are designed to show interest and finance charges, direct or indirect, in consumer loan, mortgage, or revolving credit account transactions in terms of the annual percentage rate of interest. Credit life insurance charges must be explicitly revealed and accepted by consumers. Exclusions were narrowly defined, and include title examinations and insurance, escrow accounts for future payment of taxes, insurance, water, sewer or land rents, notary fees, and fees for appraisals and credit reports, and not much else. Exclusions from TILA have been expanded to some extent by the Economic Growth Act of 2018, but these are mainly restricted to relatively small and mid-sized financial institutions.[21]

---

[21] For discussion of the Economic Growth Act, see pages 83–85, *supra*.

11. CREDIT CARDS AND ELECTRONIC BANKING

The growth of credit card and debit card use greatly affects financial institutions and banking. It allows speedier, less expensive transactions, with some vulnerability to mistakes and irresponsibility like any other "human" mechanism. Through amendments to TILA, liability of credit card holders has been limited to accepted cards, and no more than $50 of charges before notification that a card was lost or stolen. Billing procedures for credit cards are regulated by the Fair Credit Billing Act of 1974 (FCBA) as amended. Full disclosure of terms, interest rates, and penalties must be provided, along with a 14-day period between mailing of bills and their due dates. In addition, this legislation limits tying arrangements, whereby card issuers might require merchants to maintain deposits with the issuer or subscribe to other services as a condition for participating in the card issuer's payment system.

Debit cards are regulated by the Electronic Funds Transfer Act of 1978 (EFTA), Title XX of FIRA (1978). Cardholder liability is limited to $50 only if a customer notifies the financial institution within 2 business days after learning of the loss or theft of the card or its access code. Liability expands to $500 when more than 2 business days is taken for notification. And if a cardholder should fail to report unauthorized transfers on the monthly statement within 60 days after the statement is mailed, they risk unlimited losses of the entire account (including maximum overdrafts). The act requires notification to customers of card transactions, but more than 60 days delay in response after the statement is mailed may waive rights of objection to erroneous transfers. Debit cards must be accepted by the customer or holder before they become effective to create liability for that person.

12. FAIR CREDIT REPORTING AND PRIVACY

Banks and savings associations have been vital sources of credit information on their depositors and borrowers, which they tend to share with related institutions and potential creditors. The Fair Credit Reporting Act of 1970 (FCRA) gives some protection to an individual injured by obsolete or inaccurate information in reports circulated by credit rating agencies, when access to credit, insurance or employment may be affected. The act does *not* apply, however, to reports used for business, commercial or insurance purposes. The FCRA provides individual access to report information (except investigative sources and medical data), and it creates some rights to replace incomplete or obsolete data with more accurate material, and the right to file brief explanatory statements. Civil actions for actual damages with attorney's fees may be brought when the credit reporting agency is shown to be negligent regarding non-compliance with the Act. This statute tends to make financial institutions more careful in providing credit information, and reinforces, hopefully, a tendency to be reasonably discreet and cautious in these matters.

The Right to Financial Privacy Act of 1978 (Title XI of FIRA) generally provides individuals with notice of government agency requests for their bank or financial institution records (within U.S. jurisdiction). Such requests normally require proper subpoenas, summons, or search warrants when relevant to legitimate law enforcement. Individuals seeking to resist such disclosure may oppose them by motions in court or special challenge procedures. Customers may authorize such disclosures by signing written and dated waivers to this effect. However, search warrants may be issued under the Federal Rules of Criminal Procedure to obtain customer account information confidentially, and without the special notice required by this act. (Subsequent disclosure to the individual normally would be required unless a court orders delay in such notification.) Individuals enforcing their rights under this act have access to injunctive relief, where appropriate, along with costs and attorney's fees in the court's discretion.

Some countries, notably Switzerland, have gone further with customer account privacy for banking institutions. Swiss customary practice on bank privacy were strengthened in 1934 by special legislation responding to Nazi Germany's brutal methods of investigation, with respect to refugees, or people suspected of flight or removal of assets. Under present Swiss law violations of bank secrecy are a serious criminal offense, and this applies to anyone inducing such breach of secrecy as well as the bank officials involved. Only in situations of criminal misconduct or conspiracy under Swiss law (normally held not to include tax avoidance) would Swiss authorities collaborate with foreign governments in obtaining bank account information. This means that Swiss bankers, who normally enjoy strong reputations for financial integrity, accept accounts created, in part, to avoid taxes or exchange controls in other countries. These practices are controversial in countries suffering significant capital flight, but Switzerland firmly insists upon its traditions of respect for the rights of refugees and foreign investors.

However, in 1998, Switzerland enacted a law requiring expanded reporting of suspicious transactions to include not only banks but also asset managers, lawyers, insurers, credit card companies and foreign exchange bureaus. The reports have resulted in the blocking of accounts by the Swiss Government while investigations of money laundering proceeded. More recently, under pressure from other jurisdictions, Swiss authorities have been more cooperative with foreign investigative efforts, particularly in tax enforcement cases. Furthermore, in 2018 the Swiss Supreme Court ruled that a Swiss bank executive located in an offshore office did not break Swiss secrecy rules, because they did not have extraterritorial effect.

Nevertheless, many other nations have tried to emulate Swiss bank secrecy practices (including numbered accounts that restrict knowledge of owners to a few bank officials.) With the recent changes in Swiss bank secrecy laws, these other jurisdictions may now have greater importance in attracting foreign accounts.

13. DISCRIMINATION IN CREDIT

Traditional banking practices have allocated credit according to the strength of collateral, earnings, and risk of default, with interest rates and fees reflecting these differentials and some bargaining between borrowers and lenders. The greatest protection for borrowers has been active competition among lenders, which helps ensure adequate alternatives in bargaining for loans and interest rates. Hence, the antitrust laws, bank merger and holding company legislation, and other regulations limiting excessive concentration play an important role in preventing unreasonable discrimination or exploitation with respect to terms and conditions of credit.

In addition, however, recent federal law prohibits discrimination in granting credit with respect to sex, marital status, race, color, religion, national origin, age (provided the applicant has the capacity to contract), receipt of public assistance benefits, or exercise of rights under some consumer credit laws. An important law on discrimination is the Equal Credit Opportunity Act of 1975 (ECOA), implemented by Regulation B of the Federal Reserve Board, 12 C.F.R. pt. 202, as well as Regulation B of the Consumer Financial Protection Bureau (CFPB), 12 C.F.R. pt. 1002. A major purpose of the original legislation was improved access to credit for women, married and unmarried, and those involved in matrimonial litigation, divorce, or separation proceedings. Amendments have extended ECOA scope to include other forms of discrimination.

Anti-redlining legislation is another effort of recent years to suppress discriminatory practices in credit transactions. Redlining is the systematic refusal to extend home mortgage loans by banks and savings institutions in certain areas, usually run-down neighborhoods with significant levels of poverty, and largely inhabited by low-income minorities or changing in that direction. The term "redlining" refers to the actual marking of real estate maps by financial institutions to exclude such areas from consideration. More subtle forms of discrimination involve less favorable terms, higher interest rates, greater difficulty in approval, and perhaps, the shifting of deposit funds from "bad" neighborhoods to more promising areas and suburban tract housing through loan allocations. Redlining activity can be an aspect of urban decay, reflecting blight, and to some degree tending to reinforce it.

An important law on redlining and discrimination was the Home Mortgage Disclosure Act (HMDA) of 1975, followed by the Community Reinvestment Act (CRA) of 1977. The HMDA required depository institutions with assets of $10 million or more in standard metropolitan statistical areas to disclose their mortgage loans and maintain records for 5 years so that "redlining" patterns could be identified. Under the Economic Growth Act, some HMDA requirements no longer apply to certain fixed mortgages (so-called "closed-end mortgage loans") or open-end lines of credit undertaken by an insured depository institution or insured credit union that does not normally handle a significant amount of this kind of lending. (The act speaks of fewer than 500 closed-end mortgage loans or 500 closed-end lines of credit in each of the two preceding calendar years.)

The Community Reinvestment Act (and other related legislation) provides a rather general mandate to the federal financial regulatory agencies to investigate and discourage discriminatory practices. Policies implemented by these agencies have led to banks and savings institutions making extra efforts to solicit loans in minority neighborhoods, and the location of branches so that all sections of a city can be effectively served. Between 1993–1996 the Clinton administration tried to strengthen CRA enforcement with tougher regulations and supervision, including limits on merger and expansion activity by institutions lacking good compliance records. But complaints erupted over paperwork burdens and ambiguous mandates. Most large BHCs with extensive branching accepted "some" responsibilities in this direction, but smaller and niche market institutions wanted relaxed obligations, insisting that serious inequities and disproportionate burdens affected them. Meanwhile, exemptions for mortgage and finance companies were particularly controversial.

14. CONSUMER FINANCIAL PROTECTION

Prior to the financial crisis that arose in 2008, consumer financial protection was in an anomalous state. Though many would view this as an area of typical state-law concern, federal preemption was often invoked against the application of state consumer protection laws to federally regulated depository institutions or their affiliates. Indeed, prior to the crisis, the Comptroller and the OTS each adopted broad preemptive policies against such laws. The problem, however, in the view of many critics was that federal regulators did not develop and enforce strong and effective consumer protection policies of their own.

This situation eventually led to the Supreme Court's 5–3 decision in *Watters v. Wachovia Bank, N.A.* in April 2007, holding that the mortgage business of a national bank conducted by a non-banking operating subsidiary of the bank was subject to the exclusive (and preemptive) supervisory jurisdiction of the OCC, and not to the licensing, reporting, and visitorial authority of any state in which the subsidiary operated. Preemption of the state law regime was required because of the "unduly burdensome and duplicative" nature of the state regulation.

This broadened preemption policy created serious tension with respect to the effectiveness of *state* consumer protection policies. If national banks and their operating subsidiaries were significant participants in a state's financial services market, not only was application of the state's policy rendered less effective; application of the state policy to state-chartered institutions also became an inequitable competitive burden on those state institutions. This consequence arguably could lead to the elimination of the state policy, or migration of state institutions to federal charters.

In the year following the decision in *Watters*, the mortgage market in the United States collapsed as a result of abusive and deceptive practices winked at by the federal regulators. By 2009, in *Cuomo v. Clearing House Ass'n, L.L.C.*, the Supreme Court held that—despite *Watters*—a state had the power to initiate a criminal investigation into the activities of a federal regulated financial services company. What a difference financial collapse makes to legal analysis!

In direct response to this collapse, the Dodd-Frank Act established the CFPB within the Fed to create and enforce effective consumer protection principles with respect to financial services at the federal level, transferring most such authority away from the federal regulators who were oblivious to the growing danger prior to the 2008 collapse. Title X of Dodd-Frank also appears to repudiate the broad preemptive effect of *Watters* and its progeny. The act insulates state consumer protection law from much of the preemptive effect that had otherwise frustrated state consumer protection policy. While the CFPB continues to implement consumer financial protection policies, it has been under continuous attack in litigation, and the Economic Growth Act of 2018 has limited the application of some federal consumer protections to many relatively small or regional financial services firms.

F. CONSTRAINTS UPON BRANCHING, HOLDING COMPANIES AND MERGERS

Banking laws in the United States set constraints on the growth of banks and bank holding companies. The legislation reflects a strong tradition of federalism and decentralized banking. The major policies involve chartering and branching limits, bank holding company restrictions, and merger regulation. As a result, the U.S. banking system still has more banks, about 4,200, than most other countries relative to population. This fosters competition and broadened economic opportunity in American society.

However, U.S. branching, merger, and holding company restrictions have been greatly relaxed over the last 40-plus years. As a result, U.S. banking concentration increased greatly between 1980–2008, which reflected the growth of large and expansionist U.S. multinational and regional banks. Between 1980–2003 the 10 largest U.S. banks grew from 18 to 41 percent of U.S. bank deposits, the top 25 from 29 to 55 percent, and the top 100 from 46 to 72 percent of U.S. bank deposits. By 2008 the top four U.S. bank holding companies held 64 percent of commercial bank assets. This is a massive consolidation. (Concentration is higher if foreign deposits are included.)

In recent years, this area of law—branching, holding companies and mergers—has become controversial. It represents a battleground of conflicting interests among financial institutions. Public policy should encourage healthy competition, efficient savings and investment flows, minimize distortions, foster reasonably decentralized enterprise and social mobility, and prevent undue concentration of economic and political power in the banking and related financial industries. However, increased automation, data processing, and electronic flows of information and funds transfer offer real cost-savings. Economies of integration and scale have become more important, and yet, reasonable access and pricing of new technology for smaller firms still allow considerable decentralized, competitive rivalry to continue. Much will depend on the evolution of law and oversight with respect to branching, holding companies and mergers, along with access, pricing and sharing of automated and EFT systems.

1. BRANCHING LAWS

When the second Bank of the United States (a multi-state branching organization) was terminated in 1836, the states were left as the exclusive chartering authorities for banks. Single-site banks or "unit banking" became the overwhelming pattern in the free banking era that followed. This practice was extended to the new nationally chartered banks shortly after Congress authorized them in 1864, and national banks were prohibited from having any branches. This policy tended to keep most banks relatively small by confining their deposit collecting areas to a single town or city. Only bigger banks in a few major cities, especially New York and its emerging Wall Street money market center, collected substantial deposits over broad areas from large corporations, smaller correspondent banks, and wealthy business interests. As a practical matter, few state banks developed branching networks until around World War I and the 1920s.

The growth of branch banking by state banks in the prosperous 1920s forced a change upon Congress for national banks. For many years, the states divided into roughly three major camps insofar as branching laws were concerned: (i) unit banking, *i.e.*, no branches allowed; (ii) county-wide branching; or (iii) state-wide branching. As branching proliferated for some state banks, the national banks demanded more latitude. The McFadden Act of 1927 gave national banks the same leeway in branching as their state chartered rivals enjoyed under the law of each state. Thus, the problem of branching, with its conflict between urban and rural interests, was resolved separately in each state's legislature (until the Interstate Banking and Branching Efficiency Act of 1994 (Riegle-Neal Act) allowed widespread interstate banking and branching.)[22]

With the rise of electronic funds transfer (EFT) technology in recent years, and particularly automated teller machines (ATMs) that dispense cash, accept deposits, and provide balances to customers, additional questions on branching policy have had to be resolved. Generally, ATM units were considered branches under the McFadden Act, so

---

[22] The Riegle Neal Act followed a widespread trend of state enactments (often with reciprocity requirements) that allowed interstate bank holding company acquisitions into their states (especially in the mid-late 1980s).

that state branching laws regulated the scope for such ATM expansion activities along with the normal "brick and mortar" branch buildings. See, for example, *Independent Bankers Association of America v. Smith*, 534 F.2d 921 (D.C. Cir. 1976). Most states enacted specific compromise legislation that allocated opportunities for ATMs for banks and savings institutions. However, the growing use of debit cards from many different banks (or other institutions) among integrated, multi-institution EFT networks was not considered branching activity under state law. Thus, the law allowed collaborative networks of debit card use that link member institutions even across state lines. But the banks (or other financial institutions) that participated in such networks were allowed ATMs within their market areas only according to each state's branching law (including specific legislation on ATMs).

Meanwhile, however, bank holding companies became increasingly important in the 1970s as a route by which restrictive branching laws were evaded *within* many states, by creating "chains" of separately chartered banks. Although the Bank Holding Company Act of 1956 was intended to curtail the anticompetitive excesses of chain banking, more liberal interpretations by the Supreme Court and Federal Reserve Board in recent years allowed bigger statewide banking chains or holding companies. See, especially, *United States v. Marine Bancorporation*, 418 U.S. 602 (1974). Unless a state enacted separately its own limitation on bank holding company expansion, most large banks faced little difficulty in extending their operations within each state by acquisition of independent banks through the holding company device.

However, for many years (1956–1994), *interstate* "branching" through bank holding companies had been almost entirely prohibited by the "Douglas Amendment" to the Bank Holding Company Act of 1956 (BHCA § 3(d), 12 U.S.C.A. § 1843(d)). This law prevented any approval by the Federal Reserve Board of bank holding company acquisitions in other states, unless the state in which the acquired bank is located explicitly authorized acquisitions by out of state banks. For many years, no state allowed such acquisitions. Aside from a few interstate bank holding companies that were grandfathered under the 1956 Douglas amendment, this meant that bank holding companies had been prevented generally from making bank acquisitions across state lines.

More recently, however, the majority of states have allowed interstate bank holding company acquisitions on a reciprocal basis, and some without reciprocity requirements. Maine was first in 1975, followed later by Alaska and South Dakota. Each of these states wanted to attract new banking capital for development and more jobs. New York enacted such a law in 1982, but its purpose was to facilitate large N.Y. city bank acquisitions in other states. Massachusetts responded the same year with a more restrictive law that allowed reciprocal bank acquisitions only in New England, and prevented "leap-frogging" into Massachusetts through Maine or any other state. The Massachusetts plan was to encourage a New England banking region that limited entry by the big New York banks. Although Citicorp challenged the constitutionality of New England regional interstate banking, the Supreme Court upheld such statutes. *Northeast Bancorp, Inc. v. Board of Governors*, 472 U.S. 159 (1985). Soon afterwards a majority of Southern states enacted at least regional interstate banking, along with a majority of Northeastern, North Central, and Southwestern states. Resisting this trend were many Plains and Mountain states, with strong community and independent bank traditions.

But once most states allowed interstate BHCs to acquire banks within their territories (at least to some extent), the stage was set for the Riegle-Neal Act in 1994. This legislation allowed interstate BHCs to make bank acquisitions in all states after 1996, but states were permitted to set limits on acquisitions of "de novo" banks (less than 5 years old), and to restrict *branching* activity by out-of-state BHCs to a substantial extent. Caps on banking concentration also were specified, but at relatively high levels. Thus, acquisitions of banks were prohibited only if the resulting bank controlled more than 10 percent of all U.S. insured depository institution deposits, or 30 percent or more of such deposits in any state. This law in effect allows a broad consolidation movement for U.S. banking and depository institutions, *i.e.*, through chain banking.

Nonetheless, some kinds of banking activity already were allowed across state lines. Lending had long been a nationwide market for the larger corporate borrowers. Loan production offices were generally permitted throughout the country. And Edge Act subsidiaries were allowed in other states since 1919 to service international banking operations, including loans, investment, export-import finance, and even non-domestic deposit gathering. Nationwide advertising for deposit customers had been considered proper, and is increasingly employed by major multinational banks (including "800" toll free telephone numbers). What remained localized, however, was most ordinary deposit activity and smaller loans to households and regional business enterprises.

The full implications of the Riegle-Neal Act could still become controversial, although not for the reasons initially anticipated by many commentators—namely, the antitrust and federalism concerns implicit in any marked increase in U.S. banking concentration. Significant concentration has become virtually a given in U.S. banking, but its exacerbation of the "too-big-to-fail" phenomenon—the impracticability of managing and resolving major bank failures—was not fully appreciated until the deep crisis that emerged in the period 2007–2009. It remains to be seen whether policymakers and regulators have absorbed the lessons of this crisis and are prepared to act decisively against large concentrated banking enterprises in danger of failure.

2. BANK HOLDING COMPANIES

Under the Bank Holding Company Act of 1956 as amended, the Federal Reserve Board is the principal regulatory authority. Bank holding companies are subject to the Board's jurisdiction, require its approval for their creation, and there is Board supervision for some activities. Bank holding companies (BHCs) are defined as those that "own or control" one or more banks. Ownership or control of 25 percent of the voting shares is enough for this purpose, and somewhat less if the Board finds a controlling influence is exercised. A presumption of no control operates if the BHC owns less than 5 percent. Federal Reserve Board approval is needed: (i) to become a BHC; (ii) for a bank to become a subsidiary of a BHC; (iii) for a BHC to acquire more than 5 percent of the stock in a bank; (iv) for a BHC to acquire the assets of a bank, or (v) for a merger of BHCs. The holding company framework has become extremely popular for larger banks. BHCs already owned most of the commercial bank assets by the late 1980s, and there were more than 6,000 BHCs.[23] This left only a fringe of mostly smaller banks that were independent of BHCs. Hence, supervision of BHCs governs the great bulk of banking resources in the country.

The principal criteria for Board review of BHC transactions are convenience and needs of the public, financial condition, management resources of the BHC and its subsidiaries, and anti-competitive effects that might flow from BHC activities.

---

[23] In contrast, when the BHCA of 1956 was enacted, there were only 47 registered BHCs with 7.6 percent of the nation's bank deposits. By 2001 6,318 BHCs held 94 percent of all bank assets. In 2003 there were 630 Financial Holding Companies (FHCs), most of which had grown out of BHCs.

Generally healthy capitalization and sound management are preconditions for BHC expansion and growth. The convenience and needs of the public normally tends to be served by broader BHC activities with strong finances and good management. But when BHCs become too large, they may inhibit competition, or restrain trade in financial or other markets. Such anticompetitive consequences have led to constraints upon BHC expansion.

The major legislative limits on growth of BHCs applied to diversification and merger activity, but some historical background is needed to understand the development of these limits. The original Bank Holding Company Act of 1956 was designed to limit chain banking (networks with more than one bank), to restrict indirect branching activity (especially across state lines), and to prevent excessive concentration in banking through holding companies. Left open was an opportunity for "one-bank" holding companies to diversify into nearby financial activities, or perhaps other industries.

Merger limitations developed first, with the Bank Merger Act of 1960, the Supreme Court's decision in *United States v. Philadelphia National Bank*, 374 U.S. 321 (1963), and the Bank Merger Act of 1966 (discussed in the next section.) As these constraints upon bank merger expansion developed, they tended to channel large bank growth and merger aspirations into diversification (or international banking). Major horizontal mergers among sizeable banks within the same cities became unlawful, and substantial chain banking networks between different cities were limited, too.

Meanwhile, increasing prosperity in the 1960s and a "Bull Market" for stock price appreciation made bank leaders (and stockholders) more eager for growth and diversification prospects. In 1967–1969 there was a surge of bank holding company formation, involving a large proportion of the bigger banks in the country, comprising one third of the nation's commercial bank deposits. This was part of a tide of conglomerate merger activity in the economy as a whole, which peaked in the later 1960s, and resumed in the 1980s and 1990s.

Congress responded with the Bank Holding Company Amendments of 1970, which confined BHCs and their subsidiaries to activities which were "a proper incident to banking or managing or controlling banks." In applying Section 4(c)(8) of the BHCA, as amended, the Board was required to "consider whether . . . performance by an affiliate of a holding company can reasonably be expected to produce benefits to the public, such as greater convenience, increased competition, or gains in efficiency, that outweigh possible adverse effects, such as undue concentration of resources, decreased or unfair competition, conflicts of interest, or unsound banking practices." 12 U.S.C.A. § 1843(c)(8). Under Regulation Y, implementing this provision, the Board allowed the following: the making and servicing of loans, such as by finance, mortgage, factoring, or industrial loan companies; fiduciary and trust account activities; closed-end investment companies; financial and investment advisory services; leasing personal and real property as a financing activity; bookkeeping and data processing services; courier services for banks; check verification and handling services; management consulting for banks; credit card operations; foreign exchange, gold and silver trading; issuing travelers checks; underwriting some federal, state, and local securities; underwriting credit life insurance; and even real estate and business appraisals. The Board allowed securities transactions for the account of customers (and affiliations with discount securities brokers). In the later 1980s, the Federal Reserve and OCC allowed some of the largest BHCs to underwrite commercial paper, securitized mortgage-backed instruments, and even corporate bonds and stocks, so long as these activities were carried on in separate affiliates (see Section D-6. Securities Marketing, supra). Subsequently, banks have been allowed to market mutual funds, and some BHC affiliates are even developing "fleets" of funds. (See Chapter V, infra.) And some banks and BHCs were poised to widely market insurance policies and underwrite insurance, provided that their regulatory and legislative authority could be clarified. But this insurance question was strongly contested by insurance interests from the mid-1980s into the late 1990s; conflict over insurance was a major battleground in Glass-Steagall "reform" efforts.

On the other hand, the Board had excluded, for many years, land development and real estate syndication, real estate brokerage, property management services, management consulting (defined broadly for all kinds of businesses), most ordinary insurance underwriting (not credit life insurance), and travel agencies. Industries threatened by competition from bank holding companies, especially insurance, securities brokerage, mutual funds, savings and loans, etc., fought in Congress, in the courts, and with the Board to keep banks and the banking industry confined to the more traditional roles of bank finance and services,[24] up-dated to allow for automatic data processing and EFT technology.

Finally, in 1999 Congress settled many aspects of a 20-year boundary war among financial industries. The Gramm-Leach-Bliley Financial Services Modernization Act of 1999 provided that financial holding companies (FHCs) could operate in banking,

---

[24] It should be emphasized, however, that the Board had authority (since 1956) to grant exemptions for small bank holding companies:

> (1) to avoid disrupting business relationships that have existed over a long period of years without adversely affecting the banks or communities involved, or
>
> (2) to avoid forced sales of small locally owned banks to purchasers not similarly representative of community interests, or
>
> (3) to allow retention of banks that are so small in relation to the holding company's total interests and so small in relation to the banking market to be served as to minimize the likelihood that the bank's power to grant or deny credit may be influenced by a desire to further the holding company's other interests.

12 U.S.C.A. § 1843(d). These provisions were used recently to allow a considerable number of BHCs to be involved with greater diversification activities, such as insurance or real estate, that had been excluded fields for larger BHCs (and not traditional for banking). But use of this loophole remained controversial.

insurance, and securities markets. By 2003 there were 630 FHCs in the U.S., which controlled 78 percent of BHC assets (supervised by the Federal Reserve Board). Banking activities in bank holding companies are regulated and supervised mainly by the Federal Reserve Board. Insurance activities are regulated largely by the state insurance departments or commissioners. Securities activities are largely regulated by the SEC. Important ambiguities, mutual access to data, and the coordination of oversight must still be worked out in the coming years. The extent to which failures, fraud, money-laundering and other problems occur will have a great impact on this evolving area of financial holding company regulation. Unfortunately, the financial and banking crisis of 2007–2009 showed insufficient supervision of investment banking and various kinds of derivatives and "securitizations." The effectiveness of the legislative responses to these problems included in the Dodd-Frank Act remains untested in practice. These responses include direct regulation and supervision of systemically significant financial institutions by the Financial Stability Oversight Council (FSOC),[25] the Federal Reserve, and the FDIC, and mandatory "stress testing" that requires financial institutions to run simulations reflecting their likely response and resilience in the face of major economic crises.

---

[25] For discussion of the FSOC, see pages 10–106, *supra*.

3. BANK MERGERS

Bank merger regulation has gone through three different stages: (1) *Between* ***1950–1974*** bank mergers were restricted to limit consolidation and preserve the traditional, largely decentralized U.S. banking market structure. Competition among depository institutions was maintained, and even enhanced by growth of savings banks, S & LS, and credit unions. (2) *Between* ***1974–1993*** these limitations on bank growth and mergers were relaxed in a gradual, incremental pattern. But no drastic increases in concentration or reduced competition occurred, even though the numbers of U.S. banks slowly declined over these 20 years from 14,600 to 10,500, savings banks and S & Ls from 5,400 to 2,200, and credit unions from 21,000 to 12,500. (3) *After* ***1994*** there has been more drastic relaxation of bank merger and BHC restrictions, which allowed much larger consolidation mergers, big chains of megabanks, and substantially weaker competition in many regional and local banking markets. By 2008 the number of U.S. banks fell further to 7,300 with only 1,260 savings institutions, and 8,238 credit unions (CUs), and the decline in these numbers has continued to the present. In 2008 the top 4 U.S. BHCs held 64 percent of U.S. bank assets. Current banking and BHC regulation fosters even more consolidation into a limited number, say 15–20 very large bank chains and BHC networks, with most becoming Financial Holding Companies (FHCs), initially authorized under the Bank Holding Company Act in 1999. There remains a fringe of regional and/or state banking chains, and a scattered survival of independent community banks, and savings associations. An extensive range of credit unions still operates, although many CUs are *employer related* and not able to accept depositors from everyone in their communities.

Merger restrictions began in 1950 with the Celler-Kefauver Amendments to Section 7 of the Clayton Act (1914). The original Section 7 outlawed acquisitions of the "stock" of other companies when they "might tend to substantially lessen competition in any line of commerce in any section of the country." Unfortunately, this provision was emasculated at the outset by a blunder in draftsmanship; not covered were acquisitions of the "assets" of companies. This allowed large mergers to be carried out as "asset" acquisitions, *i.e.*, exploiting the "asset" loophole. Considerable merger activity occurred in the 1920s, even a few bank mergers, but the original Section 7 was ineffectual as a limitation. Then the stock market Crash of 1929 and the Great Depression choked off merger activity, but mergers revived substantially in the later 1940s. Fearing a "rising tide of economic concentration," Congress enacted in 1950 an amended Section 7 as a major strengthening of U.S. antitrust policy—to limit large mergers that could substantially lessen competition. New Section 7 governed mergers in most of the economy, although its application to bank mergers was not clear.

In 1956 Congress enacted the Bank Holding Company Act to explicitly limit chain banking and interstate banking activity (see previous sections). The BHCA regulatory standard was twofold—to prevent "substantial lessening of competition," but with "convenience and needs" of the community to be considered as well. This was supplemented by the Bank Merger Act of 1960, which used the same two factor standard—substantial lessening of competition offset by convenience and needs.

In the leading case of *United States v. Philadelphia National Bank*, 374 U.S. 321 (1963), the Supreme Court held that Section 7 Clayton alone governed bank mergers, because "[i]mmunity from the antitrust laws is not lightly implied . . . [T]here is no indication in the legislative history to the 1950 amendment of § 7 that Congress wished to confer a special dispensation upon the banking industry . . ." Id. at 348. With respect to the merits, the Court held that the merger of the second and third largest banks in Philadelphia, comprising 36 percent of bank assets and deposits of the metropolitan area, would have substantial anticompetitive effects. This decision set a strong precedent, and indicated that "anti-competitive effects" were the primary concern in bank mergers.

Yet the Court clearly accepted the need for absorption mergers in failing bank situations, and even suggested in dicta that the "failing company defense" for mergers "might have somewhat larger contours as applied to bank mergers because of the greater public impact of a bank failure as compared with ordinary business failure" *Id.* at 372 n.46.

Congress responded several years later with the Bank Merger Act of 1966. The statute employed the Section 7 Clayton Act standard, *i.e.*, prohibiting *inter alia* any merger "whose effect in any section of the country may be substantially to lessen competition ... unless ... the anticompetitive effects of the proposed transaction are clearly outweighed in the public interest by the probable effect of the transaction in meeting the convenience and needs of the community to be served." 12 U.S.C.A. § 1828(c)(5)(B). These guidelines largely accepted the *Philadelphia National Bank* decision, but allowed convenience and needs to be considered as well.

Procedurally, the BMA of 1966 established the independence of the Justice Department to challenge the legality of a bank merger on anticompetitive grounds in the courts, except that "the standards applied by the court shall be identical with those that the banking agencies are directed to apply." 12 U.S.C.A. § 1828(c)(7)(B). In other words, a Justice Department action *under the antitrust laws* based on the anticompetitive nature of a bank merger would be subject to a convenience and needs defense drawn from *the federal banking laws*.

For some years, the Supreme Court extended the strong policy of *Philadelphia National Bank* and the BMA of 1966 to smaller bank merger combinations. The ultimate development of the rule was illustrated in *United States v. Phillipsburg National Bank & Trust Co.*, 399 U.S. 350 (1970). In this case the relevant market was Easton, Pa.-Phillipsburg, N.J., a twin city area on both sides of the Delaware River (with about 90,000 population.) The merging banks ranked first and second of three banks in Phillipsburg alone with 76 percent of its deposits, and third and fourth of seven banks in the twin cities area with 23.4 percent of combined deposits. The Supreme Court sustained the Justice Department's challenge under the Bank Merger Act of 1966. In the *Phillipsburg National Bank* decision the principle of preventing sizeable market share mergers was applied to relatively small cities.

According to strict Department of Justice Merger Guidelines issued in 1968, applicable to most industries, sizeable horizontal mergers (in the same market area) normally would be challenged under Section 7 of the Clayton Act. In substantially concentrated markets (normal in banking), the Department announced it would ordinarily challenge mergers with any sizeable market shares. (These guidelines were relaxed greatly in 1982–1984.)

Market extension mergers were regulated by branching laws in some states where significant restrictions had been placed on branch activity, *e.g.*, unit banking or county-wide branching. However, in many cases the holding company device represented an important loophole for indirect branching or growth by market extension merger. The BHCA of 1956 required Federal Reserve Board approval for such mergers by holding companies, thus its policies became important in shaping the latitude for market extension acquisitions. And after *Philadelphia National Bank* and the Bank Merger Act of 1966, the antitrust authorities had a role in challenging mergers that might have anticompetitive effects.

The Justice Department sometimes argued that preventing a proposed merger between a bank outside a particular market with a bank inside the market might result in the outside bank to enter the market on its own, thus increasing the number of banks competing in the market. This approach was known as the "potential competition" doctrine. However, in *United States v. Marine Bancorporation, Inc.*, 418 U.S. 602 (1974), the majority rejected this argument and allowed a major market extension merger. In this case, Marine Bancorporation, the second largest bank holding company in the state of Washington, based in Seattle, with 20 percent of all bank deposits statewide and 107 branches, acquired the third largest bank in Spokane with 19 percent of local deposits, 8 local branches and 1.5 percent of statewide deposits. Nonetheless, the courts approved the merger, reasoning that new entry by the acquiring firm was very difficult under this state's law, and consequently, there was little potential competition to be weakened, and that convenience and needs of customers in Spokane would benefit from absorption of the "target" bank into a major state banking organization.

The next major relaxation of bank merger policy was a relaxation of the Department of Justice Merger Guidelines in 1982 and 1984. The most dramatic change in the Merger Guidelines was their redefinition of concentration thresholds in terms of the Herfindahl-Hirschman Index (HHI). The "HHI," or simply the Herfindahl index or "H" (as most industrial organization economists label it), is merely the sum of the squares of each firm's market share in the relevant market. Thus, we define

$$H = \sum_{i=1}^{n} s_i^2$$

where H is the Herfindahl index, s_i is the market share, and i is the range of 1 through n firms in the relevant market. A few illustrations will be helpful:

	"Low" Concentration	"Moderate" Concentration	"High" Concentration
Rank	(1) $15\%^2$=225	(1) $25\%^2$=625	(1) $30\%^2$=900
	(2) $10\%^2$=100	(2) $20\%^2$=400	(2) $25\%^2$=625
	(3) $10\%^2$=100	(3) $15\%^2$=225	(3) $20\%^2$=400
	(4) $10\%^2$=100	(4) $10\%^2$=100	(4) $15\%^2$=225
	(5) $10\%^2$=100	(5) $10\%^2$=100	(5) $5\%^2$=25
	(6) $5\%^2$=25	(6) $5\%^2$=25	(6) $5\%^2$=25
	others [40%] 100	others [15%] 25	others [–] —
Total	s=100 s^2=750	s=100 s^2=1500	s=100 s^2=2200

Because the squares of low market shares are small numbers (*e.g.*, $1\%^2 = 1$, $.5\%^2 = .25$, $.3\%^2 = .09$, $.1\%^2 = .01$, and so forth), the Herfindahl index has the statistical property of diminishing low market shares to relative insignificance. Hence, use of the Herfindahl index, "H", puts overwhelming weight on the market shares of larger firms (*e.g.*, $5\%^2 = 25$; $10\%^2 = 100$; $15\%^2 = 225$; $20\%^2 = 400$; $25\%^2 = 625$; $30\%^2 = 900$; $40\%^2 = 1600$; $60\%^2 = 3600$; $80\%^2 = 6400$; or $100\%^2 = 10,000$).

To compute the changes in "H" or ΔH resulting from mergers, simply add the percentages of each firm together, and square their new share (*e.g.*, if firms (3) and (5) merge, in each column, then, 10% +

10% = 20%^{2} = 400, 15% + 10% = 25%^{2} = 625, and 20% + 5% = 25%^{2} = 625). Then subtract the old shares squared (*e.g.*, 400 - 100 - 100 = ΔH = 200, 625 - 225 - 100 = ΔH = 300, and 625 - 400 - 25 = ΔH = 200) to achieve the ΔH or change in concentration produced by the merger, as measured in terms of the Herfindahl index.

The Department's new standards for evaluating horizontal mergers are framed in terms of the post-merger market concentration or H value, and the increase or change in concentration resulting from the merger or ΔH.

a. Post-Merger H Below 1000

Markets in this range have relatively low to higher concentration, collaboration among firms is not easy, and the Department would not challenge mergers in this region.

b. Post-Merger H Between 1000 and 1800

Markets in this range reflect relatively low to higher concentration, and depending upon the H value, the Department might challenge mergers producing Δ H of more than 100, but is unlikely to challenge mergers yielding ΔH of less than 100. Entry conditions, product differentiation, price-output visibility, past conduct, and historical performance will be taken into account in making this evaluation.

c. Post-Merger H Above 1800

Markets in this range are highly concentrated, and the Department might challenge mergers producing ΔH of more than 100–200.

These new merger Guidelines of 1982–1984 were a significant relaxation of horizontal merger policy. The major loosening involved less concentrated markets, and moderately concentrated markets. In markets with high concentration, sizeable mergers could still be challenged, unless failing companies are involved as the acquired firms. But relevant markets have been defined much more broadly since the Reagan era, so that high concentration occurs infrequently. Typically, commercial lending was used as the "index" for geographic markets more recently, whereas local deposits were the "index" for local market definitions in Philadelphia National Bank (1963) which governed until the early 1980s.

A substantial bank consolidation merger movement got under way by 1982–1983. It featured mergers among larger banks in regional markets (when a bank was willing to sell out), and the buying up of banks in rural-suburban areas to extend BHC chains. The wave of bank, savings bank, and S & L failures of the 1980s–early 1990s also added momentum. Regional interstate banking broadened the scope for merger activity, which was extended to the entire nation by the Riegle-Neal . In 1997–1998 a series of mega-mergers combined some of the largest BHC chains in the United States (*e.g.*, Bank America and NationsBank). Finally, Gramm-Leach-Bliley in 1999 allowed FHCs) to combine banking, insurance, and securities (like the Citicorp-Travelers merger, already approved by banking regulators and Department of Justice in 1998).[26]

How much of this greatly increased consolidation activity is necessary or desirable remains controversial. Supporters argue for wide freedom to merge. Economies of scale or integration might be involved. Fear of computerization drove many to sell out, especially when premium per share gains could be shared by merger partners. Opponents, however, insist that operating efficiencies do not require mega-mergers, and that large regional institutions are big enough to be completely efficient. Consumer groups and small business interests complain that rate competition is reduced in many areas (for both deposits and lending), bank profit margins are fattening, and that service often declines in "1–800 number" banking. Getting competent, reliable attention is often more difficult. In some areas enough banking rivalry remains, including credit unions and MMMFs. But other areas suffer inadequate banking service competition. A complication is that traditional depository institutions seem to have less growth lately and that large banks often place fewer "good" loans—as more big companies raise their capital internally or by issuing commercial paper at low cost through investment bankers. If the pie of commercial banking

---

[26] Many business analysts were questioning already the "profitability" of many mega-financial mergers. Profits often decline, and many mergers failed—despite disruptive layoffs, shedding of personnel, and difficulties of combining different cultures.

is not growing, or even shrinking, some increased consolidation was not surprising. On the other hand, allowing too much banking consolidation hurts consumers and smaller business, by reducing the options available for financial services. In addition, "too big to fail" problems are aggravated, as was shown in the banking and financial crisis of 2007–2009.

By 2007, for example, the top 12 securities firms had 88 percent of the capital owned by Securities Industry Association members (along with 65 percent of SIA member employees). The top 25 mutual funds had 63 percent of all assets under such management. The top 25 life-health insurers had 88 percent of their industry's revenues, and the top 25 property-casualty insurers had 94 percent of that industry's revenues. In the late 1990s the top 25 U.S. banks were increasing their market shares significantly. (Between 1980–2003 the top 25 U.S. banks increased their share of domestic bank deposits from 29 to 55 percent. And the top four BHCs in 2008 held 64 percent of BHC assets.) Now that Gramm-Leach-Bliley in 1999 allowed FHCs across these boundaries, more BankAmerica-NationsBank and Citicorp-Travelers combinations could be expected. How much efficiency, good sense, and wise investment can be expected in giant financial conglomerates? Failures are harder to deal with politically for financial regulators. Oversight is more difficult. The experience of other nations suggests that government bailout and "moral hazard" dangers are substantially increased for mega-financial institutions. If giantism in finance proves burdensome, and with greater risks, losses, and weaker service, how can banking, securities, and insurance regulators turn things around? How can a mandate for more decentralized competition be implemented?

4. EFT ACCESS

There are two basic types of electronic funds transfer. One type has a long historical pedigree, dating back at least to the commercial use of telegraphy. Banks and other intermediaries have long transferred funds—so-called wire transfers—by means of instructions sent to correspondent banks or affiliated firms originally by telegraphic means of communication, but increasingly by other electronic means. These wholesale transactions are still generically referred to as "wire transfers," and they are covered by industry practice and more recently by Article 4A of the UCC.

A second basic type of electronic funds transfer is a product of our digital age, and it is what we commonly refer to as electronic fund transfers (EFTs). Prevalent in the retail and down-market sectors, these transactions are governed by state and federal rules, and they have proliferated dramatically with the rise of debit cards and online banking. They are *not* subject to UCC Article 4A, but are subject to the disclosure and authorization requirements of the Electronic Funds Transfer Act (EFTA), 15 U.S.C. §§ 1693 et seq.

A vital problem for modern EFT technology and its use is the extent to which access, sharing, and pricing should be regulated by law. Digital technology makes broad, interconnected networks available to take over, or at least facilitate, a great deal of what banks and other financial institutions have accomplished in the way of fund transfers and account management.

Access to EFTs has replaced many of the functions that used to be provided by branches. ATM "branching" is now regulated by many state statutes, and interstate and international debit card networks have been implemented as well. The Federal Reserve clearing system has remained an important component of a strong, national grid for checks and EFTs. Partly because of improved computer technology, Congress mandated faster check clearing deadlines in the Expedited Funds Availability Act of 1987 (Title VI of CEBA, 1987), implemented by the Fed and the CFPB.

CHAPTER IV
INTERNATIONAL BANKING

A. INTRODUCTION

Private international banking–sometimes referred to as "multinational" or "transnational" banking–has become more important for larger U.S. banks over the last generation, and the largest international banks have spread globally in their network of deposit, loan, financing, securities transactions, and currency exchange activities. Greater affluence, thriving trade and commerce, foreign investment, and increasing use of multinational channels for tax avoidance, enhanced profits, and in some situations, flight of capital to escape regulation or even possible confiscation, have helped to create a multinational banking system comparable in size to the entire U.S. domestic banking industry. U.S. banks still play an important role in this multinational scene, but by 1995 only about 10 of the 75 largest international banks were based in the United States.[1] This reflected broadened world prosperity, more involvement in external

---

1 By the early 1990s, Japanese and European banks had moved ahead of larger U.S. banks in assets and resources. (They had higher concentration than U.S. banks, and their national economies caught up with American per capita incomes.) In 1970, a third of the world's 500 largest banks were based in the United States; in 1995 only 16.6 percent were U.S.-based. However, by 2023 U.S. banks regained some prominence, with 20 percent of the 25 largest banks being U.S. based, but China had surpassed the United States, with 44 percent of the 25 largest banks China-based. *See* Table IV-1, *infra*.

commerce, and greater concentration in many banking systems. Most major multinational banks have extended branch connections throughout much of the world, including the United States itself in recent years.

From 1996 into 2008, a wave of mega-mergers among U.S. and multinational banks, investment banks, and major insurance companies occurred among leading member nations of the Organization for Economic Cooperation and Development (OECD), including the United States, Europe, and Japan. Following the capital markets collapse of 2008, a tremor of consolidations rippled through the financial services sector, driven mainly by regulatory efforts to contain the ongoing crisis and restore public confidence. By the beginning of 2017, new patterns began to emerge. Currently, the resulting 25 largest global banks are illustrated in Table IV-1, *infra*. Remarkably, in the top 25 banks, none are Swiss-based, and only one is Russian. No Africa-based bank appears in the top 25.

Table IV-1
Global Banks by Tier 1 Capital

Rank 2022*	Bank	Home Country	Tier 1 Capital ($million)
1	Industrial and Commercial Bank of China	China	497

* As of year-end 2022, unless otherwise indicated.

2	China Construction Bank Corporation	China	407
3	Agricultural Bank of China	China	380
4	Bank of China	China	339
5	JP Morgan Chase & Co	US	246
6	Bank of America	US	208
7	Citigroup	US	169
8	Wells Fargo & Co	US	153
9	Bank of Communications	China	145
10	HSBC Holdings	UK	139
11	China Merchants Bank	China	132
12	Postal Savings Bank of China	China	117
13	Credit Agricole Group	France	114
14**	Mitsubishi UFJ Financial Group	Japan	111
15	BNP Paribas	France	110
16	Goldman Sachs	US	109
17	Industrial Bank	China	107
18	Shanghai Pudong Development Bank	China	97
19	China Citic Bank	China	96
20	Banco Santander	Spain	88

** As of 31 March 2023.

21**	Sumitomo Mitsui Financial Group	Japan	87
22	China Minsheng Bank	China	86
23	Sberbank	Russia	79
24	Morgan Stanley	US	77
25	Groupe BPCE	France	74

Although the top 25 banks may naturally draw our attention, it is important to note that multinational banking continues to extend through the next few hundred banks down to "regional banking" by international standards. Many regionals participate, to some degree, in multinational loan agreements, and some have branches abroad, either directly or through consortium banks. And many smaller banks are active in international banking, especially in places like London (although this will be more constrained since Brexit[2] took place), Switzerland, Hong Kong, Singapore, Luxembourg, Lebanon, and the Persian Gulf.

B. U.S. BANKING ABROAD

International banking has a long history of involvement with foreign trade, shipping, and investments. Italian merchant bankers were important in such finance during the Middle Ages

[2] "Brexit" is the process whereby the United Kingdom withdrew from the European Union. Because this results in limited access to the EU banking market by UK-based banking operations, there has been a movement by some international banks out of London as a European base.

and Renaissance, and this banking activity gradually spread north to the Netherlands and German towns. In the early modern period, Dutch, and later British, banking became increasingly prosperous and international. London took a strong lead as an international banking center during the 19th Century, helping to enlarge British trade and industrial development. Britain placed a substantial volume of foreign investment in many countries, including the Americas. And London remains, in some ways, the most sophisticated international banking center today, even though much of the capital collected there is no longer British.[3]

U.S. banking did not begin to flow abroad until early in the 20th Century, especially during World War I and the 1920s. Significant involvement did not begin until after World War II, servicing the needs of American companies that were expanding their activities into the newly established European Economic Communities (EEC), the precursor of the EU, and worldwide. British banking, meanwhile, pioneered in creating Eurodollar accounts that gathered increasing amounts of liquidity to finance multinational business. (The role of the dollar as a preferred reserve currency, with less inflation than most countries between the later 1940s–late 1960s was also influential.) U.K. banking regulations and tax policy encouraged London's revitalization as an international banking center. Subsequent U.S. efforts to restrict "leakage" of capital in the 1960s,

---

[3] Brexit possibly might eclipse London's standing. *See* page 212 & fn. 2, *supra*.

with its interest equalization tax and other measures, actually fostered the retention of earnings abroad by American corporations, in London and elsewhere. As the momentum of Eurobanking developed, similar deposits and lending operations expanded for many clients, corporations, and even governments, drawn from around the world. When the U.S. inflation rate increased as compared to harder currencies, like the Deutschmark and Swiss Franc, in the late 1960s and early 1970s, some accounts shifted into a broader range of "Eurocurrencies" in addition to the dollar.

Then came OPEC and the "petrodollar" recycling of 1974–1980. Oil-rich exporters placed a large volume of their liquid earnings into Eurocurrency deposits. As growth rates readjusted around the world, with some newly industrialized countries (NICs) gaining, especially Japan, Korea, Taiwan, Hong Kong, and Singapore, more Eurocurrency financing spilled into Asian banking centers and tax havens. The yen became a harder currency, and Japan became a significant creditor nation with a more active role in multinational banking. In all this expansion of banking abroad, more corporations, entrepreneurs, and governments placed liquidity deposits in multinational banks for greater freedom, and to obtain maximum earnings. More borrowing needs were financed this way for international business, and even governments in recent years.

U.S. banking law put modest constraints upon this multinational banking development. (See Regulation K of the Federal Reserve Board, 12 C.F.R. pt. 211.)

The Federal Reserve Act, 12 U.S.C. § 601, allows national banks with $1 million capital and surplus to establish branches abroad, under regulations established by the Board. State chartered member banks must obtain Board approval, and, if there are any restrictions in state law, approval at that level, too. (State non-member bank branching abroad is supervised by the FDIC, and, to a modest degree, under state law, but only a small amount of international banking occurs in these banks.) Subsidiaries of U.S. banks abroad can be established under the same patterns of supervision as branches. Although some accountability has been imposed on U.S. international branches and subsidiaries, it is fair to say that properly managed, sound U.S. banks of sufficient size find no difficulty in setting up activities abroad. Under these arrangements, by the late 1980s about 130 U.S. banks had created some 800 branches abroad with at least $300 billion in assets. However, the bulk of these activities were carried on by the largest 15 or so U.S. "multinational" banks.

Another U.S. alternative for international banking is the Edge Act corporation, authorized by 12 U.S.C. § 611 since 1919 as a vehicle through which international banking can be carried on.[4] Edge Act

[4] Note that Edge corporations are incorporated under federal law. Another possibility is an "Agreement corporation" similar to an Edge corporation, but organized under state law by a state member bank and authorized by agreement with the Board to engage in international activities. This authority, 12 U.S.C. §§ 601 (Second), 603, has existed since 1916, but few Agreement corporations exist.

corporations are domestic subsidiaries that confine their activities to international banking, export-import finance, foreign investments, or deposit-gathering abroad for these purposes. Edge Act corporations may have branches and subsidiaries in other countries, and, since 1978, branches in other states. Some Edge corporations emphasize banking; others are basically investment holding companies. The banking Edges (almost 60 of them in the early 1980s) are scattered throughout the United States, but mainly in New York, Chicago, Miami, Houston, San Francisco, and Los Angeles. Investment Edges are mostly subsidiaries of parent BHCs in their home cities. Altogether, by the early 1980s some $14 billion in assets were held by banking Edge corporations, with another $30 billion for investment Edges.

In addition, bank holding companies may invest directly in foreign companies under the BHCA, 12 U.S.C. § 1843(c)(13), subject to Board regulations. However, limitations on transactions and lending among affiliates have somewhat constrained the use of this provision.

Under American law, broadly speaking, somewhat wider latitude for U.S. banks is allowed in their international banking activities than in domestic banking. Because there was no Glass-Steagall "wall"[5] for international banking, U.S. international banks could carry on the underwriting, trading, and marketing of securities abroad. Mutual funds could be managed abroad by U.S. international banks

---

5 On the Glass-Steagall Act and its separation of banking and securities activities, see 160–166.

(provided shares were not sold domestically or to U.S. residents), along with somewhat greater latitude for insurance and business consulting activities.

Of course, U.S. banks operating abroad must conform to the requirements and law of their respective host countries, some of which are more hospitable than others. In its present condition, the multinational banking system has achieved, in many respects, substantial independence from onerous regulation, as a network of transnational enterprises. Fear of moving assets to more hospitable jurisdictions tends to inhibit restrictions that might seriously crimp international banking activities.

Since December 1981, the U.S. innovation of international banking facilities (IBFs), represented an effort to bring home some of these activities. An IBF is a set of asset and liability accounts segregated on the books and records of a U.S. depository institution, U.S. branch or agency of a foreign bank, or an Edge or Agreement corporation that includes only foreign-related time deposits and extensions of credit. The Federal Reserve Board acceded to considerable urging from major banks to allow IBFs in the U.S., so that some of their current offshore activity in shell branches overseas could be switched back to these new enclaves onshore. Under the regulations, an IBF can be set up by a U.S. bank or other depositary institution, an Edge or Agreement corporation, and by foreign banks through their U.S. branches and agencies. IBFs can accept deposits from abroad without being subject to domestic reserve requirements or interest rate regulations. Lending from these IBFs may be extended only to foreign residents or entities, other IBFs, or the parent institution. Minimum transactions, however, for non-bank dealings are $100,000. States can further encourage IBFs within their own borders with special regulations and/or tax subsidies.

The great majority of countries, however, try to confine the enclave of international banking activities in their countries to the sphere of foreign trade, lending, investment and exchange activities. Most nations prevent substantial poaching on the domestic deposit collection business of local banks. But this is not entirely enforceable against corporations and entrepreneurs with large international transactions that can gather and place substantial cash flow outside local channels. In this way, international banking may lead to leakages of liquidity and capital into the world market, beyond what is publicly acknowledged or even desirable for many nations. As governments become insecure, corrupt, or suffer depreciating currencies, these leakages may be encouraged. The modern international banking system may facilitate substantial capital flight. Exchange controls are often used to limit these flows, but they are hard to maintain with complete effectiveness.

C. FOREIGN BANKS IN THE UNITED STATES

British banking played an important role in financing the American colonies, and it helped finance trade and investment after independence.

But as the U.S. economy developed strength, domestic banking became predominant. Foreign banks mainly confined their subsequent activities to financing their own exporters, trading, and selected investments, including securities in railroads and other large corporations. Some of these investments were sold off during World Wars I and II, and a major revival of foreign investment and banking in the United States did not get under way until the 1960s, when Europe and Japan had restored economic prosperity. Gradually, this foreign activity gained impetus, and a substantial presence of foreign banking was established during the 1970s. By 1989 some 300 foreign banks from about 60 countries were operating with offices, branches, or subsidiaries in the United States

Foreign banks have a range of options in the United States that is broader, in some respects, than alternatives U.S. banks enjoy to carry on activities abroad. Representative offices and agencies are the more limited connections that are most widely employed. Investment companies are authorized for foreign banks in some states. Since 1978, Edge Act corporations have been allowed for foreign banks as well as for domestic banks. In addition, many foreign bank branches, subsidiaries, and even foreign-owned U.S. banks have been established, some of which have domestic deposit collection and lending authority comparable to U.S. banks in many states. Until the International Banking Act of 1978, foreign banks also enjoyed a special freedom from restrictions on interstate branching that applied to national banks and BHCs. The proliferation of foreign bank activities finally provoked Congress into eliminating most of these special interstate branching opportunities in the International Banking Act of 1978, under the "national treatment" principle, mandating equal treatment for foreign- and domestic-owned banks. Such a broad principle of parity is not generally granted abroad, especially by countries that fear influence or competition from giant multinational banks based in the United States or other major banking nations.

The IBA created authority for the Comptroller of the Currency to license foreign bank branches or agencies in the United States. For the most part, foreign bank branches are put under "equalized" regulatory discipline, including reserve requirements for domestic U.S. deposits and FDIC insurance. The same applies to restrictions upon U.S. domestic banking activities and diversification, but not, of course, to the foreign bank's operations outside the United States and its territories. Also, the Glass-Steagall Act brought complications for foreign banks in marketing securities with U.S. residents, so they needed to keep their activities segregated into a restricted U.S. domestic market category, and unrestricted operations abroad. U.S. and foreign customers adapted easily by doing business with the most appropriate division of foreign banks in the United States or abroad.

This legal regime allows foreign banks liberal access to many U.S. banking markets. A variety of motivations has prompted considerable investments, subsidiary banks, Edge or Agreement corporations, branches or agencies in the United States by foreign banking interests. Many want stronger multinational banking networks, access to U.S. clientele, and more opportunities for international investment. Access to U.S. EFT technology, banking management and practices has also been useful. When the dollar weakened relative to other currencies, the opportunity for investment and branching activity, broadly speaking, became something of a bargain. Finally, investments in U.S. banking have been a route toward greater safety in an insecure world, when risks in many countries are often alarming. For these various reasons, foreign banks have found it attractive to take part in the U.S. banking market. The major U.S. multinational banks have not opposed this evolution, because it tends to cement stronger links for these institutions in other countries, and very likely, because international branching in the United States helped to erode the barriers to interstate banking.

D. RECENT CONTROVERSIES AND PROBLEMS

In spite of the obvious benefits to multinational banking, trade and investment in many countries, this rapid growth trend has brought uneasiness and controversy about international banking developments. These concerns involve: (i) extensive tax avoidance and encouragement of capital flight from many countries; (ii) thinner capital, liquidity mismatching, and fragility; (iii) excessive (or insufficient) liquidity and possible speculation strains; (iv) undue lending to doubtful countries with political risks; and, (v) lack of limitations on loans to weaker countries, with excessive borrowing and dangers of default. Until the 1980s, these worries were not sufficiently alarming to cause any significant restriction upon the international banking system. But since the early 1980s, widespread distress, reduced export earnings in many debtor nations, and high interest rates (resulting from inflationary momentum and tighter monetary policies) caused a serious rescheduling "crisis" affecting many debtor nations significantly involved in the multinational banking network. This led to a reappraisal of these issues, with some additional regulatory supervision. Among other things, the regulators now have supervisory authority, pursuant to the International Lending Supervision Act of 1983, with respect to U.S. banking exposure to risks of loan defaults. In situations in which long-term nonperformance or default by foreign borrowers is threatened, the regulators may require a bank to establish "allocated transfer risk reserves" to cover the default risk. The systemic crisis that arose in 2008 exacerbated these risks, or at least prolonged their effects.

1. TAX AVOIDANCE AND CAPITAL FLIGHT

Extensive tax avoidance and leakages of private capital have become an awkward problem in many countries. International banking, in its present, highly developed form, with many points of access and tax havens around the world, facilitates these flows. But the incentives to avoid high taxation, onerous regulation, possible confiscation, imprisonment or worse, are reflections of "bad" national policy, demoralization, or lack of social cohesion. The international banking industry disclaims responsibility for these underlying problems and asserts that each country should limit leakages with healthy self-discipline. Governments suffering leakages find this explanation somewhat self-serving, and often lack the administrative capacity to prevent significant tax evasion or capital flight. Unfortunately, this may leave them with unhappy dilemmas—accepting capital flight, reduced business incentives, or drastic nationalization measures that weaken productivity. Only the healthy countries, with sound morale, broad prosperity, lower inflation, and credible, honest government are likely to minimize tax evasion and possible capital flight. However, since the Mexican-Asian crises of 1994 and 1997–1998, provoked by excessive capital inflows and speculation, many now favor precautionary taxes on short-term capital inflows, to limit "hot money" speculation.

2. CAPITAL, LIQUIDITY, AND FRAGILITY

Reserves and net capital held by many international banking operations, even by U.S. multinationals, had become leaner than most domestic U.S. banks by the early 1980s. Competition in international activities is keen, and legal reserve and capital requirements were often less demanding. In international banking, customer confidence for deposits or lending comes from the size, reserves, capital, and reputation of their parent banks at home, and the evident determination of governments to support their financial integrity. Thus, domestic banking regulations and resources actually support international banking, its deposits, lending, and profitability. Most national governments found it necessary to back up their major international banks, or so people generally believe. Where banking systems were substantially nationalized, as in France (during the Mitterrand government) and many other countries, or where central banks or governments subsidize credit (especially for exports), margins in international lending may be artificially reduced. As international banking became more crowded and competitive, and surplus liquidity built up with international trade, a situation of reduced margins with thinner reserves could be somewhat risky. (This led to the development of risk-based capital requirements by ten major banking nations (the Group of Ten), among others, under the auspices of the Bank for International Settlements (BIS) in 1987, the so-called Basel Accord.) Continuing concerns about capital adequacy and recapitalization measures were highlighted again in the global banking and financial crisis that erupted during 2007–2009.

Liquidity mismatching is inevitable for banking activities. Banks take demand, short term, or at least "mobile" liquid resources on deposit, and convert them into loan assets, securities, or other investments earning a sufficient margin to compensate for interest paid to depositors and other operating expenses. With thinner reserves and lower net capital ratios, the tolerance for error in liability-asset management is reduced. Some countries, most notably Switzerland, developed liquidity ratio regulations designed to limit the risks of mismatching maturities to some degree at least. But the more important safeguards seem to be two-fold: (i) floating rate deposit liabilities that move with loan assets using floating rates; and (ii) confidence that national governments and central banks in the major banking nations will stand behind, and support financially, their significant international banks in a crisis situation.

3. LIQUIDITY AND SPECULATION

Deposits and lending in the multinational banking sector have grown at a faster rate since the 1970s than domestic banking for most industrial countries. This led some economists to argue that international banking, with reduced reserves and high-powered monetary expansion, may be contributing to (or at least reflecting) increased international inflation and/or speculation. Others said that increased flows into multinational banking merely reflect special advantages, avoidance of taxation and regulation, OPEC earnings "recycled," and the attraction of greater deposit interest rates in this sector of banking. Also, a substantial part of international banking deposits reflects interbank transactions, not necessarily involving real shifts from domestic into international deposits and lending. Some of those alarmed at this expansion of international bank liquidity urge the application of domestic monetary controls and disciplines to world banking. But this is easier said than done, when a large part of this liquidity prefers the freedom of international banking and can quickly switch to other havens in the multinational basing system. Of more interest for some countries, and more amenable to control, would be the prevention of excessive flows of speculative liquidity into domestic economies. This kind of "sterilization" operation has been feasible in strong banking centers like Switzerland, when they enjoyed good productivity, fiscal and monetary restraint, and lower inflation rates. However, the surge of OECD investments into many emerging markets, especially in 1990–1998 (*e.g.*, Mexico), showed that sterilization was more difficult in developing countries. Many economists cite these experiences, and the lack of sufficient fiscal, monetary, and/or trade-balance discipline in a large number of countries, to conclude that major problems of macro-economic coordination and instability remain unsolved.

Nonetheless, increased concern for inflation, speculation, and other disturbances have led many central banks, including the U.S. Federal Reserve, to develop more careful accounting for deposits, assets, and lending by their respective multinational banks. Detailed estimates are needed for the flows of liquidity into international banking, and the spillover effects upon domestic money markets. This implies fairly close supervision of exchange and interest rate movements, along with the balance of payments, reserves, current accounts, investment flows, and trade balances. Monetary targeting practices should take these subtleties into account, as some central banks (*e.g.*, the Swiss National Bank) already do. It is a misconception to think that monetary developments in major industrial countries (with substantial involvement in multinational banking, investment, and trade) can be understood without appreciating the role of foreign exchange rates, capital flows, lending, investment, and trade. Increased monitoring of multinational banking is unavoidable for these and other purposes.

4. LENDING AND POLITICAL RISK

Excessive loans to doubtful economies with heavy government deficits and monetary stimulus, excessive wage-price inflation, and increased demand for international credit have become a growing concern for many observers. This has provoked an extensive literature of country and political risk assessment for the international banking industry. Informally, major international banks are now setting limits on their lending commitments to specific countries, which have been strengthened as a result of central bank coordination among leading banking and creditor nations (*i.e.*, the United States, Japan, U.K., Switzerland, Germany, etc.) However, capital flows, lending, and trade are difficult to supervise. It has been hard to ban, embargo, or put ceilings on such flows, or to use formalized quotas. Instead, there has been broad support in many nations for gradually increased International Monetary Fund (IMF) quotas and lending support to many debtor nations. Still, problems of supervision and sustaining confidence in the international banking system remain serious difficulties, at least until the world's prosperity is more broadly distributed.

5. LOANS TO WEAKER COUNTRIES AND THE DANGER OF DEFAULT

Gradually, between 1982–1990, the leading banking nations (including the United States, Japan, U.K., West Germany, Switzerland, France, Italy, the Low Countries, and Canada), worked closely with the IMF and the International Bank for Reconstruction and Development (popularly known as the World Bank) to fashion a series of rescheduling agreements for most of the over-loaded debtor nations. Obligations were stretched out over time, with reduced interest rates and fees. Some new lending flowed, especially for short-term trade finance, although net new capital flows were reduced greatly (in some countries even reversed, when capital flight was included). Loans to over-loaded less developed countries (LDCs), especially in Latin America, became less secure, and they were discounted substantially (to the extent a secondary market developed). Large loan loss reserves were created (or provisioned) by the creditor banks, and appreciable losses were gradually recognized from many countries during the 1980s. For large U.S. multinational banks with sizeable assets used for LDC lending (and some other major creditor banks in other countries) this posed a continuing problem for regulatory supervision, central bank support, and IMF-aided rescheduling. But by the mid-1990s, many debt-overload countries had substantially improved their situations, reduced debt service burdens, and restored economic growth. Increased capital was flowing again into many "emerging markets" in the 1990s.

Meanwhile, during the 1980s the multinational banking community was gradually improving its prudential supervision, partly in response to the softness of lending to many LDCs. Under the Basel Concordats I (1975) and II (1983), developed by 10 major banking nations (the Group of Ten) with the Bank for International Settlements (BIS) to coordinate rules for resolving institution failures, central bank collaboration has been improving in other respects. Consolidated supervision was strengthened further between 1983–1987. Parent country responsibilities for their own banks were stressed, and the need for ample lender-of-last resort support. Another important step was the December 1987, twelve-nation agreement (adding Italy and Sweden to the G-10) that harmonized risk-adjusted capital requirements. This was a break-through toward a more level playing field, with greater financial soundness for international banking.

Unfortunately, the Bank of Commerce and Credit International (BCCI) failure in 1991 illustrated a gap in the Basel Concordat support system. BCCI, a major bank that began in Pakistan and became well-established in the Persian Gulf Emirates, was not sufficiently supported by its relevant parent nations. BCCI was designed to make supervision and accounting difficult; two linked holding companies were based in tax havens, the Cayman Islands and Luxembourg. In retrospect, it was only surprising that so many host countries (including the U.K., France, Switzerland, Luxembourg, Saudi Arabia, and others) could let such a bank develop into more than a $20 billion operation in at least 32 countries.

When BCCI failed, many depositors lost substantially (although the U.S. affiliates were soundly capitalized and made good on deposits in this country). Implicit in the Concordat regime are financial parent countries that are strong enough to stand behind their banks and guarantee international deposits.

In response to BCCI's collapse the Basel Committee established stronger Minimum Standards: (i) All international banks should be capably supervised by a home country authority with consolidated accounting; (ii) Host countries should impose restrictive measures on unsound operations in their territories that are not well supervised. Thus, home and host countries should make effective arrangements to prevent other failures like BCCI. In this way prudential practices can be improved for banking in the global marketplace.

Also in the early 1990s, as Communism collapsed in Eastern Europe and the U.S.S.R., international concern shifted toward their problems. As these "transforming" nations applied for membership in the General Agreement on Tariffs and Trade (GATT) and IMF membership, receiving considerable support from European Community and OECD nations, their large needs for additional capital, credit, and trade potential became evident. Most Western countries were inclined to be supportive, but mobilizing large resources quickly was a difficult challenge.

In 1997–1998 a wave of financial crises, with heavy capital flight and currency devaluations hit many countries, including Thailand, Malaysia, Indonesia, S. Korea, and later Russia and Brazil, together with some smaller nations (Mexico was hit earlier in 1994). Japan and China also were strained, although they continued their strong export efforts. Lessons drawn from these experiences were that prudential regulation of banks needed strengthening, along with greater disclosure and transparency, and, in many situations, precautionary taxes on short-term capital inflows to limit "hot money."

International debate resumed on the need for stronger requirements for the IMF, multilateral development banks, international banking, exchange rates, and capital and trade flows. Consensus was difficult on any stronger measures. Few wanted to cut back on global prosperity and trade flows, but the global euphoria toward freer trade and financing suffered an important setback. The World Trade Organization (WTO) financial services agreement (FSA) of December 1997 was more limited than many had been hoping for in the early 1990s. The FSA was limited by strong reciprocity requirements and prudential safeguards imposed on emerging markets by the United States, E.U., and Japan. Thus, most emerging markets were unwilling to open up their financial sectors to heavy participation or takeover by OECD nation banks and financial institutions; in response, the United States, E.U., and Japan would not open their financial markets much to "third world" banks and institutions. Ironically, this mutual caution proved wise, for a rapid opening to more BCCIs in the mid-to late-1990s would have brought more disruptions, failures and political strains. An over-riding lesson seems to be that fully open capital flows should be confined to strong, prosperous, and comparable economies (like the OECD nations) that have the fiscal and regulatory resources to provide full guarantees for the activities of their banks and other related financial institutions (under Basel Concordats I and II).

Another complication since the mid-1980s has been rising trade and current account deficits for the United States. Increasingly heavy U.S. capital inflows, with surging imports and more slowly growing exports for the United States were problems. Unfortunately, in 2007–2009 a major banking and financial crisis did hit the United States and Europe, which morphed into a widespread trade recession. It began with real estate booms and slumps. Losses developed in sub-prime mortgages and a variety of derivative securities (including quasi-insurance products). Toxic asset problems spread into many institutions, and default risks increased substantially. Government bailouts, guarantees, and recapitalization measures were needed.

Under the circumstances, many governments, including the United States, much of Europe, and some of Asia, felt that preemptive actions and Keynesian budget deficits were essential. Improved banking supervision and a recapitalization of major financial institutions were critical.

6. MERGING PROBLEMS

As a practical matter, national regulators have continued to confront these issues, and now must also take into account new global crises that seem to pull regulatory policies in contrary directions. The continuing need for stability in the international banking system calls for strong and consistent supervision by national regulators. However, the international crisis caused by the ongoing coronavirus pandemic illustrates a situation in which policy makers and regulators must respond flexibly to a threat to economic and financial stability arising out of a health crisis. So, for example, the Federal Reserve eased restrictions on loans to bank insiders otherwise eligible for such relief, and other U.S. bank regulators took similar steps to ease regulatory strictures. In addition, in March 2020, the Coronavirus Aid, Relief, and Economic Security Act (CARES Act) was enacted with, among other things, provisions intended to facilitate lending to small businesses affected by the pandemic.

Pulling the international banking system in a more stringent direction, the recent invasion of Ukraine by Russian armed forces triggered, among other responses, the imposition of economic sanctions on the Government of Russia, its officials, and many Russian nationals. U.S. sanctions included the blocking of bank assets of these sanctioned parties. These initial sanctions have been followed up by a continuing series of executive orders and proclamations imposing sanctions in response to the extended invasion of Ukraine by Russia. These presidential actions have been followed by a cascade of implementing regulatory measures and an almost daily stream of specific designations of Russian officials, affiliates, and property that have been subjected to sanctions. The transnational aspects of modern banking and financial services unavoidably expose participants to political and physical forces far beyond the supervision of a safe and sound banking system.

CHAPTER V

THRIFT INSTITUTIONS

Savings banks, savings and loan associations, credit unions, and similar entities—referred to collectively by the informal term "thrift institutions"—originally were created to meet needs for saving, credit and loans of people whose resources and income were modest. Commercial banks, merchants, money lenders, and pawn shops often did not serve this demand for loans or savings as well, or with interest rates as favorable, with respect to such individuals and families. During the last two centuries, thrift institutions were gradually developed, therefore, by social reformers, philanthropic benefactors, religious and fraternal organizations, trade unions, employers, and thrift entrepreneurs (in most countries of the world) as a collateral type of banking or financial intermediation. With expanded prosperity and broader affluence, these thrift institutions grew more sizable, and many became more like banks in their offerings of deposit accounts and check-writing services, and they sought a wider range of investment and lending alternatives for their deposit resources. This trend created a need for more flexibility in regulating thrift institutions, especially in an era of electronic fund transfers.

A. HISTORICAL BACKGROUND

The regulation of thrift institutions can only be understood historically, as a response in every country to their humane origins, and partial rivalry with commercial banking. In the United States, mutual savings banks (MSBs) were the first thrift institution to prosper. Beginning in 1816, MSBs slowly became active in most Northeastern states before the Civil War. MSBs grew stronger for the next two generations, mostly in the Northeast, although their relative influence declined since World War II, with only $175 billion in assets for 1981.

Savings and loan associations (or building societies) began in Pennsylvania in the 1830s, but expanded more rapidly after the Civil War, when they spread all over the nation. But the great heyday of S & Ls came since World War II, with VA, FHA, and other federal encouragements for housing loans. S & Ls had assets of $663 billion by 1981 (compared to $1808 billion assets in commercial banks).

Credit unions came to the U.S. in 1908, significantly later than in Western Europe. Credit unions began to grow more rapidly during the Great Depression, especially after the National Credit Union Administration and progressive employers sponsored them actively. Their postwar growth has been impressive, and credit unions accounted for $75 billion of assets in 1981, and they exceeded $1 trillion by 2012. (See Table V-1, *infra.*)

Since the S & L strains of the 1980s, which led to the bailout of the Federal Savings and Loan Insurance Corporation (FSLIC) in 1989, thrift institutions in the U.S. have grown much less rapidly than commercial banks. However, thrifts are still a major factor in financial markets, particularly in serving consumer households and families.

Table V-1
Development of U.S. Thrift Institutions: Mutual Savings Banks, Savings & Loan Associations, and Credit Unions, 1816–2022
(amounts in millions of dollars)

	Mutual Savings Banks (and Savings Banks)		Savings & Loans		Credit Unions	
	Number	Assets	Number	Assets	Number	Assets
	1st Mutual Savings Banks Founded 1816					
			1st Savings & Loan Founded 1831			
1880	629	832				
					1st Credit Unions Founded 1909	
1890	921	1,743				
1900	626	2,328	5,356	571		
1910	637	3,598	5,869	932		
1920	618	5,586	8,633	2,520	191[a]	—
1925	610	7,831	12,403	5,509	419	—
1929	598	9,873	12,342	8,695	974	—
1935	559	11,046	10,266	5,875	3,372	50
1940	542	11,925	7,521	5,733	9,023	253
1945	534	15,924	6,149	8,747	8,683	435
1950	530	22,252	5,992	16,893	10,591	1,005
1955	528	30,382	6,071	37,656	16,201	2,743
1960	516	39,598	6,320	71,476	20,047	5,653
1965	505	56,383	6,185	129,580	22,119	10,522
1970	497	76,373	5,669	176,183	23,656	15,523
1975	476	121,000	4,931	329,000	21,608	38,013
1981	448	175,000	4,347	663,300	21,119	74,700
1985	353[b]	216,800	3,552[c]	1,070,000	17,581	137,200
1991	451[d]	218,000	2,216[e]	921,000	14,549	221,000
1995	604[f]	258,000	1,478[f]	780,000	11,836	301,000
1999	462	270,000	1,110	947,000	10,841	407,000
2003	418	354,000	944	1,073,000	9,504	599,000
2007	429	347,000	836	1,504,000	8,238	740,000

	Mutual Savings Banks (and Savings Banks)		Savings & Loans		Credit Unions	
2012	440	340,000	547	719,000	6,819	1,022,000
2017	483	268,000	269	929,000	5,573	1,378,892
2022	579	1,280,560	35	12,619,224	4,760	2,710,000

[a] 1921.

[b] FDIC insured.

[c] Stock associations 1,087, stock savings banks 306, and mutual associations 2,159; all FSLIC insured.

[d] BIF insured.

[e] Federal S & Ls 628, state S & Ls 770, and stock savings banks; all SAIF insured.

[f] BIF insured 604; SAIF insured 1478. But some 200 institutions were allowed to convert from SAIF (OTS supervised) to BIF (FDIC supervised).

Sources: *Historical Statistics of the U.S.: Colonial Times to 1970,* Bureau of Census, U.S. Dept. of Commerce, 1975; *Statistical Abstract of the U.S.*, various dates, Bureau of Census, U.S. Dept. of Commerce; 1986 and 1995 Savings and Loan Sourcebook U.S. League, Wash., D.C., various dates; *Credit Union Report 1986 and 1990,* CUNA, Inc., Madison, Wisc.; *1986 National Factbook of Savings Institutions,* Nat'l Council of Savings Banks, Wash., D.C.; *Federal Home Loan Bank Board News,* April 16, 1987; *Annual Reports,* Federal Financial Institutions Examination Council, *various dates;* 1995 Sourcebook, *America's Community Bankers; Federal Reserve Staff, various dates.*

Note: Histories of specialized thrift institutions record the first Mutual Savings Bank in Switzerland 1787, the first Building Society (or Savings & Loan) in England 1781, and the first Credit Union in Germany 1850. These institutions had common origins in attempting to encourage saving by people of modest means, and often were sponsored philanthropically in their formative periods by wealthier patrons and trustees.

The Great Depression provoked a large part of modern thrift legislation in the United States, and much of the federal regulatory structure that supervises and insures most thrift institutions. Savings banks (mostly MSBs) had been authorized by 17 states, and since 1982 they could also obtain federal charters. Their deposit insurance came from the FDIC, FSLIC, or state insurance programs (*e.g.*, Massachusetts). In 1982 almost all 448 savings banks were state-chartered and supervised by their respective states, plus the FDIC or Federal Home

Loan Bank Board. Thereafter, many stock savings banks were chartered by the Federal Home Loan Bank Board, its successor agency (the OTS), and some states. By 2017 there were 483 FDIC-insured savings banks.

Savings and loan associations were chartered by every state or the federal government (originally the Federal Home Loan Bank Board, from 1989 to 2011 by the OTS, and since then by the OCC). Deposit insurance coverage was originally provided by the FSLIC, or by a few state insurance programs; now the FDIC is the primary insurer. There were 3,200 S & Ls at the end of 1985, though this number had shrunk to less than 270 federally insured S & Ls by 2017.

Credit unions are chartered by the National Credit Union Administration (NCUA) or by the states. Of all the types of thrift institutions, credit unions have been the most resilient over time. There were slightly more than 5,500 credit unions based in the U.S. in 2017, with some of the largest operating worldwide. Since 1970 federal deposit insurance has been available from the National Credit Union Share Insurance Fund (NCUSIF), which covers the great majority, while state and private insurance programs are used by most of the remaining credit unions.

Thrift institutions grew more rapidly than commercial banks between 1946–1985, as S & Ls and MSBs helped finance a large expansion in the housing industry. Greatly increased market interest rates and inflation brought an end to this long boom in the 1980s. This, combined with Regulation Q (12

C.F.R. pt. 217) ceilings on deposit interest rates and a lack of flexibility on mortgage loan earnings, put the majority of S & Ls and many MSBs into an awkward financial squeeze. Their cost of funds exceeded earnings, and net worth began eroding. In this crisis, tough new competition came from money market mutual funds that offered higher market interest rates to smaller depositors, taking away some $200 billion in deposit growth from these thrift institutions. Credit unions were less seriously damaged, because their interest rates on deposit accounts and member loans enjoyed more flexibility. This crisis for S & Ls and MSBs between 1978 and 1982 helped provoke major new laws, the Depositary Institutions Deregulation and Monetary Control Act of 1980 and the Depositary Institutions Act of 1982. This legislation allowed more direct competition between banks, thrifts, and money market funds for deposit accounts, and somewhat more rivalry in lending as well. Since the late 1980s and into the 1990s, mutual funds again took extensive deposits from thrift institutions.

This new legal environment, together with money market accounts, NOW accounts, cash management accounts, EFT technology, and continued inflation for many years, put thrift institutions into a period of severe challenge, particularly the savings banks and saving and loan associations. When many of the S & Ls suffered weakened capitalization in the early 1980s, and then received broader lending authority—especially for commercial real estate loans—hundreds of them got into big insolvency troubles with a large volume of bad loans. Those losses badly strained FSLIC insurance reserves. A $250–350 billion FSLIC "bailout" operation was required between 1985 and 1995. And under the Financial Institutions Reform, Recovery, and Enforcement Act of 1989 (FIRREA), most Federal Home Loan Bank Board supervisory functions were moved into the Office of Thrift Supervision (OTS) in the Department of the Treasury, and the FSLIC was absorbed into the FDIC. Not surprisingly, higher FDIC insurance premiums were then imposed on FSLIC insured institutions. Until the merger of the Bank Insurance Fund (BIF) and the Savings Association Insurance Fund (SAIF) into the Depository Insurance Fund (DIF) pursuant to the Federal Deposit Insurance Reform Act of 2005, most former FSLIC institutions were insured, post-1989, by the SAIF portion of FDIC rather than the BIF portion of FDIC. But higher SAIF premiums were a competitive disability for many savings banks and most S & Ls.[1] Further dramatic changes in the regulation of savings institution would occur in 2011, after the 2008 collapse of the savings associations industry. (See V.E., *infra* at 277–278.)

[1] BIF insurance premiums were raised substantially between 1989–1994 because of widespread commercial loan problems among larger banks, and BIF insurance reserves needed replenishment. But by 1995–1996, bank capital had been largely rebuilt for BIF insured institutions, and accordingly, BIF premium charges were lowered to minimal levels for soundly-rated commercial banks. For years, SAIF premiums were more expensive. This differential was a cost disadvantage for SAIF insured savings banks and S & Ls.

B. SAVINGS BANK REGULATION

Mutual savings banks for people of modest means emerged in many Western countries during the later 1700s, including Britain, Germany, Switzerland, and Italy. The utilitarian philosopher Jeremy Bentham suggested "frugality banks" in 1797, for example, and in Britain benevolent societies for savings, mutual support, and insurance developed in many communities in the early Nineteenth Century. In 1816 the first U.S. savings banks were chartered, the Philadelphia Savings Fund Society and the Provident Institution for Savings in Boston. In the early years, typical features were limitations on the size of deposits, wealthy or philanthropic trustees, relatively small loans, and investments in the most reliable public bonds, private securities, or mortgages available. Religious and community leaders often played a key role in setting up these savings banks, and in spreading the concept to other communities. These institutions were "mutual" in the sense that depositors rather than shareholders approved basic policies and elected the principal managers.

Mutual savings banks spread throughout the industrial Northeast fairly rapidly in the 1820s–1830s. The Panic and Depression of 1837 depleted their ranks, but MSBs became more numerous and prospered during the 1840s–1850s. By 1860 deposits in about 200 MSBs were $150 million, whereas assets in the 1600 commercial banks totaled $1 billion. But savings banks operations were concentrated in the more industrial states, especially Massachusetts and

New York. In the agrarian Midwest and South, banking remained overwhelmingly commercial and farming oriented, and MSBs were relatively rare. In many areas state commercial banks were also smaller, less pretentious, and served some of the functions of savings banks. Savings and loan associations (or building societies) largely took over the remaining role for mutual savings banks in the rest of the country.

Even so, the growth of MSBs was impressive in the Northeast. The majority of MSBs were in New York, Massachusetts, and Connecticut, which accounted for three-fourths of MSB deposits by 1915.

A significant reform came in Massachusetts in 1907, when MSBs were allowed to issue small life insurance policies. Louis Brandeis was a leader in this effort. New York and Connecticut later authorized comparable life insurance authority for MSBs in 1938 and 1941, respectively. This was helpful competition towards lower-cost life insurance, though it did not lead to a big volume of life insurance business for MSBs. Nor did life insurance premiums become a large part of MSB income or resources. Still, this broadening of the competitive range for MSBs was suggestive, and should be considered a precursor in expanding consumer product lines, such as NOW accounts which were offered in the 1970s and money market accounts in the 1980s.

The Great Depression was a problem for mutual savings banks, but less so than for commercial banks or savings and loan associations. While 9,000 (out of

25,000) commercial banks closed between 1929 and 1933, and 526 (out of 12,000) savings and loans failed, only eight MSBs closed during this period. Although deposit growth slowed and mortgage assets declined in value, New Deal relief measures helped ease this difficulty considerably, and greatly reduced the number of MSB failures.

Limited Depression relief came in 1932, with the creation of the Federal Home Loan Bank system, a network of 12 regional Home Loan Banks (FHLBs) supervised by the five-member FHLBB. The FHLB System was patterned, in some respects, after the Federal Reserve System for commercial banks, with lending authority to support member S & Ls and savings banks. Short-term loans without security and long-term mortgage loans to member institutions were authorized. Members had to purchase capital stock in their regional FHLB equal to one percent of their mortgage loans. This lender-of-last-resort assistance was strengthened by the availability of loans from the Reconstruction Finance Corporation (RFC), although not much help came to the thrifts before the Roosevelt administration came into office.

The FHLB System was designed mainly for the nationwide S & L and home loan mortgage industry, which suffered heavy strain as many depositors reduced thrift institution deposits in the Depression, and more real estate mortgages fell into default, with substantially increased foreclosure rates. Meanwhile, property values for homes and other real estate sagged in these hard times, and some of these defaulted mortgages led to losses for thrift institutions. But most MSBs had become substantial real estate mortgage holders along with S & Ls, though not usually with the same overwhelming dependence on this kind of loan portfolio. Ultimately most S & Ls joined the FHLB System, whereas only about one-third of the MSBs became FHLB members.

The New Deal brought more relief for thrift institutions. In 1933 the Home Owners Loan Corporation (HOLC) was created to target much larger government support to the distressed mortgage markets. During 1933–1936 the HOLC disbursed $2.7 billion in exchange for mortgages, which included $410 million to savings banks, $770 million to S & Ls, $685 million to individuals (and various trusts, estates, etc.), and the remainder to mortgage companies, insurance companies, and commercial banks. The Federal Housing Administration added substantial new mortgage money over a longer period of years, so that the revival in housing finance could be sustained. In 1934 the Federal Savings and Loan Insurance Corporation (FSLIC) was created to offer deposit account insurance for S & Ls and savings banks.

Meanwhile, MSB operations gradually revived along with the economy as a whole. World War II gave a strong boost to government-financed expenditure, and MSB deposits increased by half during these years. Postwar expansion followed through the 1970s, though at a slower pace than S & Ls. This reflected the faster growth of housing and mortgage finance outside the Northeast, together with the fact that MSBs were confined to geographic areas where they also faced competition from S & Ls.

After World War II, however, MSBs began to put more of their assets into real estate mortgages, resuming a trend evident in the 1920s. By 1960 MSBs held two-thirds of their assets in real estate mortgages, and by 1966 three-fourths of MSB assets had become real estate mortgages. Eventually, MSBs became more like S & Ls, except that MSBs tended to be bigger institutions, with more deposits than S & Ls, and MSBs were concentrated mainly in the Northeast.

But a broader latitude for investment activity, along with savings bank life insurance in key states like Massachusetts, New York, and Connecticut, proved significant in encouraging a bolder attitude toward innovation and expansion outside real estate finance. The most important development by the savings bank industry came from Massachusetts, where these thrift institutions developed the Negotiable Order of Withdrawal (NOW) account.

NOW accounts were developed in the early 1970s in Massachusetts, where the MSB tradition was strongest, and many institutions were as large as sizeable commercial banks. The NOW account was a modified savings account, which paid interest, but on which checks could be written. It was more convenient than an ordinary passbook or time deposit account, and closer to a commercial bank checking account. Congress enacted authority for NOW accounts in 1976 for all federally regulated institutions, including commercial banks, in the six

New England states. This was later extended to New York and New Jersey. Some variations developed in practice, with respect to required minimum balances, charges for checks, and the allowed number of checks. But the competitive advantages from NOW accounts were somewhat helpful in gathering new depositors for thrift institutions, which enjoyed the ¼ percent higher interest rates allowed by Regulation Q, a differential applicable from 1973 until 1982.

NOW accounts were not desired by all thrifts (especially smaller ones) in most parts of the country, but once introduced in an area by large MSBs or S & Ls, they were normally offered by the other institutions. Competitive pressures were building up when the Depository Institutions Deregulation and Monetary Control Act of 1980 (DIDMCA) authorized nationwide use of NOW accounts, effective January 1, 1981. However, as part of a tradeoff package, Congress imposed uniform reserve requirements for all transactional accounts (checking and NOW accounts) to be phased in during five years, and an end to Regulation Q ceilings and differentials on deposit interest rates within six years. Thus, thrift institutions and commercial banks would be treated more alike, and would be more directly competitive to this extent. In addition, under the DIDMCA federally chartered S & Ls could invest up to 20 percent of their assets in consumer loans, commercial paper, and corporate debt, and federally chartered MSBs could make business loans up to 5 percent of their assets. These enhanced powers were less important for MSBs, which enjoyed most of this latitude already, and some thrifts felt the DIDMCA was a net loss for them in phasing out the Regulation Q interest rate advantage over commercial banks, despite the nationwide extension of NOW account authority. It should also be noted that that NOW accounts did not bring in much new money to thrift institutions as a whole; only $2.3 billion were in NOW accounts by the end of 1981 or 1.5 percent of MSB deposits.

Meanwhile, the most serious disintermediation crisis for MSBs and S & Ls was building up in the late 1970s, and hit with full force on their earnings in the early 1980s. Although Regulation Q kept deposit rate ceilings firm, market interest rates went 5–10 percentage points higher. Money market mutual funds offered more competitive deposit rates, and $200 billion of new deposits were diverted to them and away from other institutions. MSBs and S & Ls lost substantial deposits, and began suffering an earnings squeeze when their rising cost of funds (especially from larger denomination CDs, with higher interest rates) exceeded their mortgage interest revenues (weighted down with a substantial inventory of lower yield, long-term mortgages). The majority of MSBs and S & Ls fell into a period of negative earnings in the early 1980s. This prompted efforts at self-help, such as variable interest rate mortgages, widespread conversion from mutual to stock forms of ownership, switching from state to federal charters, merger activity among thrifts, some acquisitions by banks, closer relations with mortgage bankers, and government relief, including broadened thrift powers, new liability instruments and accounts, and emergency financial assistance. This situation led to the restructuring of competitive relations among banks, thrifts, money market funds, the securities industry, and financial institutions generally.

C. SAVINGS AND LOAN ASSOCIATION REGULATION

Savings and loan associations (or building societies) were another kind of cooperative thrift organization that focused lending upon the desire for home ownership and construction by families of modest income. Building societies had been developed in Britain around 1781, and had become widely established. The first S & L in the U.S., the Oxford Provident Building Association, formed in 1831 at Frankford, Pennsylvania, a small town on the outskirts of Philadelphia, was patterned on the British model. Its founders were two local manufacturers, a physician, and a schoolteacher-surveyor, together with 33 other local resident members. Members were required to contribute $5 initial deposits and $3 monthly dues. Accumulated savings would be offered as loans among the members, though restricted to nearby residents within five miles. Withdrawal was permitted after a month's notice, but with a 5 percent penalty charge on accumulated contributions. Small fines were imposed for a failure to make monthly contributions.

A modest spread of building societies occurred in eight states before the Civil War, but a more permanent type of organization was needed. The original prototype in Frankford, Pa., only operated for ten years, when it wound up, distributed the accumulated resources, and a new association of similar name succeeded for another decade, and so on. This early type of "terminating" association had inherent limits on growth potential, and was supplanted by two varieties, the "serial plan" and the "permanent plan." The serial plan issued successive blocks of shares to provide more continuity, and allowed continuous operation with no disruption or need to terminate. Most serial plans strongly encouraged regular contributions or dues, both to accumulate enough savings for home loans, and to enforce thriftiness. But the serial plan was less suitable for larger organizations, and was inconvenient for irregular savings or withdrawals.

The "permanent plan" proved to be readily expandable and more successful in most parts of the country. In the permanent plan, shares are issued (or accounts opened) at any time, net earnings or dividends are paid regularly. The most widely known prototype developed in Dayton, Ohio, about 1880, although a few precursors can be found even earlier, including one in Charleston, South Carolina. The modern "S & L" is an outgrowth of the permanent plan, with larger resources, often with branches, a variety of deposit accounts, and lending potential extended into multi-family housing, or even other kinds of credit in recent years.

Savings and loan associations spread through the entire country between the Civil War and 1890, and by 1900 there were 5,356 S & Ls with $571 million in assets. (See Table V-1, *supra*.) By contrast, only 626

MSBs (or savings banks) were concentrated in the Northeast, with much larger assets of $2,328 million in 1900. At the turn of the century, an average sized S & L held a bit less than $100,000 deposits, whereas the average MSB or savings bank had nearly $4.5 million deposits. S & Ls were more informal, and often had only part-time offices without regular employees. Also, S & Ls assets consisted almost entirely of smaller home mortgages, while MSBs held more corporate securities (mainly bonds) than real estate mortgages at that stage.

Regulation of S & Ls was largely non-existent in this early period. Once the problems of continuity and permanence had been solved, this kind of building society had broad appeal.

Unfortunately, this appeal led to some exploitation by irresponsible promoters, and in particular, the rise and fall of the so-called "nationals." The first of these was the National Building, Loan, and Protective Union, which began in Minnesota around 1887. This outfit sold shares of "$100 par value," with monthly dues of 85 cents, from which 10 cents went to "expenses," 15 cents to "insurance," and 60 cents to the "loan fund." In addition, there was a $2 membership fee which paid sales commission agents. There was no withdrawal or surrender value, so a member lost everything contributed with a lapse in payment of dues. Liberal commissions and expenses for promoters, however, encouraged growth in the early years. The success of such promoters led to 11 other "nationals" in Minnesota within a year, and more were set up around the country. By 1893, 240 "national" associations existed in the U.S., as compared to 5,598 local building and loan associations. Between 1887 and 1895, the nationals collected an estimated $250 million, and loaned $150 million, a lower percentage than the locals.

The local building and loan organizations naturally felt outraged at the high promoter expenses and unsound finance in these "national" operations. The United States League of Local Building and Loan Associations in 1893 (later U.S. League of S & Ls) was prompted in large part by the need to organize this opposition. State legislation on S & Ls was mainly inspired by this controversy. Some states required $100,000 cash deposits (or in mortgage assets) as a condition for the nationals to do business in their jurisdiction. In other states bonds were required for the sales agents to secure against fraud. Some states made formal investigations, which tended to be unfavorable to the "nationals," their selling practices, and financial soundness. But what ultimately destroyed the "nationals" was a series of failures, beginning in 1896 with the largest, Southern Building and Loan Association of Knoxville, Tennessee. Within several years none of the significant "nationals" remained. And yet, most S & L experts believe this episode was, in the end, constructive, for it led to some sensible regulation, helped teach the importance of sound accounting and actuarial techniques, and emphasized the positive benefits of community knowledge, reputation and cooperation that caused the spread of local S & Ls in the first place.

Serious supervision of S & Ls began in New York in 1875 (along with MSB regulation) with a requirement of annual reports. This was enlarged to "visitation" authority (*i.e.*, the power to conduct on-site examinations as needed) in 1887, and annual inspections in 1892. During the late 1880s–early 1890s such regulation spread to many other states, and this supervision had become near universal by the 1920s. The main objectives were to minimize fraud and embezzlement, and to enforce reasonable prudence and care on the part of trustees and directors, many of whom served merely part-time, and were not necessarily experienced business people. Results were uneven, but local interest normally served to sustain reasonable honesty and competence.

Savings and loan institutions prospered in the period 1900–1929. The number of S & Ls grew from 5,356 to 12,342, and their assets mushroomed from $932 million to $8.7 billion. This compares with a slight decline in the number of MSBs, *i.e.*, from 626 to 598, and a slower growth of $2.3 billion to $9.9 billion in MSB assets. Meanwhile, commercial banks trebled in number from 10,800 to 30,000 between 1900–1921, although shrinking to 25,000 in 1929. Commercial bank assets grew from $9 billion in 1900 to $62 billion in 1929. As a whole, these thrifts roughly maintained their share of financial institution assets as compared to commercial banks, but S & Ls grew more rapidly than MSBs, and approached the MSBs in total assets—even though the average S & Ls $700,000 assets was still much smaller than the average MSBs $15 million assets.

The Great Depression brought widespread distress to the S & L industry, more severe than that suffered by MSBs, though not so drastic as the fate of 9,000 failing banks. Some 536 S & Ls failed in the years 1929–1933, but the FHLBB, the FSLIC insurance system, and the HOLC were created in time to save the industry from epidemic closures.

The initial problem for S & Ls brought on by the Great Depression was liquidity. Cash and liquid reserves had never been very large for S & Ls. But as the economic crisis deepened, with business failures and growing unemployment, withdrawals increased, and some associations suffered the loss of their bank deposits when the latter failed. A considerable number of S & Ls became "frozen", *i.e.*, withdrawals were no longer allowed, except as limited amounts of new deposits flowed back in. Gradually, as liquidity resumed flowing through an S & L, its situation began to unfreeze, and more new deposits were added to the association.

More serious solvency problems developed later for S & Ls in communities plagued by heavier unemployment, losses of job income, and heavy foreclosure rates on home loans. Less attractive or poorly constructed homes tended to depreciate more rapidly, and this often applied to multi-unit and lower-grade income properties. The fraction of S & L assets consisting of "real estate owned" gradually rose from less than 3 percent in 1930, to 20 percent in 1936 and 1937, and did not fall back below 5 percent until World War II. Foreclosed assets moved slowly, and market prices for real estate declined substantially during the depression, not recovering fully until the latter part of World War II.

What proved essential for the survival of many S & Ls in the Depression was generous and sustained support from the federal government. First, there was emergency refinancing support through the RFC, FHLBB, and, especially, the HOLC. RFC emergency loans to S & Ls totaled $118 million in 1932, with another $275 million of capital loans to S & Ls between 1933–1942. HOLC support to S & Ls absorbed $770 million of mortgages between 1933–1936, which refinanced 13 percent of the outstanding mortgage holdings of S & Ls (commercial banks took $525 million from the HOLC to refinance 26 percent of their mortgage portfolios). FHLB loans added another source of short- and long-term lending to member S & Ls. In these circumstances, more than 90 per cent of the nation's S & Ls survived the Depression, and did not have to terminate operations.

Second, there was regulatory support through the FHLBB, created under the Federal Home Loan Bank Act enacted in 1932 towards the end of the Hoover Administration. The FHLBB had an initial capital subscription of $125 million from the U.S. Treasury, with another $600 million of FHLB debenture authority. Both unsecured short-term loans and secured long-term loans were authorized, which could be made to member S & Ls (or MSBs). Savings associations became members by subscribing with payments for stock in their regional FHLBank worth 1 percent of their home mortgage loans outstanding.

Each FHLBank had an eleven-member board of directors, nine representing member institutions and two being public representatives.

By the end of 1933, almost 20 percent of savings associations were FHLB members. Gradually, membership increased as more S & Ls regained the liquidity to subscribe, and as membership advantages became more evident. Ultimately, by the end of 1981, about 93 percent of the nation's S & Ls and almost one-third of the MSBs were FHLBank members. (Note that in 1989 the Financial Institutions Reform, Recovery and Enforcement Act of 1989 (FIRREA) replaced the FHLBB system with the Office of Thrift Supervision, discussed in section E, *infra.*)

The third major development was deposit insurance from the FSLIC. This was offered in 1934, paralleling FDIC deposit insurance for commercial banks and MSBs. Initially accounts up to $2,500 were insured; currently the limit is a "standard maximum deposit insurance amount" of $250,000, to be adjusted periodically for inflation. By the end of 1981, most S & Ls (representing more than 98 percent of the assets) had FSLIC insurance. The remainder, mostly smaller institutions, were under state S & L insurance plans in Massachusetts, Maryland, North Carolina, and Ohio. A few savings banks were also FSLIC insured. This insurance protection was emphasized increasingly by S & Ls in marketing their deposit accounts against the strong new competition from money market funds. (Again, note that FIRREA abolished the FSLIC in 1989 and transferred its insurance functions to the FDIC.)

A fourth development was federal chartering of S & Ls. Until the Great Depression, the chartering of S & Ls (along with MSBs) was exclusively a state activity, with considerable variation from state to state. Federal chartering standards became a significant part of S & L regulation by the FHLBB. Gradually, the proportion of S & Ls with federal charters increased. By the end of 1981, 44 percent of all S & Ls had federal charters.

Additional support for the housing industry came from the Federal Housing Authority (FHA) between 1934–1942, which subsidized a substantial minority of the mortgages issued in those years. The U.S. Housing Authority, created by the Housing Act of 1937 within the Interior Department, also began a program of public housing in 1937, building 10 percent of the new homes constructed between 1939–1942. These programs enlarged the supply of housing activity, and the HOLC and FHA led the way in lengthening mortgage maturities to 15 and 20 years, breaking older, more conservative traditions of 10- to 12-year limits on mortgage finance. Interest rates also declined in these years, partly as a result of government policy, and because of the continuing depression and high unemployment.

These government programs began to revive the housing industry in the late 1930s. But the financial strains of the Depression caused a very substantial consolidation or merger movement among S & Ls. The number of S & Ls declined from 12,342 in 1929 to 6,093 in 1946. Most of those associations disappeared by consolidation or merger with existing associations. Less than 600 failed in the Depression, though many more troubled institutions were consolidated under strong encouragement from the Federal Home Loan Bank Board. Significant S & L consolidations and mergers continued during the postwar prosperity, offset largely by a considerable flow of new S & L entrants from the late 1940s through the 1980s. Policies varied among the states, and some states experienced more consolidation and branching activity by larger S & Ls.

World War II brought a temporary consolidation of housing programs (including the FHLBB, FHA, and U.S. Housing Authority) into the National Housing Agency. War-time controls limited new construction, restricted credit, and included some rent ceilings. As the war ended, plans were developed to support housing more strongly, including housing loans for veterans. After a brief adjustment period, a post-war housing boom took off.

Federal housing policy encouraged and helped sustain this boom in home construction and ownership. FHA loans were supplemented by Veterans Administration (VA) loans, both subsidized by the Treasury, Federal National Mortgage Administration (FNMA), Government National Mortgage Administration (GNMA), and the Federal Home Loan Mortgage Corporation (FHLMC). VA loans provided a powerful boost of subsidized lower interest, longer maturity, and low down payment lending to veterans. Since so many young men and women had served in the war, this gave support to family home construction and liberalized conventional mortgage terms substantially.

FNMA ("Fannie Mae") was created in 1938, but became more significant after the war in providing a secondary market in which VA, FHA, and conventional mortgages could be auctioned off for their yield value on a reliable basis, thus assuring liquidity to financial institutions that emphasize mortgage asset portfolios. When FNMA became a completely private corporation in 1968, part of its role was taken over by GNMA ("Ginnie Mae"), a government owned corporation operating within the Department of Housing and Urban Development (HUD). GNMA markets mortgages acquired from other agencies, and supports mortgage programs that subsidize low- and middle-income housing and other targeted activities. FHLMC ("Freddie Mac") was organized under the Emergency Home Finance Act of 1970 as a corporation making a secondary market for government-supported and conventional mortgages, with its capital owned by the twelve regional FHLBs. This accumulated network of federal support, securities issues, and financing was coordinated, more or less, over the years with FHLB, FHA, VA, and HUD regulations. This effort promoted and encouraged home ownership, construction, and financing beyond the level of private market activity, and these policies broadened prosperity and participation in the private enterprise system.

This support of housing markets became an important dimension of national financial and banking policy. Money and credit markets were significantly affected, and it became customary for fiscal, monetary, and banking policies to be worked out consciously in the light of housing finance and the various institutions involved. The U.S. House and Senate Banking committees included these matters as part of their detailed work and jurisdiction, and regular lobbying shaped legislative and regulatory policies, budgets, and credit support in their favor.

Tax policy was also used to encourage and complement housing policy, along with other sectors of the economy. Until 1951 most thrift institutions had been exempt from federal income taxes, because they were mutual savings institutions. Although Congress removed this special treatment in the Revenue Act of 1951, thrifts continued to be largely exempt, for practical purposes, under very liberal bad debt accounting provisions until 1962. Thereafter, income tax treatment for commercial banks, S & Ls and MSBs became more comparable. (Some even complained that commercial banks received somewhat better treatment.)

More importantly, tax law encouraged substantial investment in real estate financed by mortgages, with the expensing of interest payments, and through liberal depreciation treatment. But interest charges are expensed generally for business borrowing, and depreciation is often quite liberal for capital equipment and other investment outlays. Thus, the encouragement of housing finance through tax policy is hardly unique, and its consistent congressional support is not really surprising.

In this postwar housing era, typical mortgage maturities lengthened to as much as 25 or 30 years (when credit markets were not being restrained, as in the Korean War 1950–1952), loan-value ratios were increased, and low down payments became customary, and FHLBB supervision of standard mortgage contracts became generally accepted. Some mortgage supervision proved unfortunate in later years, however, when housing market and thrift institutions adapted too slowly to increased inflation rates, and the growing severity of disintermediation strains in the late 1960s, 1973–1974, and the most serious crisis recently, 1978–1982. Nonetheless, a large part of this housing support and financing system has been worthwhile, beneficial to the economy, and helped broaden the distribution of wealth.

D. INFLATION, DISINTERMEDIATION, AND CRISIS

When the economy approached full employment in 1965–1966, and the Vietnam War brought an additional surge of government spending and a deficit, the Federal Reserve significantly tightened monetary policy. Growth of the monetary aggregates was halted in the second half of 1966, and interest rates rose sharply. Significant disintermediation began to occur from savings accounts, which shifted towards T-bills and other investments paying higher interest. In this context the Interest Rate Control Act of 1966 extended rate ceiling controls to the thrift institutions, under coordination of the Federal Reserve Board through Regulation Q (and involving the FHLBB and FDIC). As a stop-gap measure, it was hoped that "temporary" upward pressures on interest rates could be contained, the cost of funds for thrifts and housing credit kept down, without much need to choke off the 1961–1966 economic prosperity. In this way, Regulation Q was transformed from a loose rein on excessively generous bank interest rates that might endanger bank solvency into a general, seriously restrictive, and protectionist effort to keep savings account and mortgage interest rates below market levels, at least briefly.

As the economy slowed, the Federal Reserve eased restraint late in 1966, but the broadened Regulation Q limitations were retained, with some slight easing for large CDs over $100,000. This policy allowed banks and thrifts to get some additional "price sensitive" funds by paying more for them, and yet hold the larger portion of existing deposits at somewhat below market rates. At this stage, the Vietnam War surtax closed the budget gap, which eased the fiscal pressures toward inflation. Unfortunately, in the meantime wage-price discipline broke down, the administration's guidelines were increasingly disregarded, and the inflationary spiral gradually increased momentum.

In 1969 monetary policy was tightened significantly, stock market prices fell off appreciably, and some slack developed in the economy. Yet inflationary momentum eased only slowly, and interest rates did not fall much. But Regulation Q ceilings were raised slightly, and disintermediation was less serious. In the Summer 1971 a run on the dollar developed in foreign exchange markets (reflecting a buildup of Eurodollars abroad and weakening confidence in the U.S. economy). Nixon was forced into the first U.S. devaluation since 1933–1934. The administration reversed course, imposed wage-price controls, and switched to more stimulative monetary and fiscal policy. The economy improved with reduced inflation and falling unemployment. But after successful re-election, the administration abandoned most controls, and inflationary momentum rebounded in 1973–1974, aggravated greatly by world market food scarcities and the OPEC oil price increases. Inflation rates quickly reached double digit levels, the worst since the end of World War II.

In 1973–1974 short-term interest rates rose very sharply above Regulation Q ceilings, and another serious disintermediation period developed (a flow from savings and thrift accounts into higher interest alternatives). This time the Regulation Q ceilings on large deposits over $100,000 were raised more significantly. Once again, however, this was designed to allow banks and thrifts some additional high-cost CD funds for liquidity and new lending purposes, while trying to keep the bulk of their lower interest deposits intact. This assumed that inflation and higher interest rates were brief, transitory phenomena, and any disintermediation would be limited and bearable.

If inflation rates had been brought quickly under control, and reduced to low levels in the mid-late 1970s, these two disintermediation episodes might have been passed off as limited disturbances, with no significant, lasting impact on thrift institutions. Unfortunately, inflation and higher interest rates developed stronger, renewed momentum in the later 1970s–early 1980s, and only began to abate after severely restrictive monetary policy (between 1979–1982), record high interest rates, and the worst recession of the postwar era. This third, higher round of inflation and elevated interest rates built upon an increased underlying inflation rate, that lasted much longer, leaving residual inflation after 1982 at 3–4 percent annually, which would have been considered unacceptably high in the late 1960s–early 1970s. Interest rates began declining in 1982, yet remained unusually high into 1986, sustained by increased federal budget deficits (reaching 5 percent of GNP for 1983–1986, with fears of a possible renewal of higher inflation). This situation led to a worldwide recession, and a sustained period of strain for international banking, as many debtor nations found it hard to pay increased debt loads at high rates of interest.

This third round of disintermediation also produced the worst crisis for thrift institutions (S & Ls and MSBs) since the Great Depression, with far-reaching consequences. In 1978 major withdrawals began from thrift institutions, aggravated the rapid rise of MMMFs. By 1982 MMMFs had accumulated more than $200 billion in deposits, much of which would have gone to savings accounts, especially in thrift institutions. For MSBs there was a net outflow of $25 billion in 1978–1982, and for S & Ls a net outflow of about $50 billion in 1979–1982. This loss of deposits by itself might have been manageable, but the cost of funds for thrifts (with increased rates on CDs and other high-rate deposits) began to exceed asset earnings (weighted down with older, low-yield mortgages, and not sufficiently increased with a smaller volume of new, high-rate mortgages) during 1980–1982. For the majority of S & Ls (at one point nearly 85 percent of them) earnings became negative for a while, and their net capital or reserves declined appreciably. Many were forced into consolidation mergers as a result. For MSBs, this distress was not so widespread, because their reserves were normally larger, but severe financial distress did occur in some of the largest MSBs.

There was belated recognition that mortgage interest rates for S & Ls and MSBs should have floated upwards with their increasing costs of funds. Although the FHLBB eventually began liberalizing mortgage terms, and even encouraged variable interest mortgages in one form or another, this relief came late. A large majority of older mortgages in thrift portfolios had been fixed-rate conventional mortgages. These low-interest mortgages could not be floated, and, in fact, turned over (were paid off) less frequently as new mortgage rates went higher. In retrospect, this failure to develop floating rate mortgages earlier was a blunder. But government officials in charge during the late 1960s, 1973–1974, and even the mid-late 1970s, did not expect such strong inflation and elevated interest rates, and were reluctant to mandate a substantial increase in mortgage costs for consumers (with immediate inflationary impact).

In the end, the U.S. effort to hold down mortgage interest costs and savings account rates was a failure for thrift institutions. Market forces, with increased inflationary pressure, proved too strong. Thrift institutions were saddled with asset portfolios that could not move up sufficiently with market rates, and, while ordinary passbook rates were kept artificially low throughout, net disintermediation greatly reduced the volume of these low-cost accounts as a source of funds. Instead, thrift institutions had to get more and more of their funds through higher interest CDs, retail "repos,"[2] and ultimately, after the Depositary Institutions Act of 1982, money market accounts. In other words, thrift institutions had to pay market rates of interest in the end, but were stuck with too many low-yielding mortgages that squeezed their earnings, and brought widespread distress, forced mergers and consolidations.

E. REGULATING THRIFTS IN TRANSITION

Thrift institutions during the early 1980s experienced a painful transition, with increased rivalry for deposits from money market funds and commercial banks, and serious strains on net capital resulting from low-earning mortgage portfolios. A

---

[2] Typically, a retail repurchase agreement is actually a borrowing by a bank (or other "seller") from its customer, collateralized by government-issued or guaranteed securities that the bank characterizes as "selling" securities from its portfolio with a contractual obligation to repurchase them at a stated time at a premium to the customer. *See* Malloy & Pitts, *Post-Mortem on Retail Repurchase Agreements: Where were the Regulators*? 3 ANN. REV. OF BANKING L. 89 (1984) (discussing legal implications of retail repurchase agreements).

large minority—including many that had converted from mutual to stock form of ownership—got into serious trouble managing their loans. Asset quality problems became especially widespread in Texas and other energy "boom" areas after oil prices collapsed in 1986, and in parts of the Sunbelt where excessive real estate speculation occurred. By the end of the 1980s, hundreds of these thrifts had become seriously insolvent, with hundreds more in trouble. This led to an emergency FSLIC "bailout" in 1989 under FIRREA, and a transfer of S & L supervision and insurance responsibilities to the banking regulators (the OCC and FDIC respectively).[3] Massive FSLIC liabilities had developed that required a huge clean-up operation. By early 1992 at least $160 billion in outlays had accumulated to close or merge insolvent thrifts (and to dispose of "assets" taken in receiverships). Another $200–300 billion in ultimate interest costs were projected by some experts.

How did this situation get out of hand? First, many S & Ls had suffered weakened capitalization by 1982 as a result of interest rate "squeeze"—losses caused by limited earnings from lower-rate mortgages and a rising cost of deposits in the 1978–1981 inflation surge. The FHLBB tried to help weakened S & Ls by allowing lower capitalization, and more relaxed

---

[3] The Financial Institutions Reform, Recovery, and Enforcement Act of 1989 (FIRREA) folded the FSLIC into FDIC, and the FHLBB into a new Office of Thrift Supervision (OTS) within the Department of the Treasury. The new OTS Director became another member of the FDIC Board (joining the FDIC Chairman, Comptroller, and two independent FDIC members). FIRREA also created the Resolution Trust Corporation (RTC) to manage and sell off the assets of failed institutions.

accounting (especially for "good will" derived from seriously troubled thrifts that had been merged into somewhat stronger thrifts). Before 1980, the capital/assets ratio for FSLIC insured thrift institutions had been 5 percent. The DIDMCA of 1980 relaxed this to a range of 3–6%, with the FHLBB setting the specific ratio. The FHLBB reduced the required ratio to 4 percent in 1980, and later to 3 percent in 1982. Meanwhile, the Garn-St. Germain Act of 1982 allowed all thrifts and banks to borrow medium-term from the FSLIC and FDIC, respectively, to replenish net worth, if their mortgage portfolios equaled 20 percent or more of outstanding loans. Between 1986 and 1989, the FSLIC was overwhelmed with too many troubled and increasingly insolvent thrifts.

Second, the FHLBB relaxed accounting rules by allowing deferral of loan loss recognition and by allowing many insolvent thrifts to be absorbed into acquiring institutions with unrealistic "good will" valuations. Both accounting devices were extensively employed to somewhat overstate the asset or capital values in troubled thrift institutions, and to delay full recognition of their actual or impending insolvency. By 1984, these loose accounting devices allowed some 600 institutions, with over one-third of the industry's assets, to avoid reporting insolvency.

Third, the widespread encouragement of new thrift entrepreneurs in the early–mid-1980s, with additional capital (converting mutuals into stock institutions or chartering new stock savings banks) brought many aggressive, high-growth oriented managers into commercial real estate lending. Conversion of thrifts from the older, traditional mutual forms into stock S & Ls or stock savings banks had become a priority in the early 1980s. The advantages of conversion were three-fold: (i) additional equity capital, with the potential for greater earnings for stockholders; (ii) extra profits and stock-option benefits for managers who themselves became equity shareholders; and (iii) the potential for more easily arranged mergers with other stock associations or savings banks. In the context of weakened net capital for thrifts, with many mergers and consolidations inevitable, the advantages of conversion seemed important. A great many conversions occurred quickly, such that there were 1,285 stock S & Ls by the end of 1988 (1,644 remained as mutuals). More stock thrifts followed in later years, some by conversion, and others by new entry, with others by acquisition over the years as well.

Fourth, the Garn-St. Germain Act gave S & Ls broader commercial real estate lending powers and allowed unrestricted interest rates on deposits. This was designed to help troubled thrifts make more money, and attract more deposits. A few key states, Texas, Florida, and California, went even further with much broader lending authority for state-chartered S & Ls and/or savings banks. These states offered great potential for speculative real estate investments, and many of the worst-case institutions developed in these states. Unfortunately, giving troubled thrifts a much longer leash allowed many of them to get into much bigger trouble.

Fifth, regulatory supervision relaxed somewhat in 1982–1985 under a deregulation-oriented administration, and with budget constraints on staffing and excessive turnover among examiners. When oil prices slumped heavily in early 1986, many more substandard, doubtful loans quickly accumulated in many S & L and new savings bank portfolios in the Southwest-Sunbelt States. At the same time, a potential landslide of risky commercial real estate loans had been building up. More of the substandard loans were concentrated in a few hundred institutions, often with the most aggressive growth strategies, while attracting deposits with premium interest rates through deposit brokers.[4] The biggest concentration of this questionable loan expansion was in Texas, and to a lesser extent Louisiana and Oklahoma.

During 1985–1987 the FHLBB and FSLIC gradually began to realize that more insolvencies and troubled institutions were developing. In 1984, the FHLBB attempted to limit riskier thrifts by restricting deposit brokers, but the courts promptly held this regulation illegal and unenforceable. In 1985 the FHLBB began to restrict deposit growth slightly for under-capitalized thrifts, and raised prospective capital ratios in 1986, and somewhat

---

4 A "deposit broker" is an intermediary who solicits and consolidates funds of prospective depositors and negotiates *en bloc* with a depository institution for a jumbo rate for placement of the consolidated deposits. For an early case involving a "solicitor" of deposits for a national bank, see *Case v. First Nat'l Bank of City of Brooklyn*, 109 N.Y.S. 1119, 59 Misc. 269 (Sup. Ct. 1908) (permitting the practice on a short-term basis).

further in 1987. Supervisory staff was significantly expanded after 1985, but a mushrooming number of thrift insolvencies quickly overwhelmed the FSLIC's net deposit insurance reserves.[5]

Constrained by limited FSLIC reserves, the FHLBB developed the Management Consignment Program (MCP) in early 1985—a provisional holding status for insolvent thrifts under new caretaker managers that tried to contain further financial losses, so that mergers or other less expensive resolutions could be worked out later. More than 100 insolvent thrifts were put into the MCP during 1985–1988; 26 still remained for disposal at the end of 1988. But additional FSLIC resources were needed to properly close or assist disposal for the expanding roster of insolvent thrifts.

In early 1986 the FHLBB had proposed a $15 billion borrowing program for the FSLIC (based on future deposit insurance premiums, and $3 billion current net worth in the FHLBs). The Administration and Congressional leaders were slow to appreciate the seriousness of thrift insolvencies,

---

[5] By the end of 1984 FSLIC reserves were only $5.6 billion, and 71 institutions with $15 billion assets were already insolvent under relatively lenient regulatory accounting principles, which departed from generally accepted accounting principles (GAAP). Under traditional GAAP accounting, 374 thrifts with $95 billion assets were insolvent at the close of 1984. Meanwhile, FSLIC and FDIC insurance premium rates had been modest; only 1/12 of one percent for deposits. Previous failures had been few and involved relatively small losses before the early 1980s. Although the FHLBB levied special assessments that increased FSLIC premiums 150 percent in 1985, this yielded only $1 billion in additional reserves.

and 15 months passed without significant action. Then the General Accounting Office reported FSLIC itself insolvent, since its contingent liabilities for unresolved thrifts exceeded reserve assets. Meanwhile, the thrift industry resisted extensive closures, preferring more forbearance. This led to more caretaking of operating but insolvent thrifts. Finally, in July Congress enacted the Competitive Equality Banking Act (CEBA) with $10.8 billion additional borrowing authority for FSLIC.

With this funding, the FHLBB and the FSLIC tried to dispose of more thrifts quickly. By the end of 1987, there were 351 insolvent thrifts with $99 billion assets (and net worth of $21 billion). Texas thrifts alone accounted for roughly half these losses. Accordingly, the "Southwest Plan" received top priority. Of 205 thrifts "disposed of" in 1988 (with $100 billion assets), 81 were Texas thrifts.[6] Sixty percent of the $30 billion disposal costs that year went for Texas thrifts. These disposals were controversial, however, because of substantial losses incurred by the FSLIC, and relatively generous terms conceded to thrift purchasers—often with guarantees against loss by the FSLIC.

Neither Congressional nor Administration leaders chose to highlight FSLIC problems during the 1988 election year. But by year end, despite many disposals, about 500 thrifts with $300 billion in assets were insolvent on a tangible net worth basis, and a third of the industry was still unprofitable.

---

[6] Most of these involved assisted mergers, or 179 acquisitions with $27 billion in FSLIC costs.

Once elected, President George H. W. Bush felt obliged to clean up the FSLIC mess promptly. Congress went along, because the FSLIC crisis was now obvious.[7]

A significant FSLIC bailout through massive borrowing was authorized by the FIRREA, which was enacted in August 1989. The FHLBB and the FSLIC were abolished, and their powers and authority were transferred into the new OTS in the Treasury Department and FDIC, respectively.[8] The OTS took over supervision, while the FDIC's deposit insurance funding was divided into separate parts—the Bank Insurance Fund (BIF) and Savings Association Insurance Fund (SAIF). Deposit insurance premiums were raised substantially, though more rapidly at first for thrifts. Ironically, within several years FDIC bank deposit insurance premiums were as high as thrift premiums, because of increasingly expensive commercial bank failures in 1989–1992. Many larger banks got into trouble with bad real estate loans and highly leveraged corporate lending.

Heavy FSLIC bailout borrowing began in 1989 ($20 billion *on budget* from the Treasury, and $30 billion *off budget*). By early 1992, $160 billion in FSLIC liabilities had accumulated, with some

---

[7] Political observers noted that "blame" for neglect of thrift insolvencies could not be assigned on a partisan basis. Leaders in both parties, regulators and most industry lobbyists had all played roles in not facing up to thrift problems earlier.

[8] Only a modest remnant of the FHLBB survived, a new Federal Housing Finance Board (FHFB), to provide oversight for the Federal Home Loan Banks (owned by the thrift industry through its District Banks).

experts projecting another $200–300 billion in borrowing costs. (The majority of costs will be borne by taxpayers—a lesson in the social costs of excessive forbearance with insolvent institutions.) Meanwhile, the RTC became responsible for collecting bad loans and foreclosed assets from failed thrifts. The RTC took over the role of the Federal Asset Disposal Association (FADA), an FSLIC affiliate between 1985–1989. By the mid-1990s, it was hoped, most of the RTC's assets, largely real estate mortgages and assets, would have been sold off or liquidated.

FIRREA had important effects in other areas: (1) Mergers and acquisitions by banks of S & Ls and savings banks were generally allowed under FIRREA. Under the Garn-St. Germain Act of 1982, only failing institutions had been allowed to merge across these traditional boundaries, with clear preferences for mergers among institutions of the same type and, as far as possible, within the same state.

(2) Higher net worth or capital standards were to be phased-in over several years under FIRREA, so that S & Ls, savings banks, and banks would operate together under the same "leverage" (3 percent) and "risk-based capital" requirements (8 percent) as established for banks in 1987–1989. There were some anomalies in this new capital system. For example, under the risk-based capital requirements, *residential* real estate (*conservatively appraised*) carries only a 50 percent risk rating. Thus, effective capital needed for *residential* real estate lending is only 4 percent under international standards.

Commercial real estate, however, would carry the full 8 percent capital requirement for *these* loan assets.

(3) Enforcement powers, civil penalties, fines, and criminal sentences were strengthened under FIRREA, with enlarged authority to remove officers and directors, and explicit FDIC power to suspend or terminate deposit insurance for thrifts or banks.

(4) The "Qualified Thrift Lender" (QTL) test was strengthened in FIRREA, so that to enjoy some tax, credit, and accounting advantages, S & Ls and savings banks must hold at least 70 percent of their assets in housing-related assets. The earlier CEBA of 1987 had initiated the QTL test with a 60 percent requirement. This QTL test was designed to encourage and reward more conservative, traditional thrifts that did not get into overly risky, dangerous, and speculative diversification. (Some questioned these QTL restrictions, however, wondering whether diversification had been the main problem—as opposed to under-capitalization and weakened supervision. But many felt that an excessive, sudden surge of commercial lending by inexperienced thrift managements was a major part of the FSLIC fiasco.)

(5) Because a limited number of thrifts got into very serious trouble with heavy investments in "junk bonds," thrifts were generally prohibited under FIRREA from investing in corporate debt securities below "investment grade." Transition rules were provided to phase out most of such low-grade investments by mid-1994.

(6) Many of the worst managed, most costly thrifts were state-chartered (in Texas, Florida, or California), where much wider investment latitude had been allowed. Therefore, FIRREA generally prohibited state-chartered thrifts from any investment activity not allowed to federally chartered institutions, unless the FDIC determines there is no risk to its reserve fund, and the thrift is fully complying with capitalization standards.

Clearly, a major consequence of the FSLIC fiasco, and the heavy costs of cleaning up nearly 1,000 insolvent or seriously troubled thrift institutions, was an increased consciousness of the need for supervision, prudential regulation, and adequate capital for financial institutions generally. Attitudes in Congress, the press, and the public shifted somewhat away from the deregulation enthusiasm of the early–mid-1980s. The FDIC Improvement Act of 1991 (described at length in Chapter 3) reflected the new mood.

More recently, however, much of the thrift industry recovered their financial health. Generally, the "problem" institutions had either failed or recovered by the mid-1990s. But the consolidation movement that hit the U.S. banking industry since the mid-1980s continued throughout the full range of depository institutions. Commercial banks declined in numbers from 14,285 to 7,338 between 1985–2008, while bank assets grew from $2,350 billion to $11,806 billion in these 24 years. Savings banks and S & Ls declined from 3,905 to 1,265 between 1985–2008, but thrift assets (S & Ls, savings banks, and credit unions) grew modestly from $1,414 billion in 1985 to $2,591 billion in 2008.[9] Substantial numbers of thrift institutions, and their assets, had been acquired by commercial banks in these years. Also significant was a disparity in FDIC insurance premium assessments for BIF institutions—as compared to SAIF-insured S & Ls and savings banks—prior to the merger of the BIF and SAIF into the consolidated DIF, pursuant to the Federal Deposit Insurance Reform Act. Meanwhile, other cost pressures, computerization, and increased competition from mutual funds (especially money market mutual funds) adversely impacted some S & Ls and savings banks. This squeezed their profit margins, which encouraged some mergers and consolidation among thrifts and by banks.

In the aftermath of the financial crisis that began in 2008, more dramatic changes occurred in the thrift sector. The Dodd-Frank Act transferred the functions and responsibilities of the OTS to the OCC, except for authority over savings and loan holding companies and affiliate transactions, which was transferred to the Federal Reserve. The transfer was effective July 21, 2011, and the OTS and the position of its director were to be abolished 90 days after that effective date. This transfer triggered a lengthy process in which the OCC and the Federal Reserve began amending their regulations to assimilate and adapt OTS rules governing the supervision of thrift institutions and their holding companies.

---

[9] Credit unions declined substantially in numbers, *i.e.*, from 17,581 in 1985 to 8,238 in 2008.

F. CREDIT UNION REGULATION

Credit unions were the last major thrift institutions developed in the United States. They began as another type of small scale, cooperative borrowing and savings institution in Germany during the 1850s. These credit cooperatives spread to other countries including Scandinavia, Switzerland, France, and Italy, but became especially strong in Germany. The credit union concept spread to the United States, and the first U.S. credit unions were founded in 1909. The first general statute was the Massachusetts Credit Union Act of 1909, and that state quickly became the pacesetter in credit union development.

What distinguished credit unions from MSBs and S & Ls was their emphasis on a common bond of workers, church members, or people in a local area, wanting to borrow relatively small amounts at reasonable interest rates from each other, and help each other save to meet short-term needs. Their goal was to provide a low interest rate alternative to loan sharks or pawnbrokers. In the United States, credit unions developed mainly among urban or smaller town workers, but did not do so well among farmers as in Northern Europe. The credit union became the smallest and most informal of thrift institutions. And the credit union objective of making installment loans at modest rates with their deposits was quite different from MSBs or S & Ls, whose asset portfolios stressed security and good returns to savers. Many early credit unions emphasized borrower needs more than saving, although some diversity among credit unions developed in the growth of this movement.

During the next decade credit unions spread unevenly on a modest scale. Philanthropic backers were important in some early credit union societies, although democratic self-rule and elected officers were an organizing theme, along with virtues of thrift, regular work, and mutual assistance. By 1920 there were 64 credit unions in Massachusetts, 68 in New York, 33 in North Carolina (all rural), and relatively few elsewhere. The next year the nation had 190 credit unions altogether, with a total of only 72,000 members.

By 1929 there were about 1,000 credit unions with 265,000 members, spreading into more states (with credit union chartering laws in a dozen states). Members were mostly employees with some local or occupational common bond. Yet the aggregate resources of credit unions remained modest, only $54 million in outstanding loans to individuals. The Great Depression reduced the deposits available to credit unions, and their total loans dropped to $16 million in 1932. However, the number of credit union societies had grown to 1700 by that year, and a broader cooperative movement began to strengthen interest in credit unions.

When Roosevelt's New Deal came to Washington in 1933, a push began for a federal credit union law. Congress passed the Federal Credit Union Act of 1934, which provided federal chartering authority, and a small staff to facilitate organizing efforts, and a Credit Union Section of the Farm Credit

Administration (FCA) was established in the Agriculture Department. Shortly thereafter the Credit Union National Association (CUNA) was founded. One of its first priorities, apart from organizing efforts, was an insurance affiliate, CUNA Mutual Insurance Society set up in 1935. This offered credit life insurance for CUNA loans, and it helped to strengthen the reliability of installment credit assets. A few years later an independent CUNA Life Insurance Co. was established to offer smaller life insurance policies to members.

There were controversies in the credit union movement as it grew. There was conflict over the proper interest rate charges on loans to members, *i.e.*, borrower-oriented 6 percent versus a saver-oriented 7–10 percent. There were also disputes as to how expansion was to be financed, *i.e.*, through CUNA dues, income on CUNA affiliate insurance, or federal FCA staff budgets? CUNA dues for credit unions became the main resource for expansion. By 1941, there were 9,891 credit unions, with 3.3 million members and $320 million assets, and credit unions held 3.3 percent of consumer installment loans.

During World War II, installment credit loans by credit unions were restricted, along with other policies to control war-time inflation. This reduced credit union lending by roughly 50 percent. However, improved wages and earnings expanded credit union deposits and assets by 50 percent, even though membership and the number of credit unions declined slightly. Another complication proved awkward, when the credit union section of the FCA was transferred to the FDIC. CUNA soon began to complain of FDIC restrictions, delays in chartering, and a prohibition of CUNA credit life insurance. Therefore, CUNA sought to move the credit union section, and its chartering responsibilities to a more friendly agency, the Federal Security Agency (social security). The transfer was achieved in 1948, and the section became the Bureau of Federal Credit Unions, which facilitated chartering activity.

CUNA added automobile insurance to its offerings for credit unions in 1949, through private insurance company contracts that it sponsored. Yet CUNA opposed any federal credit union guarantees on accounts (like FDIC or FSLIC insurance), preferring to maintain CUNA affiliate bonding insurance for credit union officers responsible for funds. CUNA saw this as a sufficient safeguard against the risk of theft, embezzlement and fraudulent credit union managers, while allowing lower cost borrowing by credit union members.

By 1960 there were 20,047 credit unions, with 12 million members and $5.6 billion assets. These societies were becoming more mature; many had full-time staff and offices, and some were sizeable institutions. The common bond for most credit unions was still the employment relationship, but credit unions were becoming commonplace among employers, especially those with a larger work force. Some kinds of employees were especially prone to credit unions, including government workers, the military, teachers, aerospace, universities, hospitals, IBM, and some public utilities. In the late 1960s, some new credit unions were organized with the Office of Economic Opportunity (part of the "War on Poverty" program), but by this time credit unions were no longer oriented mainly to poorer workers, and this new drive did not become a major part of the credit union network. By 1969, 23,731 credit unions were in operation, with 21 million members and $16 billion assets. At this stage regulatory maturity was established, with basic new legislation.

In 1970 the National Credit Union Administration (NCUA) was created, which took over the chartering, supervision and examining function for federal credit unions. State authorities continue to supervise state-chartered credit unions. Congress also established the National Credit Union Share Insurance Fund (NCUSIF), administered through NCUA, to insure credit union accounts. By 1981, 12,000 federally chartered credit unions, and the majority of nearly 9,000 state-chartered credit unions, were insured by NCUSIF, with limits on insurance raised to $100,000 per account. By 1995, 97 percent of credit union savings were NCUSIF insured, with most of the remainder insured under state plans or privately. Like the Federal Reserve and the FHLBB, NCUA is self-financing, with income from chartering, examination, supervision, and insurance fees. NCUA is now administered by a three-member board, appointed by the president with the confirmation of the Senate. The term of each member is six years, staggered so that one member's term expires every two years. One member is designated by the President as Chairman of the NCUA Board, and one as Vice Chairman.

In 1978, Congress added another feature to NCUA, a National Credit Union Central Liquidity Facility. This provides discounting and loan support to credit unions, and supplements previously established mutual support arrangements and borrowing. Among the latter institutions is the private U.S. Central Credit Union, with $22 billion assets, which provides support and financial services to the "corporate" credit unions (most of the stronger credit unions became members of the "corporate" credit union network).

The distribution of common bonds in the credit unions active in 2003 was 70 percent occupational (or employer-related), 15 percent associational, and 15 percent residential. Within the employer-related group, 10 percent of all credit unions were in manufacturing, 11 percent governmental, 10 percent educational and health, and the remainder scattered through other sectors. The NCUA later adopted a policy allowing an application filed by a credit union to expand its field of membership to include employees of various small businesses that were unaffiliated with credit union's existing membership base. In 1998, the Supreme Court in a 5–4 decision held that the common bond provision of Federal Credit Union Act (FCUA) required that *all* members of an occupational credit union share a *single* common bond. *NCUA v. First National Bank and Trust Co.*, 522 U.S. 479 (1998). Congress promptly and overwhelmingly passed corrective legislation, the Credit Union Membership Access Act of 1998, that reinstated the NCUA multiple group policy, with some modifications.

In 2008 there were 8,064 credit unions (according to CUNA, Inc.), with 90 million members and $814 billion assets. This represented a large minority of the entire U.S. population, and accounted for $424 billion in loans to members. Aggregate assets of U.S. commercial banks at $11,806 billion still dwarfed the credit unions, and the $1,851 billion for S & Ls and savings banks were greater, too. But credit unions have become significant financial institutions, with more substantial growth in the last decade than S & Ls and savings banks.

Fortunately, credit union failures have been relatively infrequent, and involved only small institutions. For the most part, credit unions maintained their traditional lines of business and avoided serious trouble. They continued consumer-family loans, *e.g.*, cars, furniture, home renovations, house mortgages, etc., and avoided risky new areas—like commercial real estate, which became the downfall of so many S & Ls and savings banks. Because of relatively high customer loyalty, they also seemed to be able to avoid the severe disintermediation that threatened so many other thrift institutions. The average capital/assets ratio was 11.2 percent in 2008, appreciably stronger than for commercial banks, savings banks, and S & Ls. (The only significant exception to this pattern was a group of credit union failures in Rhode Island, with a state funded deposit insurance scheme that became overwhelmed in the 1980s, much like the FSLIC. Their problems stemmed largely from bolder lending activities, including real estate, which got some credit unions into deeper waters where some of them foundered.)

Credit unions (like banks, MSBs and S & Ls) vary greatly in size. The largest, Virginia Navy Federal Credit Union of Merrifield, Va. held $8.4 billion assets in 1996, and in 2003 around 250 credit unions had more than $500 million assets, and another 400 credit unions at least $200 million assets. But the average credit union in 2003 held only $60 million assets; the great majority, 63 percent of credit unions, were still small operations, with $50 million or less assets.

This varied size, with different mixtures of educational background, income, and outlook among members, leads to somewhat divergent policies, expectations of service, and management capacities. The large, more affluent credit unions normally offer a wider spread of financial services, and may emphasize saver perspectives more than borrowers. Small credit unions, on the other hand, confine themselves to one or a few basic accounts, and more limited loans for automobiles, furniture, and other personal or family needs. However, most credit unions include a range of members, some older, others younger, with more or less income, so that a portion will be substantial savers, while another will be borrowers. Most credit unions are net savers overall, with surplus invested in various assets, whereas others may be net borrowers for their members. Their asset and liability structures reflect these variations in emphasis, with more or less investment outside the credit union, some liquid reserves, and perhaps, limited borrowing to meet service needs. This helps explain why the mutual support, borrowing, and lending operations among credit unions, through the U.S. Central Credit Union and the National Credit Union Central Liquidity Facility, and other external borrowing and investment activities, have become so useful to the credit union network.

Supervision, examination, and correction of credit union malpractices by the NCUA and state regulatory authorities is comparable to the supervision of other thrift institutions. Thus, NCUA employs rulemaking authority, along with powers to suspend charters, remove officers and directors, and impose involuntary liquidation for insolvency or violations of charters, by laws or regulatory requirement. In this way, misconduct by irresponsible officers and directors, and misappropriation of funds can be minimized. Bonding requirements for officers and directors, and NCUSIF insurance provide further safeguards.

Charters for credit unions are either federal or state, with similar requirements. Compared to banks and other thrift institutions, the process of chartering credit unions is simple and relatively inexpensive. Perhaps most important, chartering does not encourage protestants to resist increased competition. Rivalry among credit unions is limited normally by the fact that each common bond group is served by only one society. Provided that an employer company, institution, locality, or government agency is agreeable to a credit union, minimum requirements for members, initial contributions, and bylaws provide no real barrier to entry for sizable groups of employees. Employers usually find the credit union helpful as a fringe benefit of employment, and it tends to improve employee morale. The main requirements for a charter are a showing of (i) a common bond (occupational, associational, or locational) that provides an adequate foundation, (ii) sufficient economic prospects, and (iii) an initial group of responsible leaders and sample subscribers. Federal and state chartering agencies are helpful in explaining charter procedures, and CUNA, Inc. has a network of fieldworkers in every state to provide instruction and chartering kits, along with expert advice. In contrast to other financial institutions, entry into the marketplace is facilitated for new credit unions.

There has been extensive consolidation activity among credit unions, as when mergers occur among companies, or for other reasons of convenience, and liquidations occur (usually voluntary) for credit unions that do not catch on or retain adequate membership. The peak in numbers of credit unions was reached in 1970 with about 23,700, and the figure for 2003 had declined to 10,841 (according to CUNA data). However, the overall membership in credit unions, and assets held by them, have increased steadily over these years, from 22.7 million to 85 million members, with assets growing from $18 to $599 billion in the same period 1970–2003.

A modest employer "subsidy" was typical for credit unions, at least in their early stages. Office space, equipment, and supplies are frequently furnished. Officers and directors elected from employee ranks (often personnel administrators, accountants, or engineers) are not discouraged from these responsibilities, for the benefit of the company or institution involved. As assets and earnings build up most credit unions hire part- or full-time employees for filing, bookkeeping, and member services. Eventually, full-time salaried managers take over as earnings justify overhead expenses. Among the important advantages of a credit union is being part of the personnel system of a responsible employer. This involves access to personnel records, and the employment relation greatly facilitates reliable debt collection.

Interest rates paid by credit unions reflected more flexibility than passbook savings accounts in commercial banks, S & Ls, or savings banks. On the other hand, credit unions normally charge somewhat lower interest rates to borrowers than consumer finance companies or other institutions for small loans. This thinner margin is justified by low default rates, reduced credit risks, and lower cost operations in credit unions.

Although the growth of new deposits for credit unions slowed somewhat in 1978–1982, there was no disintermediation or outflow from credit unions comparable to that suffered by other thrift institutions (S & Ls and MSBs). Nor did credit unions suffer as serious a squeeze on earnings. Three factors explain this contrast: (i) greater loyalty of credit union members to their institutions; (ii) somewhat higher interest rates and more flexibility for credit unions; and (iii) much less involvement by credit unions in real estate mortgages, generally speaking.

PART C

REGULATION OF OTHER FINANCIAL INTERMEDIARIES

CHAPTER VI
SECURITIES MARKET REGULATION

A. ROLE OF SECURITIES MARKETS

Securities markets and financial intermediaries help to mobilize the savings, loanable funds, and resources available for investment in society. These resources are gathered by appropriate incentives, interest payable, and profits shared (or some kind of taxation), through financial intermediaries, securities markets, and government operations. Although some saving and investment occurs internally within households, business enterprises, other institutions, and government, the larger portion of savings in a complex industrial society flows through financial intermediaries and the securities markets. (*See* Chart VI-1 *infra.*) In this way, specialized information, talent, and risk pooling makes safer, more productive allocations for many investments than would otherwise be feasible within households (or other direct resource holding organizations). The allocations within each alternative channel for intermediation and investment should be optimized by free market price competition. The constantly adjusting network of markets, supplies, demands, and prices tends to equilibrate real rates of return, adjusted for risks and uncertainties. Thus, every decision-making unit in society (whether a household, business, institution, or element of government) tries to make the most efficient and productive use of resources, and this allocates the optimum flow of resources through each channel for savings and outlays—internal investments, financial intermediaries, securities markets, and government.

Chart VI-1
Financial Intermediation and Securities Markets

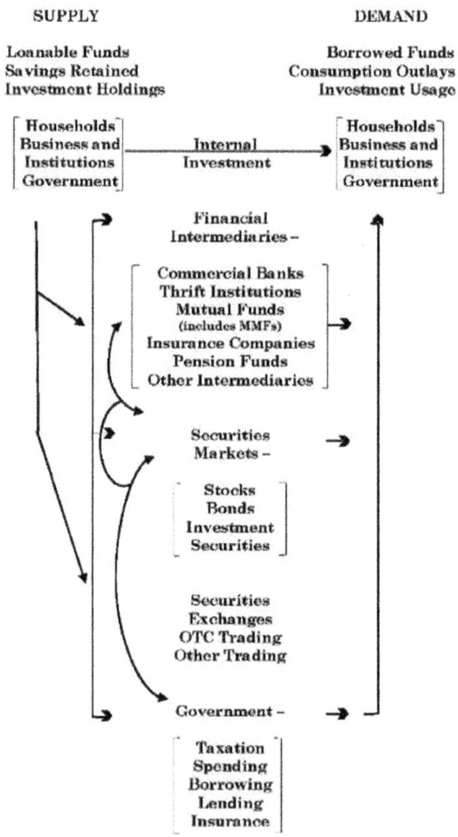

Securities markets are an outgrowth of mercantile prosperity. Whenever trading flourishes there is opportunity for joint venture deals and investments. Joint stock companies and modern business corporations evolved over the last few centuries as a further refinement in this process. Trading in stock, bonds, and other investment securities developed naturally in the larger mercantile centers. Stock exchanges merely formalize this trading more efficiently. They provide buyers and sellers of securities a convenient focal point, where trading takes place quickly, with better information, more reliable brokers, and competitive prices. Britain created the first modern stock exchange in London in 1773, and similar stock exchanges spread through the more prosperous countries of Europe and America in the Nineteenth Century. The London Stock Exchange set a pattern for the New York Stock Exchange (NYSE), the American Stock Exchange (AMEX), and regional exchanges. Characteristic features of organized exchanges are: limited membership for professional traders, specialists ("market makers") inside the exchanges for many securities, self-regulation for the convenience and protection of members, restrictions on outside dealing in listed securities, and policies enforcing integrity of traders for the public's benefit. In most nations, these standards were developed privately by the exchanges, but government regulation has tended to reinforce and supplement them, especially since the Great Depression.

Financial and securities markets have become increasingly "internationalized" over the last 50 years. Broader prosperity followed, but bigger risks of booms, disruptions, inflations, and slumps are natural complications of this prosperity. Accordingly, national governments, central banks, securities market regulators, insurance supervisors, and legislative bodies became more active in monitoring, regulating, and supporting the markets. In addition, a larger role is now played by international institutions like the International Monetary Fund, the Bank for International Settlements, the International Association of Insurance Supervisors, the International Organization of Securities Commissions (IOSCO), and the World Bank.

B. UNITED STATES SECURITIES REGULATION SYSTEM

Securities market regulation in the United States was prompted mainly by the Great Depression. Earlier securities trading had developed informally, regulated by contract and corporation law (mostly at the state level), and through the evolution of the NYSE, AMEX, and regional exchanges. The Stock Market Crash of 1929, and the Depression that followed, were traumatic events that led to the present system of regulation. (*See* Chart VI-2 Summary, *infra.*) Its main elements comprise: (i) statutory registration and disclosure requirements to enforce more complete, accurate information for market participants; (ii) Securities and Exchange Commission (SEC) supervision and regulation of the disclosure process, the stock exchanges, over-the-counter market, the National Association of Securities Dealers (NASD) and its successor, the

Financial Industry Regulatory Authority (FINRA); (iii) enforcement of disclosure and anti-fraud policies by the SEC and private litigation encouraged under the law; and (iv) Securities Investor Protection Corporation (SIPC) insurance for accounts held for customers by brokerage firms, though not for securities owned directly by the public.

In contrast to the banking and thrift regulatory systems, where federal and state regulatory authorities impose trustee-like accountability on such institutions and their managers, with strong efforts to preserve and regulate growth of the money supply, SEC supervision of securities markets is much more limited. So long as adequate disclosure is assured, and deceptive practices and market manipulation minimized, the securities regulation system assumes investors should take their own risks. Investments, for the most part, are considered to be more risky, hopefully more profitable, and not deserving of government safeguards to the same degree as demand or other liquid deposits in financial institutions like banks and thrift institutions. Thus, the major theme of securities regulation is registration and disclosure enforced by SEC and private remedies. The firms participating in the securities business, exchanges, underwriters, dealers, brokers, investment companies, mutual funds, and their sales forces are subject to much lighter, though not inconsiderable, supervision than financial institutions.

Money markets, liquidity, and their regulation (discussed in Chapters II–V), clearly impact securities markets, especially through interest rates. But monetary policies do not attempt, with very limited exceptions, to regulate securities directly. And, for many years (1933–1999) the Glass-Steagall Act provisions largely separated commercial banking from securities distribution and marketing. Hence, securities regulation is quite distinct from banking and insurance regulation.

Chart VI-2
Securities Regulation System

Scope

Stocks, bonds debentures, investments certificates, variable annuities, and profit sharing interests.

Exemptions for deposits, accounts, and CDs in financial institutions; ordinary life insurance and annuity policies; and many pension funds, along with most IRAs and Keoghs in exempt categories.

Registration and Disclosure Disciplines

[Securities Act of 1933; Securities Exchange Act of 1934, Trust Indenture Act of 1939, Investment Company Act of 1940]

Underwriting and Distribution—
- Federal registration requirements
- State Blue Sky laws
- Administrative enforcement
- Private remedies

Publicly Held Companies—
- Periodic disclosure and reports
- Proxy solicitations
- Takeover bids and tender offers
- Insider trading and "short swing" profits*

Trading—
- Securities exchanges—

---

* Pursuant to Securities Exchange Act § 16(b), 15 U.S.C.A. § 78p(b), which applies to directors, officers and principal shareholders of publicly traded issuers registered under the act.

Self regulated under SEC supervision
Members and specialists

Industry Regulation

Investment Bankers and Underwriters—
- Disclosure discipline
- Separation from commercial banking (eroding)
- Domestic underwriting
- International underwriting

Broker-Dealer Network (NASD)—
- Responsibilities
  - Net capital rules
  - Segregation of customer funds and securities

SEC supervision

Securities Investor Protection Corporation (SIPC)—
- Account insurance
- Assessments and borrowing authority
- Protective supervision and remedies

Investment Companies (including Mutual Funds)
- Regulated operations
- Registration and reporting
- Assets and capital
- Management restrictions
- Selling and price restrictions
- Money market mutual funds

Investment Advisors—
- Registration requirements
- Advisory contracts and compensation restrictions

Antifraud, Deceptive Practice and Manipulation Remedies

Administrative enforcement
- Private remedies**
- Margin regulation
- Arbitration remedies

** Pursuant to SEC regulations issued under the authority of Securities Exchange Act § 10(b), 15 U.S.C.A. § 78j(b), which applies to "any security registered on a national securities exchange or any security not so registered, or any securities-based swap agreement. . . ."

Commissions

OTC Market—

NASD trading outside exchanges

National Market System (computer linkages)

Other Trading—

Institutional trading

Other private transactions

1. SCOPE OF SECURITIES REGULATION

Registration and disclosure requirements administered by the SEC apply to "securities." The term is defined under the Securities Act of 1933 as

> any note, stock, treasury stock, security future, security-based swap, bond, debenture, evidence of indebtedness, certificate of interest or participation in any profit-sharing agreement, collateral-trust certificate, preorganization certificate or subscription, transferable share, investment contract, voting-trust certificate, certificate of deposit for a security, fractional undivided interest in oil, gas, or other mineral rights, any put, call, straddle, option, or privilege on any security, certificate of deposit, or group or index of securities (including any interest therein or based on the value thereof), or any put, call, straddle, option, or privilege entered into on a national securities exchange relating to foreign currency, *or, in general, any interest or instrument commonly known as a "security"* . . . .

15 U.S.C.A. § 77b(a)(1) (emphasis added). Especially in light of the highlighted phrase in the definition, this is a very broad definition. Similar, but not

identical, definitions of the term "security" appear in the Securities Exchange Act, Investment Company Act, and most state securities laws. But most accounts in banks or financial institutions, trust accounts, share accounts in thrifts, or certificates of deposit in such institutions are exempted from the securities laws.[1] Likewise, ordinary insurance policy contracts (not involving variable annuities or profit sharing) are not considered securities.

Limited categories of securities are exempted from registration requirements under the securities acts, including federal, state, and local government obligations. The 1933 Act (but not the 1934 Act) also exempts securities issued by banks, savings and loan associations, and religious and charitable organizations. Short-term notes (with less than 9-month maturity), known as commercial paper, are *in effect* exempted securities under both acts.[2]

To deal with the gap for government obligations, Congress created the Municipal Securities Rulemaking Board in 1975, and after June 30, 1983, there was a registration process for new municipal (state and local) securities. Considerable information

---

[1] On the other hand, banks received more authority in recent years to sell securities or mutual funds to their customers. These products are not exempt—despite the bank involvement—and must be registered with disclosures like other securities under the law.

[2] Strictly speaking, these notes are only *exempted* from the registration requirements of the 1933 Act. They are *excluded* from the definition of the term "security" for purposes of the 1934 Act. In practical terms, this means that fraudulent statements about the notes might be punishable under section 17 of the 1933 Act, but *not* under section 10(b) of the 1934 Act.

had already been disclosed, however, and forms the basis for privately published ratings on these securities. Some reporting is also required under the Internal Revenue Code to obtain tax-free status. Subsequently in the mid-1990s, the SEC began some anti-fraud enforcement in the municipal bond area. The December 1994 municipal bankruptcy of Orange County, CA also added to public concerns, with a highly publicized insolvency proceeding.

Finally, federal registration requirements for securities do not apply to private placements, intrastate offerings (though these may be regulated by state "blue sky" law[3] requirements), and certain small offerings. Thus, investments among relatively small groups of investors, often involving limited partnerships, are routinely made without the cost, disclosure, or safeguards of formal registration. They are still subject, however, to the antifraud provisions of federal law, because these provisions apply to all securities, whether or not subject to registration requirements.

---

[3] The expression "blue sky law," referring to state securities statutes, was reportedly first popularized by Kansas bank commissioner J. N. Dolley during his successful efforts to have Kansas enact the first such statute in 1911. One of the earliest uses of the expression in the case law is *Hall v. Geiger-Jones Co.*, 242 U.S. 539, 550 (1917) (explaining that Ohio securities statute was referred to as "blue sky law" to indicate "the evil at which it is aimed; that is, . . . 'speculative schemes which have no more basis than so many feet of 'blue sky'").

2. REGISTRATION AND DISCLOSURE PROCESS

Under the Securities Act of 1933, unless an exemption applies, no "security" (as defined previously) may be offered or sold to the public unless it is registered with the SEC. This requires a "registration statement" meeting SEC requirements, and acceptable disclosure has become a precondition for general marketing of such securities to the public. The registration statement comprises a prospectus, a copy of which must be furnished to every purchaser, and other information filed and available for inspection with the SEC. The method of offering, description of security, business of issuer, management and control, and appropriate financial statements must be included, according to SEC regulations, guidelines, and staff approval. This means, in practice, that statements required by SEC staff as to "risk factors" might be needed. This disclosure discipline is applied to the initial distribution or flotation of the securities by the issuing company, the underwriters and dealers, or in secondary offerings by those persons who control the issuer.

These disclosure requirements impose legal responsibility for material misstatements of fact or omissions. The most important enforcement discipline is civil liability to purchasers, either individually or as a class, for any resulting damage or losses. Those responsible may include the issuer, its principal executive, financial and accounting officers, the directors involved, along with each accountant, appraiser, engineer, or other expert named as having prepared or certified the registration statement, and every underwriter. But the issuer is generally liable for damages, and the others for breach of their duty of due diligence in discharging particular responsibilities. In addition to these liabilities, dealers and salespersons may be liable for their written or oral misrepresentations or omissions of material fact, but only for the consideration paid by customers.

These civil liabilities for failure of disclosure are supplemented by SEC authority to make investigations, conduct hearings, bring injunctive actions, obtain cease and desist orders, and achieve ancillary relief (including rescission, return of profits, and even receivership for corporations suffering pervasive mismanagement). Willful violations may lead to criminal sanctions, fine or imprisonment, in cases recommended by the SEC to the Justice Department.

3. PUBLIC COMPANIES AND TRADING LIMITATIONS

Once securities have been distributed, additional responsibilities for disclosure and the avoidance of misrepresentation apply to publicly held companies. Most of these requirements come from the Securities Exchange Act of 1934 as amended. Annual reports, quarterly reports, and solicitation of proxies for shareholder voting are the major requirements. These disclosure duties have been extended to any issuer engaged in interstate commerce (or in a business affecting interstate commerce, or whose securities are traded by mail or through interstate commerce) if it has total assets over $10 million and a class of equity securities held of record by 2,000 persons or 500 persons who are not "accredited investors." Enforcement by the SEC through regulations and administrative proceedings applies to material misstatements or omissions of material facts, along with private rights of action for damages or other appropriate relief. However, dissident shareholders are limited in their rights to injunctions, and normally would have to show injury to the company or shareholders as a whole in order to change corporate policies (unless minority interests are being unfairly prejudiced).

Special disclosures and restrictions apply to corporate "insiders," defined as officers, directors, and owners of more than 10 percent of a class of equity securities, other than an exempted security. Under Section 16 of the 1934 Act such insiders must report their purchases and sales of equity securities. In order to inhibit unfair insider trading in these securities at the expense of other shareholders, the "short swing" profits (resulting from sale or purchase within less than six months) can be recovered by the corporation involved, or through derivative suits brought by any shareholder on behalf of the corporation. However, this provision is not enforceable by the SEC itself.

In 1968, the Williams Act added disclosure requirements for possible takeover and tender-offer situations. Any person or group becoming owner of 5 percent or more of any class of registered securities must file a statement with the issuer and the SEC within 10 days. This statement must set forth the background of the person, corporation or group making the acquisition, along with their purpose, source of funding, number of shares owned, and any relevant contracts or understandings. Private rights of action enforce these disclosure obligations, including those brought by the issuer (or target company) and its management.

Manipulation of markets in securities by underwriters, the issuer, and others with the purpose of artificially encouraging purchases or sale of securities is regulated under Sections 9 and 10 of 1934 Act. However, some efforts which are limited to stabilizing the offer price as part of the initial distribution for the securities are specifically permitted. See SEC Rules 10b–6 through 10b–8. In general, however, these prohibitions on manipulation may be interpreted as attempts to limit unfair, deceptive, and distortive interventions (upwards or downwards) in the market for a security by powerful economic interests. Such manipulations are subject to SEC administrative remedies and private rights of action. But such misconduct is not easy to document or prove in practice, and there has been only limited enforcement effort.

Most of the litigation involving securities trading has concerned deception and fraud. Deceptive and manipulative practices in the purchase or sale of securities are outlawed generally under Section 10(b) of the SEA, as implemented by SEC Rule 10b–5.

Since 1946 the courts have enforced 10b–5 civil liability in private lawsuits involving securities fraud or misrepresentation, in addition to SEC enforcement proceedings. More recently, however, some court decisions have given a narrower, more conservative reading to this rule. Furthermore, the Private Securities Litigation Act of 1995 placed some additional restrictions on access to relief by private litigants. Nonetheless, it is still accurate to say that the principal goal of securities regulation in the United States has been to maintain a regime of "truth-in-securities," so that investors can allocate funds intelligently and minimize waste on undeserving investment projects.

4. REGULATION OF SECURITIES OF PUBLICLY TRADED BANKS AND SAVINGS ASSOCIATIONS

Since 1964, special rules have applied to regulation of the publicly traded securities of FDIC-insured banks and savings associations, under § 12(i) of the 1934 Act, 15 U.S.C.A. § 78*l*(i), as amended. As to these securities, the "powers, functions, and duties" of the SEC are vested in the Comptroller, the Federal Reserve, and the FDIC. Their authority covers the 1934 Act registration requirement, standards relating to audit committees, periodic reporting, proxy voting, required disclosures and restrictions on insiders, and corporate responsibility for financial reports and internal controls. Significantly, this transferred authority does *not* include power to enforce anti-fraud and anti-manipulation rules. Even though the three federal bank regulators are in effect the SEC for banks and savings associations, if the securities problem involves securities fraud or manipulation, the SEC investigates and enforces, even though the securities involved are issued by a bank or savings association.

As to the power that they do have under section 12(i) of the 1934 Act, the statute divides up the authority of the bank regulators along very specific lines. First, the authorities are exercised by the Comptroller with respect to FDIC-insured national banks and federal savings associations. Second, the authorities are exercised by the Federal Reserve with respect to all other member banks of the Federal Reserve System. Third, the authorities are exercised by the FDIC with respect to all other FDIC-insured banks and state savings associations. The three agencies have the power to issue rules and regulations to implement the statutory provisions, but section 12(i) concludes by requiring the three bank regulators to "issue substantially similar regulations to regulations and rules issued by the Commission."[4]

5. MARGIN TRADING RESTRICTIONS

In "margin trading," a broker-dealer lends an investor client cash, using the client's account as collateral, to purchase securities. Obviously, margin

---

[4] For an analysis of § 12(i) and discussion of the reasons why the division of authority was structured in this peculiar way, see Malloy, *The 12(i)'ed Monster: Administration of the Securities Exchange Act of 1934 by the Federal Bank Regulatory Agencies*, 19 HOFSTRA L. REV. 269 (1991).

trading increases an investor's purchasing power, but it also exposes the investor to the risk of larger losses. Margin credit requirements for securities trading are regulated by the Federal Reserve Board. Under legislation enacted in 1934, the Federal Reserve was empowered to prevent excessive speculation through margin account trading on securities. Excessive credit on securities trading with low margins had been significant in building the stock market boom of the late 1920s, and this vulnerability aggravated the Crash of 1929 and the ensuing depression.

More specifically, the Margin Requirements Act (15 U.S.C.A. § 78g), allows the Board to set margin credit limits within a broad range. Currently, the extension of margin credit by broker-dealers is governed through Regulation T (12 C.F.R. pt. 220), the extension of margin credit by banks through Regulation U (12 C.F.R. pt. 221), by other persons through Regulation G (12 C.F.R. pt. 207), and with respect to some additional creditors and borrowers through Regulation X (12 C.F.R. pt. 224).

The importance of margin credit regulation by the Board is that a speculative stock market boom, or even a surge in stock trading through margin credit, can be curtailed by an increase in margin credit requirements, thus reducing this kind of speculation. In contrast, margin requirements can be relaxed in a serious slump as a prod to recovery in stock market trading and prices. The Board (not the SEC) was given this authority, because it relates to monetary policy, restraint over money supply, credit conditions, and interest rates, typically concerns of a central bank.

Following the October 1987 slide in stock prices, a Presidential Commission studied these events and made recommendations. Some experts felt that computerized "program" trading (especially involving futures and options) exaggerated the severity of this slump. Many also believed that speculative optimism had driven stock prices somewhat too high in many countries, and that a substantial, downside correction was unavoidable. Greater attention was drawn to the dangers of speculation, over-leveraging, and a need for improved U.S. fiscal responsibility. Many suggested (i) better coordination among securities and financial market regulators; (ii) improved clearing arrangements and data dissemination; (iii) somewhat higher margin requirements (then only 8–12 percent) for options and futures transactions; (iv) "circuit breakers" (temporary measures that halt trading to curb panic-selling) and possible limits on daily swings in trading; and (v) a new "super-agency" to regulate national (and possibly international) securities markets.

The Market Reform Act of 1990 authorized the SEC to collect data on automated and program trading, facilitate coordinated clearing, and regulate activities that contribute to extreme volatility, including emergency powers to suspend trading under a new § 12(g) of the 1934 Act. During the market crisis in July 2008, the SEC invoked its emergency powers in response to the sharp decline in market value in the stock of Lehman Brothers, as well as 18 other companies that seemed to be the targets of unusually high volume of sales. The order was intended to protect investors, to maintain fair and orderly securities markets, and to prevent substantial disruption in the securities markets by suspected market manipulation resulting from the dissemination of false rumors. Unfortunately, this had little immediate effect on the market value of Lehman Brothers stock; the company eventually collapsed and filed for bankruptcy.

6. SPECULATIVE DANGERS

As a strong "bull market" resumed in the United States between 1993–2000 (and again between 2003–2007), concerns resumed about the dangers of U.S. speculative excess. Greater global market integration and capital inflows could bring fragility along with some resiliency. "Excessive" capital inflows reinforced a U.S. recovery, and not even the Federal Reserve was eager to halt the boom with tighter credit and sharply rising interest rates. Perhaps computerization, "globalization," and a new round of innovation explained the faster growth in the United States and Asia. But speculative excess was recognized properly in Mexico's boom-bubble-devaluation of 1994–1995. Soon afterwards boom-devaluation crises hit Asia in 1997–1998 (Thailand, Malaysia, Indonesia, Philippines, and S. Korea), and later in Latin America (Brazil, Ecuador, and Argentina). Ironically, their distress only accentuated capital flight into the United States, reinforced by the stock market boom (1993–2000), and a real estate boom that developed in many areas between 2003–2007. This super-charged the American stock market boom-bubble, which peaked at record high prices in 2000.

In the big U.S. stock market correction that followed in 2001–2003, significant corporate scandals exploded. Enron, Andersen, World Com, Adelphia, Global Crossing, Health South, and Tyco were among the worst examples. These corporate scandals involved over-stated profits, fraudulent accounting, aggravated misuse, and default on pension fund obligations. Such corporate abuse threatened global confidence in U.S. capital markets. Public and congressional outrage demanded stronger legislation. Renewed corporate accountability, government prosecutions, and private damage actions were needed to restore the reputation of Wall Street. This led to passage of the Sarbanes-Oxley Act of 2002.

The Sarbanes-Oxley Act (i) strengthened criminal penalties for fraudulent corporate executives, auditors, and lawyers; (ii) created a new Public Company Accounting Oversight Board (PCOAB) to supervise auditing standards, quality control, and ethics; (iii) imposed periodic review by the SEC of public company financial reporting; (iv) required CEO and CFO certification of public company financial reports; (v) mandated independent audit committees for publicly listed companies; (vi) required prompt disclosure of material changes in financial condition and operations; (vii) obligated lawyers representing fraudulent companies to withdraw and disclose breaches of fiduciary duty by company leaders and auditors; (viii) prohibited most loans by companies to their executive officers and directors; and (ix) protected corporate whistleblowers. In many respects, the legislation tried to mandate what had been understood as "best practice" by responsible and enlightened leadership for U.S. public companies. (Not provided were limits on "excessive and greedy" executive compensation for top level CEOs. Some critics insisted that this goal should have been included. Instead, Sarbanes-Oxley focused upon corporate responsibility, enhanced CEO and CFO liabilities, and responsibility for auditing and financial reporting.)

From a comparative law standpoint, Sarbanes-Oxley was intended to restore the integrity of U.S. corporate securities markets. While some foreign company issuers of U.S. securities might chafe at higher U.S. requirements, their securities gain the respectability of U.S. shares and bonds. Better capital access was why many foreign companies wanted to be listed in the U.S. capital markets, and the SEC made a substantial effort to be reasonable and not unduly burdensome in implementing Sarbanes-Oxley. Ironically, this brought even more foreign capital into U.S. markets in 2003–2007.

Meanwhile, IOSCO has evolved into an increasingly important multinational agency, with 131 ordinary members as of the end of 2022 (*i.e.*, national securities commissions or similar governmental bodies), 33 associate members (*i.e.*, supranational, subnational, intergovernmental, and other governmental bodies, as well as national governmental regulators that are not signatories of the IOSCO multilateral memorandum of understanding), and 70 affiliate members (*i.e.*, self-regulatory organizations and other private and non-governmental bodies with an appropriate interest in securities regulation). Only ordinary members have full participation and voting rights in the deliberations of the organization. IOSCO began as a Western Hemisphere cooperative association of securities regulators in 1983 that moved toward more universal membership between 1986 and 1998. IOSCO goals are to promote high standards of securities; responsible securities regulation; fair, efficient and transparent markets; and effective surveillance of international securities transactions. While binding consensus is lacking on international accounting standards,[5] the thrust of this harmonization effort does strengthen sound investor protection and disclosure in global markets. This could gradually improve market transparency and knowledgeability by a process of competition for international investments.

By 2012, the IOSCO Secretary General reported that the organization saw a profound reorientation in process, from bank-centric financial models in many countries towards more market-based financing in the future. With capital requirements increasing and a new emphasis on global systemically important

---

[5] International Accounting Standards (IAS), a set of rules for financial statements were replaced in 2001 by International Financial Reporting Standards (IFRS) that have been adopted by most major financial markets around the world.

financial institutions, financing gaps are becoming critical and will have to be filled by market instruments of one form or another. Thus, strong local securities market development is essential for long term economic prosperity, making the role of securities regulators and the role of IOSCO even more important for the future.

C. SECURITIES EXCHANGES AND TRADING

Stock exchanges have been convenient and efficient places to trade securities, once issued through a network of underwriters, brokers and dealers. Although securities exchanges developed as private membership organizations of merchants and bankers active in trading securities, their economic importance led to government regulation (*e.g.*, Securities Exchange Act of 1934). In the United States, the NYSE and AMEX were the dominant exchanges, with leading issues listed on the New York Stock Exchange. Regional exchanges (including Boston, Philadelphia, Chicago, and Pacific) listed some other issues. Many additional securities were traded in the over-the-counter (OTC) market (now NASDAQ market), which comprises hundreds of dealers throughout the country. (The largest have seats on the major stock exchanges as well.) This dealer network is linked together by computers and other communications in the NASDAQ (*i.e.*, the National Association of Securities Dealers Automated Quotations), through which current information on securities and trading activity is widely available. Comparable links exist among leading multinational banks and brokerage firms to other important financial and money market centers around the globe. In addition, large blocks of securities held by institutions (banks, mutual funds, insurance companies, pension funds, and others) are often bought or sold off the exchanges and OTC-NASDAQ market through negotiated transactions for greater confidentiality, and also because big trades may disrupt the market, against the interest of large block holders. But current exchange and NASDAQ prices are usually the benchmark for other transactions, so that regulation of exchanges and OTC activity affects all securities trading generally.

Self-regulation of the exchanges under SEC supervision has been a major theme of U.S. securities regulation. Continuous auction trading for listed securities is carried on through specialist-members who handle the more important securities, and by floor brokers acting on behalf of member firms and their customers. Exchange rules are largely conveniences to this trading process with elements of protection for members and their firms. The SEC exercises supervisory authority, with oversight responsibility over exchange rules and commission rates (in light of industry needs and the public interest). While the SEC exercises primary jurisdiction under its statutory mandate for these purposes, the Supreme Court has held that antitrust principles should be taken into account in reviewing the SEC's supervision of securities markets.

A major development of 1970–1975 was the gradual elimination of fixed commissions on trading at the exchanges. Under pressure of increasing competition on large trades from third market transactions, Congress and the SEC forced negotiated, competitive pricing practices upon member firms in the exchanges. A related reform was SEC elimination of the rule which prohibited exchange members from making off-market transactions for customers. This strengthened competitive disciplines for securities trading.

Memberships or seats on the exchanges had become strictly limited and increasingly valuable as scarce "property" rights. Except for some regional exchanges, institutional investors have not been allowed to obtain memberships. This added some pressure for off-market transactions, but negotiated prices for large block trades have eased this difficulty.

The role of specialists on the exchanges provoked controversy for years. Specialists are supposed to reduce erratic swings in security prices by making markets on a regular basis for the securities they handle. But competition among specialists on securities within each exchange was generally not feasible, so that their profit margins were questioned. And yet without specialists there might be wider price fluctuations in trading, with more opportunities for manipulation. In any event, long established practices on the exchanges, including the role of specialists, have been substantially retained under SEC supervision.

Some believe that securities exchanges should evolve into a national (conceivably international) grid of computerized trading that might obviate the need for existing exchanges and specialists. Congress proclaimed the goal of a National Market System in 1975 as a partial expression of this idea, but authority was delegated to the SEC for its implementation. Some steps have been taken in that direction. They include a nationwide transactions tape, a composite quotations system, and electronic links between exchanges and world markets (used by most significant broker dealers). The current trend toward enforcing more of an "open book" in computerized data processing helps encourage more efficient trading and marketplace competition.

Congress also mandated in 1975 a national clearing system for securities to improve "back office" efficiency and the securities certificate transfer process. More might be done in this direction, conceivably yielding simplified card-like security certificates, easier to handle in the mails and through automated processing (like the check clearing system).

While little significant innovation has occurred in this direction, much of the internal management and operation of settlement and clearance of securities trades is supervised and regulated on a day-to-day basis by FINRA. Furthermore, following the market collapse of 2008, the Dodd-Frank Wall Street Reform and Consumer Protection Act of 2010 made some potentially significant changes to the regulation of securities trading,[6] including new standards for the "securitization" of pools of financial instruments, enhanced enforcement powers for the SEC, SEC supervision of hedge fund and private equity fund advisers and of credit rating agencies, and comprehensive regulation of swaps and security-based swaps by the Commodity Futures Trading Commission (CFTC) and the SEC, in consultation with the Federal Reserve.

D. REGULATION OF SECURITIES FIRMS

The securities industry comprises a variety of firms. Included are nationwide underwriter-dealer-brokerage firms like Merrill-Lynch (now a subsidiary of Bank of America Corp.), major underwriters without retail distribution networks, investment advisers, exchange specialists, floor traders and brokers, regional broker-dealers, and many small brokers with varied emphasis or specialization. Since the Maloney Act of 1938 and formation of the NASD in 1939, the SEC has had supervisory authority over this self-regulatory organization, its rules and practices. In 2007, the regulatory functions of the NASD merged with the regulatory functions of the New York Stock Exchange to form FINRA. Currently, FINRA is the only "national securities association" registered pursuant to the Maloney Act. It carries out its self-regulatory functions for the securities industry subject to SEC oversight.

---

[6] The principal features of the Dodd-Frank Act with respect to regulation of securities trading are discussed at pages 28–29, *supra*.

1. UNDERWRITERS AND INVESTMENT BANKING

Underwriters support the initial distribution of new securities. They provide risk capital or "investment banking" resources for this purpose. Underwriting involves a wide mixture of risk possibilities that may go considerably beyond normal commercial banking for collateralized loan accounts. And yet, some international bank lending, especially to problem countries with default vulnerability, really involves the equivalent of investment banking risk exposure. For these reasons, a considerable part of international bank lending has been allocated among syndications much like domestic underwriters put together for securities issues.

The major underwriters in the domestic U.S. securities market comprise leading broker-dealer organizations like Merrill-Lynch, which have excellent opportunities to float large blocks of securities to the public, along with a few important investment bankers that concentrate more directly on institutions. Regional underwriters and broker-dealers may participate actively in selected issues, especially in their marketing areas. Large domestic commercial banks recently participated in this underwriting process, although restricted by Glass-Steagall Act limitations on securities distribution. However, in 1987–1990 the bank regulatory agencies allowed some of the largest U.S. banks to underwrite commercial paper, securitized instruments, and even domestic bonds and stocks, provided that such underwriting was handled in separate affiliates, and in moderate amounts compared to other activities.[7] (*See* III.E.6., *supra*, discussing securities marketing and commercial banking.) In international banking, however, there were no Glass-Steagall restrictions, and there was extensive overlap and commingling of activities between investment and commercial banking (for U.S. and foreign banks).

Apart from the securities disclosure, registration, and anti-manipulation disciplines described previously for underwriters, dealers and brokers, there is little specific regulation of investment banking under U.S. law. FINRA supervision applies, but this adds little further regulation to underwriting or investment banking. Thus, there are no comparable entry or chartering requirements, only modest capital or solvency regulation, and no merger, holding company, or branching restrictions for domestic investment banks, in contrast to the extensive supervision of virtually every aspect of the corporate and transactional life of a commercial bank that was discussed in Chapters II and III. One basic reason for this difference in treatment is that investment banking outlays are viewed as a specialized type of risk-taking entrepreneurship. Although often highly profitable, the underwriting of securities is not considered generally a normal, prudent investment for public deposits of liquidity. Commercial bankers are not allowed to take such risks in domestic banking operations with depositor

---

[7] With the Gramm-Leach-Bliley Financial Services Modernization Act of 1999, financial holding companies (FHCs) could integrate banking, securities, and insurance affiliates under appropriate supervision of their respective regulatory agencies.

funds, and investment bankers must use their own equity capital to play the trading game. Accordingly, investment bankers do not need to be constrained for the sake of depositor protection or insurance requirements.

On the other hand, some leading U.S. investment banks got into financial trouble with excessive speculation, bad investments, and under-capitalization in 2007–2009. They had become "too big to fail," and Federal Reserve support was needed for them (or their acquisition partners). This included Merrill Lynch and Bear Stearns. Some argue, with hindsight, that Lehman Bros. should have been bailed out with an assisted merger as well.

The crisis that began in 2008 with the collapse of the subprime mortgage market prompted the question, who should be supervising big investment banks? The Federal Reserve, the SEC, or the U.S. Treasury (and the OCC)? Or all of them? These issues provoked extended controversy. Some experts even suggested a re-enactment of the Glass-Steagall separation of investment and commercial banking. The Dodd-Frank Act goes only so far as to restrict, but not eliminate, "proprietary trading" in securities by banks, subject to a range of exceptions included in implementing rules promulgated in December 2013.[8]

The primary thrust of investment banking regulation has been to enforce the disclosure-

---

[8] For discussion of these restrictions—known as the "Volcker Rule," for former Federal Reserve Chairman Paul Volcker, who pushed for the restriction—see pages 127–129, *supra*.

antifraud disciplines of the securities laws, and to protect potential purchasers of the securities against incomplete disclosures or misrepresented investment opportunities. In commercial banking, borrowing liquidity on a loan basis is a more neutral, objective process, but the nature of investment banking is more entrepreneurial. Thus, underwriting and marketing securities constitute a substantially different business from commercial banking, which was separated by custom and under U.S. law by the Glass-Steagall Act.[9]

2. BROKER-DEALER NETWORK AND FINRA

Broker-dealers (along with underwriters) comprise the main marketing effort for new securities, and most of the public conduct their trading activities through broker-dealer firms. Therefore, the disciplines for disclosure and avoiding misrepresentation are logically extended from issuers and underwriters to the broker-dealer network, in order to support trustworthy securities, improve responsible securities market behavior, and encourage wiser investment activity.

---

[9] But does this differentiation of underwriting from deposit-taking and commercial lending justify a prohibition against FHCs that combine banks, securities firms, and/or insurance companies? (*See* Chapter III and Chapter IX.) In any event, Congress decided in 1999 to eliminate that aspect of the Glass-Steagall "wall." However, in the aftermath of the market collapse of 2008, of the Dodd-Frank Act included a mandate for regulatory action restricting "proprietary trading" in securities by banks, the so called "Volcker Rule. These restrictions are discussed at pages 127–129, *supra*.

Broker-dealers are subject to additional extensive regulation for the protection of customers. Most importantly, "brokers" and "dealers" must be registered with the SEC if they handle registered securities or engage in interstate commerce. Many brokerage firms, in addition, register as investment advisors. Such registrations may be revoked or suspended, or the firm may be censured, for violations of the securities laws. Along with liability for engaging in misrepresentation, manipulative, or deceptive practices, more specific rules have developed with respect to possible conflicts of interest, suitability, markups, segregation of customer funds, financial responsibility and net capital requirements. Also, since 1970 the Stockholder Investor Protection Corporation has provided further assurance that valid customer claims will be paid in the event of broker-dealer insolvency.

Many cases hold that securities broker-dealers are under an obligation not to over-reach their customers, or to exploit them. FINRA (formerly NASD) Rules of Fair Practice provide that broker-dealers should not recommend a security unless they have reason to believe it is suitable to the customer's financial situation and needs. The fair spread or profit rule has been interpreted generally to allow markups of no more than 5 percent (although in some limited circumstances up to 10 percent may be reasonable), but this 5 percent rule is, strictly speaking, a guide, not a rigid requirement. A large number of disciplinary proceedings have been brought against excessive markups. Other disciplinary proceedings have been brought against "churning," the systematic encouragement of excessive transactions. The SEC has attacked "scalping," *i.e.*, the systematic recommendation of securities purchased by an investment advisor (without disclosing this to a customer), so that extra profits could be made when the price rises after recommendations. "Boiler room" operations have been challenged where high-pressure telephone or other campaigns have been mounted to tout securities with exaggerated claims.

Some potential for conflict of interest and abuse of customers remains unavoidable, and it is built into the business model that combines independent dealing activities for the account of the broker-dealer, and brokerage activities for the account of customers. It would be difficult, politically and practically, to sever this connection between dealers and brokers. However, the SEC and FINRA have tried to reduce this conflict with rules and specific proceedings against over-reaching, excessive markups, churning, scalping, and other misconduct involving serious deception, fraud, or manipulation.

Misuse of customer funds can occur in many ways: churning of accounts where brokers have authority to manage them, misappropriation of securities owned by customers to the advantage of brokers or their sales staff, or conversion of cash held on account for customers. Such abuses have been dealt with by specific SEC disciplinary proceedings and private litigation, and by general SEC rules. Under SEC rules now in force brokers must maintain records, and properly segregate the accounts and securities fully paid by customers. (Brokers, however, may hold margin account securities as pledges for loan obligations, and brokers may commingle the cash left on deposit with them and earn interest on it along with the broker's own cash funds.)

Financial responsibility standards have been strengthened since 1969–1971, when many brokerage firms were over-extended and suffered losses in a slump of stock market prices. During that period of strain on brokerage firms the SEC informally encouraged many mergers among broker-dealers (with industry support), so that customer losses were minimized. Under SEC net capital rules, 17 C.F.R. § 240.15c3–1, most broker-dealers may not let their aggregate indebtedness exceed 1500 percent of their net capital. (A complicated list of adjustments for different circumstances is made under this regulation, based on the broker-dealer activities of each firm.) Alternatively, a broker-dealer can qualify under Rule 15c3–1(a)(1)(ii), a simpler formula, which merely requires net capital equal to the greater of $250,000 or 2 percent of the aggregate debit balances attributable to transactions with customers. These requirements are comparable to, though less demanding than, the net worth and reserve requirements of commercial banks.[10] Securities

[10] Capital "adequacy" for investment banking (wholesale) activities are not closely comparable to commercial banks. Investment banks use their own capital (and long-term borrowing) to finance deal-making; they do not hold large deposits from the public like commercial banks. And retail brokerage operations for securities customers provide transactional services and "street

underwriters have only brief capital risk exposure (days or weeks) during the sale of each issue, while brokerage activities merely require sufficient net assets or liquidity to meet customer obligations (and limit sizeable losses for the SIPC). Trading losses, however, may justify increased capital requirements to safeguard against disruptive bankruptcy.

3. SECURITIES INVESTOR PROTECTION CORPORATION

While the New York Stock Exchange established a trust fund in 1963 to pay customer claims when a member firm failed, this fund was inadequate to deal with a widespread securities brokerage crisis of 1969–1971. The SEC responded by encouraging a great many consolidation mergers among brokerage firms, using its registration authority with widespread industry support. Congress also enacted at that stage the Securities Investor Protection Act of 1970 (SIPA). SIPA created the SIPC, which required almost all registered broker-dealers to become members. SIPC is administered by a seven-member board, including one representative of the Treasury, another from the Federal Reserve Board, and five presidential appointees from the industry and the public.

---

name" accounts for customers (who assume their own investment risks). Some risk of insolvency does exist, but this seems most likely to occur in stock market meltdowns or currency devaluation crises; major fraud and embezzlement is less likely (but would be covered by SIPC guarantees). However, the crisis of 2007–2009 suggests that more capital should have been required to limit over-leveraging.

SIPC's function is to satisfy claims of customers against a broker-dealer firm when the latter's assets are insufficient. To meet these responsibilities SIPC maintains a reserve fund, which is supported by modest assessments against member firms, based on their gross revenues. In the event this fund was inadequate, SIPC may borrow from the Treasury. The SEC may levy additional charges of not more than $^1/_{50}$ of 1 percent of all transactions value in the stock exchanges and OTC markets to assure repayment of Treasury loans. Thus far, relatively few firms have failed, but the crisis of 2007–2013 was hard on the industry. As of the end of 2022, there were 3,396 SIPC member firms,[11] as compared to 7,614 at the end of 1994.

SIPC protects against the loss of cash and securities held by a customer at a financially troubled SIPC-member brokerage firm. The limit of this protection is $500,000, including a $250,000 limit for cash. While the FDIC and NCUSIF directly insure depositor accounts, SIPC is more limited and merely provides a guarantee of funds to assure satisfaction of claims. Delays of six months or more may be involved.

SIPC does have some emergency authority. When the SEC or FINRA determines that a broker or dealer is approaching financial difficulty, SIPC must be notified. If SIPC finds the firm has failed or is in danger of failing to meet its obligations to customers, it may apply for a court order, trustee, and

---

[11] Current information about SIPC is available at https://www.sipc.org/list-of-members.

receivership. The trustee's responsibilities are to return customer property, complete the firm's contract commitments, and liquidate the business. SIPC will meet the firm's deficiencies, up to the limits specified previously. Obviously, SIPC parallels, in a more limited way, the bank examination regime, and the FDIC and NCUSIF disciplines, but is less comprehensive in data gathering and oversight authority.

Some interesting case law has developed in recent years illustrating the importance of broker-dealer obligations, where pension, retirement, or health insurance funds are being handled as customer accounts.[12] Obviously, SIPC coverage limits do not go very far, since individual pensioners or employees cannot recover from SIPC if the brokerage firm fails. Yet many smaller pension plans use brokerage firms or mutual funds as their securities fund custodians. A sizeable gap in effective risk guarantee and fiduciary responsibility has developed this way.

E. INVESTMENT COMPANIES AND MUTUAL FUNDS

Investment companies are designed mainly as vehicles for smaller investors to select and diversify investments in securities. The most popular kind of investment company, the open-end (mutual fund) company, can continuously issue interests to new

---

[12] *See, e.g., In re Bernard L. Madoff Investment Securities LLC*, 12 F.4th 171 (2d Cir. 2021) (involving *inter alia* banks and funds that pooled money from customers and invested directly or indirectly with broker-dealer that eventually failed)

customers, and itself invests in the market. A variant that invests in money market instruments, the money market mutual fund (MMMF), became even more important in the late 1970s and early 1980s. The MMMF has become a major source of competition for banks and savings associations.

Investment company shares are securities, and accordingly, their distribution has been regulated under the Securities Act of 1933 and the Securities Exchange Act of 1934. Marketing efforts by registered broker-dealers are further regulated under that legislation by the SEC and NASD. Hence, the scope of securities disclosure, antifraud, and non-manipulation policies extends to investment company activities, and the marketing of shares in such companies.

In addition, investment companies and mutual funds are regulated by more specialized legislation, primarily the Investment Company Act of 1940 and the Investment Advisers Act of 1940. These laws require separate registration with the SEC of investment companies and investment advisors[13]

---

[13] The term "investment adviser" is defined in the Investment Advisers Act, 15 U.S.C.A. § 80b–2(a)(11), to mean:

> any person who, for compensation, engages in the business of advising others, either directly or through publications or writings, as to the value of securities or as to the advisability of investing in, purchasing, or selling securities, or who, for compensation and as part of a regular business, issues or promulgates analyses or reports concerning securities . . .

but usually does not include a bank. A similar definition of the term appears in the Investment Company Act. *See id.* § 80a–2(a)(20).

(even if affiliated with broker-dealer firms). Investment companies must make registration statements disclosing their investment policies. They must file annual reports, and they must maintain specified accounts and records. The company's investment advisor must be disclosed, with details of its advisory contract, including compensation arrangements. Investment advisers must report their activities, affiliations and background, and relevant financial information prescribed by SEC regulations.

Investment companies are divided into three categories: (1) face amount certificate companies, which offer fixed income bond and debenture securities; (2) unit investment trusts (similar to real estate investment trusts (REITs) covered by 26 U.S.C.A. § 856 *et seq.*), offering interests in a fixed block or portfolio of securities; and (3) management companies, which includes all others. The most important investment companies are the third type, especially "open-end" companies or mutual funds. Open-end companies offer shares continuously, with prices reflecting the current net asset value of a portfolio per share, and allow redemption at any time. Closed-end companies have a fixed number of shares outstanding at any time (like most corporations), and their value fluctuates accordingly. In terms of customer investments and popularity, "open-end" companies are much more important than the other varieties, although unit investment trusts (often corporate and municipal bonds) have had considerable play as well.

Investment company assets must be held by a responsible custodian, a stock exchange member, bank, or under other strict safeguards. Officers and employees with access to the securities or cash owned by the company must be bonded. Capital structures of investment companies must meet requirements of the Investment Company Act (*e.g.*, 15 U.S.C.A. § 80a–18), but earnings practices of investment companies, and particularly of REITs, are largely dictated by federal tax law, a subject beyond the scope of this book. For example, under 26 U.S.C.A. § 852(a)(1), at least 90 percent of the investment company's net earnings must be distributed to the shareholder's fund each year in order to avoid double taxation.

It must be emphasized that investment company and mutual fund investments (or customer accounts) are not insured. Thus, the risk of loss is real, and falls solely upon the customer-investor. There is no counterpart to FDIC, FSLIC, or NCUSIF insurance for these investments, and SIPC guarantees do not apply to mutual fund or investment company accounts. SIPC guarantees only apply to securities and funds held for customers by brokerage firms or broker-dealers.

Every investment company selects its own investment strategy at the outset, and any significant changes (or dissolution) must be ratified by the majority of shareholders at that time. There are only limited restrictions on managerial discretion within these constraints, however, and there is no obligation to produce any particular level of return (or even to avoid losses). The only enforceable general obligation is conformity with the advertised investment strategy. But investment companies may not invest more than small percentages in any other single investment company. Investment companies should not make margin purchases of securities, sell securities short, or make commitments to underwrite securities with more than 25 percent of their assets. Beyond these limits, competition among informed investors is the primary discipline to encourage and reward investment company (or mutual fund) managers. The penalties for weaker performance are slow sales of shareholder interests and reduction in growth (for open-end companies or mutual funds) of the resources available for investment, advisory fees, and managerial compensation.

Management has broad latitude within the advertised investment strategy. Most investment companies contract with an investment adviser for management services. Typical fees for this service are ½ to 1 percent annually of the net assets in the investment company's funds. The investment advisor may be a large brokerage firm or its affiliate, or a smaller corporation or partnership. Investment advisers commonly serve a number of funds, and most large brokerage firms now sponsor or use a family of funds or investment companies. A typical range might include separate funds for money market liquidity, corporate bonds, tax-free municipals, international bonds, large corporate stocks, small firm growth stocks, and so forth. Easy and low cost transfer of customer shares may be encouraged within each family of funds to provide more flexibility.

The law requires that at least 40 percent of the board of directors for an investment company be independent (for open-end companies). This means they should not be involved as officers or partners in the company, its investment adviser, a broker-dealer affiliate, as legal counsel, or employed in any other material or business relationship. (For closed-end companies only one independent director is required.) This safeguard is designed to encourage some independence and integrity of management for the fund.

More significant, perhaps, are restrictions on transactions with affiliates. There is potential for abuse in an investment company affiliated with a broker-dealer, because the fund might be used for "scalping" or "dumping" less desirable securities, since it is a captive customer. Section 17 of the Investment Company Act, 15 U.S.C.A. § 80a–17, attempts to limit such abuses, and tries to ensure fair and equal participation for the fund in a broker-dealer's trading activities.

Selling prices are restricted for fund shares to some extent under Section 22 of the act, 15 U.S.C.A. § 80a–22. For example, fund shares must be sold at the prospectus price, *i.e.*, resale price maintenance is required by the law.

A typical portfolio for money market mutual funds would comprise CDs from U.S. and foreign banks, high-grade commercial paper (short-term) from corporations, and/or short-term government securities. Average maturity of this portfolio for MMMFs would be 30–40 days. Such a portfolio is reasonably secure, reliable, and dividend yields float with portfolio yields (minus expenses). There is little danger of such a fund's liquidity or solvency failure—unless there were a major crisis in the domestic or world economy. Normal expenses for such funds average less than 1 percent on assets. This is a thin margin for operating expenses among financial institutions.

Increasingly important contributors to mutual fund activities are IRA (individual retirement account) and Keogh plan (self-employed income) tax-sheltered investments. (See Chapter VIII.) Mutual funds have taken the lead in recent years in recruiting such investments from the public, but commercial banks and thrift institutions seek IRA and Keogh account deposits as well. Insurance companies have also been active in this area, with annuity and other policies designed for tax-sheltered retirement savings and investment.

Finally, it is necessary to consider "hedge funds" and "private equity funds," investment companies that were exempt from regulation because they had, respectively, very few investors or only sophisticated investors. In the aftermath of the market collapse of 2008, these funds became subject to significant regulation. The Dodd-Frank Act requires hedge fund and private equity fund advisers to register with the SEC, and subjects them to SEC inspection and examination.

CHAPTER VII

INSURANCE REGULATION

Insurance companies are important financial intermediaries gathering large funds from the public and business enterprises. Insurance premiums paid on private life, health, property, marine, liability, and surety coverage accounted, in the United States, for roughly 10 percent of national income. Intermediation occurs when the net proceeds of those premiums are invested by the insurance companies in assets representing major blocks of institutional investment for the securities industry, real estate, and agricultural finance. The insurers' reserve assets provide, along with premium income revenues, the resources from which insurance claims are paid, and the profits or dividends taken by insurance companies for their stockholders and policyholders. Thus, insurance companies act as specialized financial intermediaries between those who contract for such risk protection and investment activity, and the business enterprises, farmers, individuals, and real estate projects that use insurance company investment (in the form of bonds, stock, mortgages, and other interests).

A. REGULATORY STRUCTURE

The regulation of insurance companies bears a strong resemblance, in certain features, to the regulation of banks, savings institutions, and securities markets. Insurers must be chartered, meet capital and solvency requirements, and conform to restrictions on their investment portfolios. Their financial adequacy is supervised by Commissions or Departments of Insurance (at the state level of government), so that the public can place greater reliance on their contractual and investment commitments. These regulatory authorities try to limit irresponsible failure of insurers. Fairness in dealing with the public is encouraged, along with limits on misrepresentation or unreasonable discrimination. Standard form contracts are supervised by these agencies to provide more reliable insurance protection, and to minimize over-reaching and fraud.

And yet, unique features distinguish insurance regulation. The wide variety of risks to be insured or protected against requires a much more complicated range of product and contract variations. Rate-making procedures have developed that sometimes inhibit pricing rivalry, although competitive forces do have impact on long run insurance rate levels. Most strikingly, perhaps, insurance regulation is almost exclusively a responsibility of state governments. This represents a dramatic contrast to the federal-state "dual" regulation of banking and thrift institutions, and the largely federal regulation of securities markets. But the state insurance regulation system enjoys substantial momentum, the insurance industry finds major advantages in this tradition, and it will not easily be displaced or changed radically in the near future.[1]

---

1 The increase of insurance premiums (of all kinds) in the GNP, *i.e.*, from 6 to nearly 10 percent between 1984–2008, has caused concern.

Nonetheless, recent competitive trends and inflationary distortions have affected insurance companies, along with other financial institutions. For these reasons, insurance company product offerings, their attractiveness to the public, and the regulation of insurance is better understood in conjunction with banking, thrifts, securities markets, and government policies affecting capital and financial markets generally. Meanwhile, the financial crises of 2007–2009 brought greatly increased losses in the financial sector (including quasi-insurance products, many toxic assets, and derivative securities).

Recent events have prompted increasing supervision of the insurance industry. Even before the market collapse of 2008, insurance companies were reorganizing and diversifying as financial holding companies (FHCs), by acquiring or establishing banking and financial services affiliates under the FHC structure, including State Farm Group (State Farm Bank), MetLife (MetLife Bank NA), American International Group (AIG Federal Savings Bank), and Allstate Corp. (Allstate Bank). Efficiencies have been achieved by maintaining banking affiliates as virtual banks accessed by customers through the Internet, ATMs, and mail. Significantly, these reorganizations open up the possibility of significant supervision of these conglomerates by the Federal Reserve as FHCs.

The financial crisis highlighted the lack of expertise within the Federal Government with respect to the insurance industry. In response, the

Dodd-Frank Act established the Federal Insurance Office (FIO) within the Department of the Treasury to provide expertise regarding the insurance business, marketplace, and regulatory environment. The following are among the FIO's authorities: (*i*) monitoring all aspects of the insurance industry, including identifying issues or gaps in the regulation of insurers that could contribute to a systemic crisis in the insurance industry or the U.S. financial system; (*ii*) monitoring the extent to which traditionally underserved communities and consumers, minorities, and low- and moderate-income persons have access to affordable insurance, except health insurance; (*iii*) recommending that the Financial Stability Oversight Council (FSOC) designate an insurer as a nonbank financial company that should be subject to supervision by the Federal Reserve (as of this writing, none are currently designated as such; *see* VII.E., *infra* at 379); (*iv*) coordinating federal efforts and developing federal policy on prudential aspects of international insurance matters; and, (*v*) recommending and approving the resolution of certain troubled insurance companies under the "orderly liquidation" authority of the FDIC.

B. DEVELOPMENT OF INSURANCE AND REGULATION

Modern insurance underwriting began with marine risk coverage by medieval Italian merchants, and it gradually spread through Europe. As British seaborne commerce expanded in the late Seventeenth Century, Lloyd's coffeehouse in London became a convenient focal point for arranging underwriter contracts with shipowners. Each underwriter at Lloyd's took a portion of the risk in a projected voyage, pledging his unlimited personal liability in support. If the vessel or cargo were lost, each underwriter would be liable up to the full amount of his portion. This type of insurance coverage was investor-underwriting, and it was well suited to a merchant city like London with many investors willing to take these risks for a sufficiently profitable premium. The rates or premiums charged reflected current risk exposure, including storm damage, war losses or piracy. The South Sea Bubble of 1718–1720, a rapid boom and collapse in joint-stock company prices, had a significant impact in strengthening the role of Lloyd's underwriters, because Parliament promptly outlawed joint-stock companies for underwriting marine insurance risks (except for two companies). In 1774 Lloyd's—no longer selling coffee—moved to the Royal Exchange, and its investor-underwriting became more routine with general form policies. Lloyd's received a parliamentary charter in 1871, which recognized and protected its dominant role in British marine insurance, mandated data collection activities (including Lloyd's register of shipping) and allowed it internal regulatory authority. In fact, Lloyd's underwriters have been willing for a long time to insure a considerable variety of risks, beyond marine insurance, including the most exotic insurable interests, at relatively high premium rates.

Meanwhile, other British and European insurers developed early fire insurance and rudimentary life insurance contracts in the Eighteenth Century. Most fire insurance developed on a joint stock company or benevolent society basis, among the more prosperous merchants of cities, and it did not much attract the higher profit-seeking underwriters of Lloyd's. Early fire insurers also helped sponsor some fire prevention measures and building codes, and local governments occasionally sponsored these insurance companies or mutual organizations. Life insurance evolved even more slowly, partly because mortality experience and survival rates were not well understood. Some tontine contracts[2] and related gambling risks were underwritten, but life insurance, generally speaking, was not really a serious business until the Nineteenth Century.

When the United States became an independent nation, insurance companies were among the first chartered corporations, especially in Pennsylvania, New York, and Massachusetts. As in Europe, marine and fire insurance developed initially, followed more slowly by limited experiments with life insurance. But because America lacked a major city with extensive merchant wealth, early efforts to transplant Lloyd's-type exchanges of underwriters were not very successful. Joint stock companies proved essential for early U.S. insurance to mobilize

---

[2] A tontine contract is an agreement in which a group of investors share in income generated by the investment until all but one has died or defaulted, at which time the entire income or principal goes to the survivor. The term is derived from Lorenzo Tonti, who first conceived the idea and put it in practice during the Seventeenth Century. Viewed as a wagering contract, it is commonly prohibited throughout the United States, with certain exceptions like insurance or annuity contracts.

enough capital. It was also somewhat more difficult to collect premiums and enforce claims in a federal republic spreading over a large territory, and this gradually encouraged the development of new insurers as other cities grew and prospered.

Early insurance regulation began with Pennsylvania, New York, and Massachusetts, and slowly spread to some other states. It started with restrictions upon out-of-state insurers, and was designed to protect local companies and citizens (Pennsylvania 1810 and New York 1814). New York added a premium tax on out-of-state insurers in 1824, and other states followed with some retaliation. Further requirements included filing of information on out-of-state companies, powers of attorney for local agents, and minimum capitalization or deposits. Some disclosure and safeguards already existed for in-state companies through the state chartering process, and the community standing of their local leaders. The Married Women's Act of 1840 in New York gave an important boost to life insurance marketing, because it allowed policy proceeds to be paid directly to widows and orphans (free of the deceased husband's creditors). In the 1840s local companies began to be regulated also, and New York passed the first general law on insurance companies in 1849. It provided for filing of information and capital requirements for local insurers, equivalent capital or bonding for out of state insurers, and the separation of life insurance from fire or marine insurance. Access to insurance company books, fines for wrongdoing, and procedures for dissolution followed several years later. Some restrictions were placed on investments to promote more reliable reserve funds. In 1859 New York set up a Department of Insurance under a bonded Commissioner, supported by filing fees to meet expenses.

Massachusetts evolved in a similar direction, with its Married Women's Act in 1844, a Board of Insurance Commissioners in 1855, state valuation of policies in 1856, visitation powers in 1858. Other states followed this trend, including Connecticut and Pennsylvania, and became centers for responsible insurance company development. By 1873, twenty states had set up insurance commissions, departments, or supervision of some sort. Gradually, other states did the same so that by World War I the state insurance regulation system had become virtually nationwide. The quality of supervision varied greatly from state to state, but the best regulated states were insurance industry leaders, for the most part, and their policies were cheaper and more reliable in nationwide competition. Capital, bonding, and information requirements for out-of-state insurers were easier for the larger, more successful companies to satisfy, so that leading companies (and, especially, mutual life insurers) that offered a better deal to policyholders were rewarded with faster growth.

Meanwhile, an important legal milestone occurred in 1868, with the U.S. Supreme Court decision of *Paul v. Virginia,* 75 U.S. 168 (1868). In this litigation an insurance agent challenged the constitutionality of a Virginia statute requiring the deposit of $30–

50,000 in bonds for out-of-state fire insurers that he represented. The Court held that neither the privileges or immunities of citizens, nor the commerce power of the federal government, would preclude regulation of insurers from other states in this manner. This landmark decision clearly allowed the states to proceed with regulation of insurance in their best judgment, even though some protection of local interests might be involved.

Insurance marketing expanded greatly since the 1840s, when mutual companies took the lead with somewhat reduced premiums (especially for life insurance), and rapidly expanded agent sales forces. Commissions for agents varied considerably in this era, with some life insurance companies offering as much as 30–50 percent of the initial premium and nothing on renewals, while others offered 10–15 percent of the initial premium and 5 percent on renewals. The latter practice tended to encourage more responsible, financially sound insurance companies, with stronger reserves, and it gave local agents an incentive to keep customers happy over the long run (because the agent's income was tied to renewals).

The number of new insurance companies increased sharply in the 1840s and 1860s, followed by more frequent failures of weaker companies. Entry and growth slowed in the 1870s–1880s, but picked up more strongly until the Great Depression. The pricing of life insurance was based on mortality tables, and increased longevity and expanding policy sales made them profitable. Fire, property, and casualty insurance grew substantially also, though in these fields rate-making bureaus became important later in limiting price competition, protecting reserves, and facilitating insurance company profits.

Insurance companies as a whole did not experience any drastic reversal of fortunes in the Great Depression, mainly suffering an increase in policy cancellations and a reduction in premium income. Although a considerable number of mergers occurred, with some discontinuance and failure of smaller companies, the reserves of sound insurance companies were not significantly affected. A reduction in policy obligations might even leave sound companies in a stronger financial position, although current expenses had to be reduced in line with lower premium revenues. Loans on life insurance policies increased somewhat, but this did not weaken investment income appreciably. For these reasons, the insurance industry and its regulation were not that seriously affected by the Depression period, and nothing comparable to the changes in banking or securities regulation occurred.

Instead, the insurance industry and its state regulatory institutions continued their evolution. World War II and the postwar prosperity brought greatly expanded sales for life insurance, though an increasing proportion of this came to be annuities and group life policies at lower rates. Health and disability insurance became increasingly important, often marketed as an adjunct to group life policies. Meanwhile, the gradual expansion of tort and legal liabilities was encouraging an expansion of property and casualty insurance coverage, with additional lines and types of insurance being written. The varieties of life insurance, endowment, and annuity contracts also proliferated, as "product innovation" became more important for insurance and its marketing.

Over the post-World War II era, there was a substantial flow of new entrants into the insurance business. Life insurance company assets multiplied forty-fold, and property-casualty insurer assets increased even faster in the last twenty years. Profitability remained strong with expanding sales and economic growth, although inflation during the last decades made life insurance less attractive for investment (though useful for protection against risk of death). Leading insurers have grown substantially larger. Many new entrants have been smaller companies, however, with limited marketing territories and impact.

The major challenge to this pattern of development came from antitrust enforcement, and *United States v. South-Eastern Underwriters Association*, 322 U.S. 533 (1944). The Antitrust Division of the Justice Department had indicted a rate-making cartel of 200 insurers for fire and allied lines under the Sherman Act, charging concerted boycotts and restraints of trade to enforce price fixing through state "supervised" rate bureaus. The insurers defended by asserting insurance was not interstate commerce (citing earlier precedents, including *Paul v. Virginia*), and the District Court granted dismissal. The Supreme Court reversed, holding that the modern insurance business is interstate commerce, and, therefore, that a price fixing cartel, boycotts, and restraint of trade could be challenged properly under the antitrust laws. Congress responded promptly with the McCarran-Ferguson Act, 15 U.S.C.A. §§ 1011–1015, which granted antitrust exemption for insurance activities to the extent that they were regulated by state law. In subsequent cases, courts have held coercive boycotts by insurance companies to be antitrust violations and not protected by McCarran-Ferguson. *See, e.g., United States v. New Orleans Insurance Exchange,* 148 F.Supp. 915 (E.D. La. 1957). On the other hand, where there is comprehensive state insurance regulation, the courts will not inquire into its effectiveness, or excessive rate levels supervised by the states. *See Ohio AFL-CIO v. Insurance Rating Board*, 451 F.2d 1178 (6th Cir. 1971). Thus far, Congress and the courts have allowed the partly industry-oriented regulation of insurance companies to continue as an area of substantial exemption from antitrust law. For the most part, sources of healthy growth and profitability for the insurance industry have remained operative throughout the postwar era.

Chart VII-1
Insurance Regulation System

Scope

Insurance Companies—

Life, Annuity, Disability Pensions and Health
Property, Marine, Liability
Surety and Fidelity

State Regulation

Key States and Industry Associations

- National Association of Insurance Comm'rs (NAIC)
- Trade Groups
- Main Themes—
  - Standard Form Contracts
  - Capital and Reserves
  - Investment Regulation
  - Authorization and Marketing
  - Rate Filing System
  - Socialized Risks

Entry, Underwriting and Marketing

- Life and Health
  - Life and Annuity
  - Groups and Pensions
  - Health Care
  - Disability
- Property, Marine, Liability, Surety, and Fidelity
- Multiple Lines and merger activity

Competition With Other Financial Intermediaries

- Banks and Trust Departments
- Investment Companies and Mutual Funds
- Securities Broker-Dealers
- Pension Funds
- Government

Industry Regulation

- Chartering and Authorization
  - Chartering requirements
  - Out-of-state insurers
  - Agent activities

Potential Regulatory Expansion

- State Regulation Problems
- Industry Influence on Regulatory Process
- Reduced Antitrust Exemption

Financial Service Holding Companies

Insurance Guaranty Funds Solvency Safeguards

- Capital, Reserves and Solvency—
  - Minimum capital
  - Reserves requirements
  - Liquidation procedures
  - Examination and valuation

- Rate Making and Filing—
    - Property-Liability
        - Prior Approval
        - Open Competition
        - Direct Writers
    - Life and Group
    - Health and Disability
- Standard Contracts—
    - Standardization
    - Limits on Harshness or Cancellation
- Socialized Risks—
    - Extreme Costs
    - Limited Incomes
    - Unaffordability
- Taxation—
    - Premium taxes
    - Assessments
    - Contributions

Federal Regulation

- McCarran Act
    - Antitrust exemption
- Socialization of Risk
    - Social Security
    - Health Care
    - Flood Insurance
    - Crime Insurance
    - Export Financing
- Dodd-Frank Act
    - Regulation of FHCs

Portfolio and investment management are more sophisticated for insurers in recent years. As insurance companies became large institutional investors, many have become more professional, skillfully diversified, sometimes aggressive, and their portfolio performance is watched carefully. Many insurers did well with higher interest rates and investment earnings. For many insurers, investment profitability became more significant as a path to improved earnings. For some insurers, however, earnings weakened, and a limited number suffered loan losses, with occasional up-surges of insolvencies.

Another aspect of insurance development is the growth and increased sophistication of risk management services. More business enterprises, particularly larger corporations, comprise a sufficient spread of activities to allow internal risk management. Developing insurance for these organizations requires skillful judgment and collaboration with management, and may require tailor-made pricing and negotiated rates, often with discounts.

C. MAIN FEATURES OF INSURANCE REGULATION

The established system of U.S. insurance regulation is comprehensive, highly developed, with much technical detail. There is a trend toward greater uniformity in statutory provisions, reflecting the influence of key states (including New York, Massachusetts, Pennsylvania, Connecticut, and more recently Wisconsin, and California), and most importantly, the National Association of Insurance Commissioners (NAIC). The NAIC serves a progressive, consensus building role, and develops a great deal of model statutory language and uniform laws in the insurance area.

1. CHARTERING, ENTRY AND LICENSING

The state insurance departments charter new insurance companies under standards set by local law. These requirements involve minimum capital, financial reporting, disclosures of initial organizers and principals, and acceptance of regulatory obligations. Groups meeting these standards are normally free to enter, without any showing of public convenience or necessity. Most insurers charter themselves in only one state as a primary legal domicile.

For out-of-state insurers seeking to market insurance policies through agents within a state, licensing requirements usually must be satisfied. Agents for service of process and litigation must be designated, capital or bonding requirements met, and any appropriate fees or premium taxes paid. Mail-order insurance may avoid these requirements, but non-compliance with other state laws could bring sanctions. In most states local agents or brokers could, on occasion, also place "surplus line" business with non-admitted insurers, but only under special restrictions: (i) unavailability of such insurance in the state; (ii) acceptance of legal process, financial data filings, bonding or trust fund requirements, and (iii) premium taxes (often higher than for admitted insurers).

Agents, brokers, and adjusters selling insurance in each state are separately licensed. Written examinations are common, and the trend has been toward some tightening of these requirements.

The effect of licensing requirements is to enforce supervision upon all insurers and sellers of insurance policies within each state. Failure to comply with state insurance laws may justify various penalties, suspension, or revocation of a charter or license. Thus, companies participating in the insurance business are subject to the laws and discipline of every state in which they do business.

2. CAPITAL, RESERVES AND SOLVENCY

A major theme of state insurance law and regulation is to enforce reasonable reserve requirements. Adequate reserves are needed to support insurance company obligations under their contracts. For life insurance companies these reserve requirements are based upon mortality tables and interest accumulation projections, so that normal premium revenues would provide a comfortable flow of resources adequate for these purposes (after expenses are deducted). For property and liability insurers, loss reserves and unearned premium reserves must be maintained. The loss reserve is an estimated liability for claims and settlement expenses. Standard formulas or loss ratios are employed. The unearned premium reserve equals the unearned portion of the gross premiums of all outstanding policies at the time of valuation. These requirements are designed to provide adequate resources for expenses and to prevent any insurer insolvency, though care should be taken to limit over-reserve buildup, for this can result in excessive rates. Competition among insurers, if vigorous and healthy, is supposed to limit excessive rates and premiums, while reasonable reserve requirements, if enforced, ensure the availability of funds to meet claims.

Examination of assets and valuation of policies is needed to enforce these reserve requirements, and to make sure that insurance company managers do not dissipate, waste, or encumber assets needed to support policy obligations and solvency. There are obvious dangers of fraud, embezzlement, or bad investment that could put an insurer into insolvency. For these reasons, insurance companies, like banks and other financial institutions, need the discipline of regular and competent examination, and financial accountability. Modern computer technology allows this to be done more effectively, although insurance company examination and valuation routines have not been developed to the same level as bank examination procedures. While insurance companies are not subject to a risk of "runs" or mass withdrawal by depositors, insolvencies do occur among smaller insurers. Most states, therefore, have guaranty funds and insolvency associations to settle claims against insolvent insurers, which assess the costs of failure among surviving companies.

Capital stock and policyholders' surplus represent the equity or ownership interest in an insurance company. The states require paid-in surplus for stock companies, and comparable surplus funds for mutual insurers. These surplus or capital requirements are another financial constraint upon the dissipation of assets, and a limit upon excessive growth of policy obligations (especially for property-liability insurance) relative to surplus and capital accounts.

Rules of thumb used for property-liability insurance are that net written premiums should not exceed several times the policyowners' surplus (ratios of 2 to 1, 3 to 1, and perhaps even 4 to 1 are employed). A major purpose of this cushion of surplus or capital is to help offset any unexpected operating losses, above and beyond the other reserves required. In life insurance there is less risk of a wide variance in loss experience, or a bunching of policy claims in any given year, so that less regulation applies to surplus as a constraint upon life insurer growth "capacity" in the short run.

Dividends payable to policyholders have been regulated in some states, along with accumulated surplus. Reserve requirements, in one form or another, can prevent overly generous dividends, but some states have found it desirable to limit surplus accumulations, and thereby encourage reasonable distribution of dividends to policyholders (or, perhaps, stockholders).

Investment regulation is another route toward protecting solvency and maintaining reserves or assets for insurance companies. Overly bold investment strategies could impair financial soundness, and state laws try to limit unwarranted risk and impose some requirements. Although state laws vary considerably, they tend to set limits for investment in different categories. For life insurance companies, earnings and growth performance are more important, so that they are allowed more equity stock investment, along with mortgages. Property-liability insurers need more liquidity, and are given less latitude for equity securities, and usually hold more bonds and government securities. Diversification rules may be employed, along with constraints upon self-dealing and insider lending. However, asset quality supervision is generally not as strict as for commercial banks, or even thrift institutions.

In situations involving fraud, embezzlement, or dissipation of assets or reserves through irresponsible management, most state insurance authorities could take action to suspend or revoke charters or licenses, and, if necessary, impose liquidation and receivership. However, insurance examination is not as systematic, well-developed, or regular as with bank examinations. Some states have enacted the Uniform Insurers Liquidation Act, which provides more fairness in allocating claims among the creditors of different states. But the NAIC was relatively late in seeking to strengthen accountability procedures.[3]

New and tougher Risk-Based Capital requirements (RBCs) were developed in the early–mid-1990s as Model Acts by the NAIC that brought significant progress, and enhanced capitalization for life, property, casualty, and later, health insurance

---

[3] Insurance company failures increased in the late 1980s–early 1990s, but were still less frequent than banks or thrifts. All 50 states now have Insurance Guaranty and Insolvency Funds financed by assessments (with more or less taxpayer backup), but not all lines of insurance are fully guaranteed. NAIC accreditation standards were being tightened in the 1990s, partly under the pressures of proposals to federalize solvency protection. Capital adequacy greatly improved as well.

companies. In addition, the NAIC developed an Insurance Regulatory Information System (IRIS), which includes Financial Analysis Solvency Tools (FAST), to flag attention on troubled companies. Increasingly used, these measures facilitate financial review and earlier corrective action, analogous to CAMELS ratings (*see* III.D., *supra*, at 133–134) and tighter capital standards for banks and thrifts (*see* III.D., *supra* at 139–140). A reduced rate of insurance company insolvencies has been achieved. In the years 1989–1994 insurance company insolvencies totaled 389; in 1995–1996 there were only 13 insolvencies each year.

Furthermore, the NAIC has pressed state insurance commissioners to improve their oversight and staffing through an accreditation program. Most state insurance departments are now "accredited," with improved capabilities.[4]

3. RATE MAKING AND FILINGS

The general guideline for insurance regulators with respect to rates has been adequate, not excessive, and not unreasonably discriminatory. Rate levels for property and liability insurance are regulated in most states under rating laws. These laws normally require "adequate" rates in light of past and prospective loss experience, reasonable margins for underwriting, and overall financial conditions for insurers. Yet rates should not be

---

[4] Increasingly, state insurance commissioners have corrective order authority, together with powers for conservatorship, rehabilitation, or when appropriate, liquidation.

"excessive" and provide too much premium income. Presumably, competition among insurers limits insurance prices, if this is allowed to operate. For mutual insurers, where policyholders get the benefits of unneeded surplus and dividends, there is a further corrective for overly generous rates. This helps explain a tendency for most state insurance departments to emphasize adequacy, which has been criticized by consumer advocates as leading to more expensive coverage (at least for ordinary policyholders). Insurers, however, stress the dangers of cutthroat competition, rate wars, and the possibility of inadequate reserves or insolvency.

Sensible classification according to risk experience is an established insurance practice, and regulatory standards take this into account. Thus, insurance regulation merely tries to prevent "unreasonable discrimination." The creation of preferred risk categories can be a means to reducing rates and premium income, so that regulators try to supervise (at least loosely) such developments. On the other hand, certain risk classifications have become controversial with consumers, such as high rates for younger automobile drivers. In these matters regulators tend to follow industry trends, and they rarely interfere with risk classification used by insurers.

Rate bureaus are employed widely for property and liability insurance. The most commonly used model rate filing law is a compromise between "prior approval" and "file and use," which allows filed rates to be used after a limited interval, unless specifically disapproved by the state authorities. Unusually low rate filings have been challenged and litigated by bureau insurers in some states. This framework has permitted reductions in rates by some insurers, when they believe this to be in their interest for expanding sales. Other states require mandatory membership in rate bureaus or insist upon regulatory approval. On the other hand, many states employ permissive rate filing laws (on some lines of insurance at least), under which insurers are free either to follow or not follow bureau rate levels. Even in these states, though, bureau rates tend to be influential.

Direct writers—insurance companies or agents that sell only a single brand—have become more important in some lines of insurance. While mail order insurance (sometimes TV advertised) is one form of direct writing that dispenses with commission agents and expenses, this is not a very substantial fraction of the insurance sold. Much more significant as direct writers are large insurance companies such as State Farm Mutual, Allstate, Liberty Mutual and Nationwide Mutual, which use exclusive agent networks, with bigger sales volume, direct billing procedures, and lower commissions. Direct writers are active with automobile insurance, and are spreading into residential, home, and some commercial property insurance.

With respect to life insurance, rate practices have been different. Generally speaking, life insurers are free to set their own policy rates and prices, except, in some states, for group rates. This reflects great variability of risk, including age, sex, and occupation, together with different sizes of policies, and other relevant circumstances. Another factor has been a strong role for mutual insurance companies in the earlier, formative years of life insurance development. Indirectly, of course, life insurance rates are regulated through reserve requirements and solvency supervision. Unduly low rates and premium revenue undermine solvency for a life insurer. But normally it is only large, strong insurance companies (often mutuals) that reduce prevailing rate levels somewhat for individual life policies. On the other hand, group life insurance is much cheaper, with lower marketing costs than ordinary individual policies. By 2003 about 42 percent of the life insurance in force consisted of group policies. Yet much of the individual life insurance sold today goes to large face value policyholders, for whom tax sheltering and estate planning is emphasized, where the role of the selling agent becomes more like investment counseling. Commission expenses can be reduced for larger policies, and this is reflected in negotiating coverage and rates.

Various kinds of annuity policies (with fixed or variable returns, perhaps linked to equity security markets) are offered as vehicles for investment/insurance. This has become an expanding part of the life insurance business; by 1998, for example, 70 million people were covered by life insurance pension plans. Banks have offered increasing competition in annuity investments, so that their share in this area has expanded, too.

Health and disability insurance is an outgrowth of the life insurance business, generally without formalized rate bureaus. Group policies and coverage are predominant in this area. Standard cost plus markups have become customary for these group policies, although discounts are sometimes conceded by insurers to obtain the group life insurance coverage commonly associated with an employers' package of fringe benefits for employees. Health Maintenance Organizations (HMOs) are increasingly important, however, as vehicles for cost control and wider affordability, although their restrictions on access to procedures are controversial with patients.

Ocean marine insurance is another branch of coverage where rating bureaus do not normally govern. This reflects diverse risks and strong international competition, where insurers want flexibility. Inland marine insurance, however, is commonly regulated through rate bureaus, along with the bulk of property-liability coverage.

4. FINANCIAL REPORTING

While state-enforced financial reporting is essential to identify insolvent insurers, some insurers, especially in the life area, would prefer more accounting leeway to show stronger growth and profit performance. Certain consumer advocates, on the other hand, want better profit data (including investment income) in order to limit premiums and rate increases, particularly for property and liability insurance. The American Institute of Certified Public Accounts has developed more liberal accounting guidelines for life insurance companies. For the property-liability portion of the industry, however, accounting procedures are more controversial, and involve the issue of rate making policies. And now that the Gramm-Leach-Bliley Financial Services Modernization Act of 1999 allows financial conglomerates into insurance, securities, and banking, there is a need for greater coordination of financial reporting across all three industries.

5. STANDARD CONTRACTS AND CONSUMER PROTECTION

A major achievement of insurance regulation has been considerable standardization of the more common insurance contracts, such as conventional life insurance and home-fire protection. Through a blend of regulatory pressure, responsible company leadership, and market competition, the harsher features of earlier insurance contracting have been eliminated. Non-forfeiture provisions and surrender values for life insurance, the standard fire policy, and limitations upon cancellation treatment are examples of this effort. On the other hand, conflicting pressures for insurance product innovation, new kinds of coverage, economical and low-cost premiums, marketing incentives and commissions encourage policy variation. While insurance departments and consumer groups can monitor basic policies fairly easily, it is difficult to review provisions for every contract and all lines of insurance, including commercial and business property, liability, marine, fidelity, and surety coverage. For business insurance, however, we presume enough competence on the part of the insured to negotiate contracts intelligently, so that consumer protection efforts are most important for basic policies widely used by the general public.

State insurance departments also regulate unfair trade practices. The NAIC Model Unfair Trade Practice Bill has been influential in defining unfair methods of competition and deceptive acts or practices. They include misrepresentation, false advertising and financial statements, intimidation, coercion, boycotts, defamation, unfair price discrimination, commission rebates to customers, questionable stock operations, suspicious advisory board contracts, and unsound self-dealing by company officials. State insurance departments have the responsibility of investigating consumer complaints with respect to rates, claims cancellations, dividends, underwriting, misrepresentation and fraudulent activities and other grievances. Limited efforts along these lines are made in most states, although some insurance regulators also believe they are responsible for limiting excessive competition or unsound practices that might undermine insurer solvency.

D. SOCIALIZED RISK COVERAGE

Not all risks should be insured. Many are bearable adversities of living, better and less expensively absorbed in the ordinary course of business or family life. A considerable range of risks has been insured, however, at affordable rates by commercial private insurers. This is the established private insurance system—with life, annuity, health, disability, property, marine, liability, surety, and fidelity coverage. But some risks are insured or compensated, in part at least, by government insurance or relief programs. This is the area of socialized risk coverage, which, in a pluralistic society, is often somewhat controversial.

Table VII-2
Socialized Insurance

Funded Government Insurance or Compensation Programs

Old Age Survivors, Disability, and Health Insurance (OASDHI)
Railroad Retirement (Federal)
Unemployment Compensation (Federal and states)
Worker's Compensation (States)
Temporary Disability Income Benefits (some states)
Government Employee Pensions
Military Pensions, Benefits
[Proposals to Expand National Health Insurance (NHI)]
Crime Insurance (Federal Insurance Administration)
FAIR plans (Riot reinsurance)
Flood Insurance (Federal)
Crop Insurance (Federal and states)
Financial Institution Insurance (FDIC, NCUSIF)
Securities Investor Protection Corporation (SPIC)
Pension Benefit Guaranty Corp. (PBGC)
War Risk Marine Insurance
Assigned Risk Plans for State Auto Insurance
State Auto Insurance (a few states)
State Title Insurance (a few states)
State Property Insurance (some states)
State Solvency Insurance Funds

Government Assistance Programs

Aid for Dependent Children (AFDC)

Assistance to the Blind (AB)
Aid to the Permanently and Totally Disabled (APTD)
Food Stamps
Black Lung Program
Veteran's Benefit Programs
Student Loan Programs
Housing and Urban Development Subsidies
Disaster Relief and Credit Subsidies
Superfund (chemical wastes)
International Aid (Bilateral)
IMF, World Bank, and IDB Contributions
Eximbank
Export Credit Guarantees

The reasons for government insurance or relief may involve heavy cost or extreme risk that most private parties cannot readily absorb, even through private insurer risk pooling. Exceptional natural disasters, earthquakes, massive floods, insurrection and war costs are examples. Other examples include social costs from depressions and heavy unemployment, export financing and international credit risks, chemical waste disposal or drastic accidents at nuclear power plants. Government insurance or relief may also be prompted by limited incomes and lack of affordability, which have prompted old age and survivors insurance, medical care and hospitalization for the elderly and poor, worker's accident or sickness compensation, aid to the blind and disabled, poverty relief and assistance, food stamps, and so on. In these government programs it may not be easy to draw neat lines between the "insurable" portion, which could be supported by reasonable assessments and contributions related to benefit and risk, and the "relief" or transfer payment portion supported by tax revenues. Politics in pluralist societies may make it difficult to set limits on socialized insurance and relief programs. There is disagreement on the extent to which they should be fully funded by intended beneficiaries, whether progressive taxes or internal subsidies should be involved, and the degree to which general budget revenues should be drawn upon for these purposes. Ultimately, though, excessive liberality for social insurance and relief increases tax loads, may strain incentives for the heavily taxed, and divert investment and tax resources from capital formation and economic growth into income maintenance and welfare programs. Social insurance also competes with other government spending priorities. In other words, there are some limits to social affordability, even for humane and beneficent purposes.

Under-funding is not uncommon in socialized insurance programs, along with a gradual expansion of benefits and beneficiaries. Thus, even with socialized insurance designed to be self-financing, such as Old Age and Survivor's Insurance (the core of Social Security), additional benefits and disability assistance were tacked on, along with generous inflation-indexed cost of living increments, that made this program more expensive. Meanwhile, increased longevity, uncertain economic growth, and a bunching of projected retirements for "baby boomers" in the Twenty-First Century, make some of the funding assumptions unrealistic. Since Social Security and Medicare are the biggest single elements of socialized risk protection and transfer payment activity, their handling carries special significance. However, Social Security financing is merely part of a continuing struggle over spending priorities, tied in with budget and tax controversies. Few doubt that government should provide a basic floor of social insurance protection. The problem is to achieve reasonable consensus upon its content and distribution among competing constituencies and their alliances. No one can deny the importance of these issues, because about 10 percent of the gross national product is involved in government insurance and relief programs (federal, state and local), which is roughly comparable to the total of all insurance premiums paid through private insurance companies.

E. POSSIBLE REFORMS AND FEDERAL REGULATION

Modern insurance protection in the United States is a blend of private insurance company activity regulated by the states, and largely federal social insurance and relief programs. Many proposals for improving this system emphasize the shortcomings of state regulation, and the need for refinement of social insurance, its size, benefit distribution, or financing support. Changes in federal programs, stronger regulation (federal or state), and greater antitrust discipline (with less exemption under the McCarran-Ferguson Act) are common proposals.

While the Gramm-Leach-Bliley Act pushed state insurance regulators in the direction of greater harmonization, it was only with the market collapse of 2008 that significant federal involvement in the supervision of insurance began to seem a practical possibility. A number of insurance companies (as well as some investment firms) became FHCs in the run up to the crisis by creating or acquiring a banking subsidiary, and this voluntary action placed them under the direct supervision of the Federal Reserve, in its capacity as regulator of bank and financial holding companies.

Post-2010, the FSOC has the statutory authority under the Dodd-Frank Act to designate non-banking financial services firms—including insurance companies—as systemically significant financial institutions, which would place them under the direct supervision of the Federal Reserve and subject to FDIC "orderly liquidation" authority if they encountered serious financial difficulty. To date, the FSOC has identified only four nonbank financial firms as systemically significant financial institutions, and three of those were in the insurance sector—American International Group Inc. (AIG), Prudential Financial Inc., and MetLife, Inc. The fourth institution, GE Capital, was "de-designated" in June 2016, after selling off its online deposits. Later, AIG also restructured itself and was de-designated. MetLife successfully challenged its designation in litigation.[5] Finally, in October 2018, the FSOC de-designated Prudential Financial, leaving no nonbank currently designated as an SIFI.

---

[5] *See, e.g.*, *MetLife, Inc. v. Financial Stability Oversight Council*, 865 F.3d 661 (D.C. Cir. 2017) (holding that FSOC designation procedures did not abrogate common-law right of public access to judicial records).

1. SHORTCOMINGS AND REFORMS

Proposals for changing insurance regulation and social insurance come from three directions: (i) consumer-oriented proposals to reduce excess profits, prices, and waste, and to expand benefits for the public; (ii) conservative proposals to reduce socialized risk protection, lower tax support, and increase contributions from beneficiaries; and (iii) technical-minded proposals from moderate experts that blend specific elements from each of the foregoing, and emphasize improved spending discipline and efficiency.

Automobile insurance, its growing cost, wasteful litigation, and limited net compensation has received criticism for many years. Auto insurance premiums accounted for 1.5 percent of the GNP in 2003 or $176 billion, and less than half of this amount goes to pay valid claims for injury and damage. Litigation costs, selling expense and commissions, fraudulent and nuisance claims, and administrative overhead use up some 50–60 percent. Various proposals for no fault liability (or at least reduced liability) are made to cut the litigation and nuisance burden somewhat, but these ideas have been implemented only to a partial degree. Major cuts in premiums probably would entail reductions in claims benefits and trial lawyers strongly resist any drastic changes in tort liability. (With perfect information, reasonable claims could be processed more efficiently, but bargaining conflicts and litigation make this difficult.) Part of the cost burden also results from inflated medical and hospitalization expenses, together with expensive automobiles, parts and repairs.[6]

Rate bureau and cartel pricing practices in the property-liability area have been criticized. While direct writer competition has helped in many states for some lines of insurance, this discipline could be broadened. Mandatory rate bureau pricing might be outlawed, either by state or federal legislation (*e.g.*, McCarran Act amendments to eliminate their antitrust exemption).

In the life insurance area, other financial institutions wanted to enter which could narrow sales margins and commissions somewhat further. Until recently, only some MSBs and credit unions offered life insurance policies, but now many thrifts and commercial banks sell annuities and/or some life insurance, and more competition has resulted. Yet, it should be emphasized, reasonable life insurance reserves have to be maintained, in any event, by new competitors. Larger banks and financial institutions will probably find it easier, therefore, simply to make acquisitions of life insurance companies, and perhaps expand their sales (and absorb their profits).[7] This is

---

6 Many states recently have tried to limit or roll back auto insurance rates, with great resistance from insurer lobbies. In some areas, costs and rates seem clearly excessive, but a serious solution requires a combined effort on expenses, broad-ranging tort "reforms", and improved insurance supervision.

7 Some states recently began in the 1990s to allow banks into insurance underwriting or marketing (some via special affiliates). Major BHCs pushed strongly for such authority as beachheads for expanded activities. But most insurers, and especially independent insurance agents, feared these incursions, and lobbied to limit them. (See Chapter IX for more discussion.)

what Gramm-Leach-Bliley achieved in allowing financial service conglomerates in 1999.

Industrial life insurance policies (small value policies, with high expenses and commissions) have been a target of criticism for several generations. But their importance has declined substantially, with increasing worker incomes and enlarged group life insurance coverage. Credit life insurance has even greater selling and commission expense, with low payout benefits, and has been extensively criticized. Some suggest minimum payout requirements to reduce credit life insurance charges.

Health insurance costs have been increasing rapidly, along with inflation in medical and hospital charges. Private insurers do not have enough incentive to resist this overall inflationary pressure, because of their cost-plus service contracts. But the problem of cost containment for health care is broader, and politically difficult. It involves larger outlays for socialized health care (Medicare, Medicaid, and government support for hospitals and medical research), specialty certification and high charges for medical services, malpractice litigation, defensive medicine, expensive drugs, and substantial waste and duplication in hospitals. Even so, many complain of inadequate health care for a minority without sufficient health insurance or government supported medical and hospitalization care. Therefore, proposals to expand socialized health

---

Bankers contended that economies of integration or scope may be involved, yet insurance interests worried about displacement effects, especially in marketing.

insurance have been made, including at least catastrophic insurance coverage and a basic floor of health insurance for all citizens. Such enlarged care would be expensive, and additional tax revenues would be required, unless the waste in present practices can be eliminated. In the meantime, HMOs have been performing some of the gatekeeper and cost-control responsibilities under "moderate" and "lower income" health insurance plans. And the federal government tried to limit Medicare-Medicaid expenses with incomplete success and considerable bickering. All of these inter-related problems make health care and insurance controversial and awkward politically, as the country learned in the Clinton, Bush, and Obama presidencies.

Another complaint of consumer advocates is that insurance company rates on policies or premium charges are not sufficiently reduced for investment income on reserves and other assets. They contend, in other words, that profits and executive compensation (even for mutual companies) are more generous than necessary for adequate reserves. They argue that the growth of insurance companies, with some new entrants, reflects this fact. Insurance industry advocates deny these contentions, and say that insurance industry returns are not exceptional, or at least that rates of return are justified by risk factors in a competitive economy. At issue is a basic disagreement over the effectiveness of price competition in this regulated industry.

From a conservative standpoint and that of the insurance industry, the present state regulatory system functions reasonably well. The main problems of cost increase are external forces, *i.e.*, tort litigation, excessive awards and risks, together with inflated medical care, auto repair, and prices generally. They view diversity in premiums, policies, and service as part of healthy market competition over the long run.

Conservatives find more problems, and greater waste, generally speaking, with socialized insurance and government relief programs. They insist that politics has carried these efforts to excess, and that Social Security, Medicare, food stamps, welfare, and other programs need pruning to offset over-spending. Hence, the major task of insurance reform is to discipline public sector insurance and relief programs, not private insurers who already meet a market test for performance.

There is sharp conflict between the opposing camps on these issues. Some experts take a middle view, finding considerable waste, overpricing, and generous profit in much of the private insurance industry, yet condemning socialized insurance for appreciable waste, under-funding, and an aggregate contribution to government deficits and inflation. The current literature on insurance regulation has ample expressions of all these viewpoints.

2. FEDERAL REGULATION

The state-regulated insurance system has strong conservative momentum, with great industry influence. It has resisted federal regulation, and even antitrust enforcement. Most insurance industry advocates question the need and desirability for any major federal regulation. On the other hand, a considerable range of federal insurance programs has been accumulated (including Social Security, Medicare, unemployment compensation, military and government employee pensions, crime and riot insurance, flood and crop insurance, disaster relief, FDIC, NCUSIF, SIPC, PBGC, export credit guarantees, and war risk marine insurance).

Under the Federal Emergency Management Agency (FEMA), the Federal Insurance and Mitigation Administration already exists to supervise flood and riot insurance, and it provides limited planning efforts, including earthquake and civil defense plans. The U.S. Fire Administration conducts training and research activities within FEMA. The Department of Transportation also does studies on automobile insurance, and the Federal Trade Commission has published a few reports on insurance.

An interesting precedent for limited federal regulation of insurance is the Product Liability Risk Retention Act of September 1981, 15 U.S.C.A. § 3901 *et seq*. This was prompted by manufacturing industry concern about the expanding burden of product liability litigation and insurance costs. This legislation facilitates the establishment of manufacturer self-insurance groups on a nationwide basis, so that risk management can be developed more efficiently, at lower costs by industries affected with product liability risks.

There have been other proposals for selective federal regulation to deal with particular problems. Federal "no fault" insurance for automobile liability claims was suggested some years ago, but the states handled this issue with a varied range of legislation, or no action at all.

The McCarran-Ferguson Act of 1946 is another example of selective regulation in a way, although its goal was largely to insulate state insurance regulation and rate bureaus from federal antitrust prosecution. The McCarran Act exemption can be reduced to allow more direct writer competition, and to provide encouragement for self-insurance groups in other areas. Mandatory participation in rate bureaus could be made unlawful this way.

Selective federal regulation, at this stage, is the most likely method by which major changes could be made in the present pattern of state regulation. However, we must recall that insurance industry groups have urged "friendly" federal regulation at times as an alternative to legislation that seemed more threatening. Such proposals were made in the later 1860s as a response to state law restrictions, but *Paul v. Virginia* inhibited that approach for many years. More recently, the Research Institute of the College of Insurance (funded by some leading insurance companies) offered a tentative suggestion for federal insurance regulation in the Fall 1976, when it seemed possible that a more consumer-oriented Congress and president could be elected. In 1975 a White House task force also had proposed repeal of the McCarran Act, and its replacement with federal standards for state regulation of insurance. In this context, the Research Institute suggested a Model Bill, with more limited revision of the McCarran Act, allowing substantial joint preparation of cost, risk, and reserve data by insurance company associations, and preserving the opportunity for state regulation at rates that were adequate, not excessive, and not unreasonably discriminatory. This suggests the insurance industry will seek to retain as much as possible of the present state regulatory system that is favorable to insurers, one way or another.

The history of other financial industries suggests that some degree of industry-friendly regulation is hard to avoid over the long run. Consumer advocates will press for their reforms, but the insurance industry's track record for influencing its own regulatory environment has been reasonably successful. The National Association of Insurance Commissioners (NAIC) moved forward as well, with stronger solvency and risk-based capital proposals, the IRIS accounting system, and a new certification program for state insurance departments. Results so far have been considerable, with capital enhanced, and the frequency of insolvencies declining.

A bigger challenge to the state oriented insurance regulatory tradition is the new opportunity for banking-securities-insurance industry holding companies. When the Gramm-Leach-Bliley Act authorized financial holding companies to have subsidiaries in all three fields together, it contemplated regulation of each field in their present form. Banking is regulated mainly by the Federal

Reserve, OCC, FDIC, and by state banking regulators; securities markets are regulated mainly by the SEC, NASD, stock and options-trading exchanges; insurance is regulated mainly by the state insurance departments and their commissioners, along with NAIC.

There is still a need to harmonize more effectively financial accounting, oversight, and responses to problems (such as financial holding company failures; mergers involving foreign banks, insurers, and/or securities firms; tax treatment for these conglomerate enterprises; difficulties posed by tax havens and claims for privacy; illegal and drug money laundering; and speculative capital flows in world markets). A serious complication with the NAIC-state insurance regulation system in its present form is the lack of speedy, national level decision-making for insurance policy. The Fed, OCC, FDIC, and SEC can work together within a few days for emergencies. The insurance industry regulators really need comparably rapid decision-making. Without a strong federal insurance agency, the banking and securities agencies dominate policy at the national level for these industries.

An interesting development over the last 30 years has been international insurance supervisory collaboration. The International Association of Insurance Supervisors (IAIS) was formed in 1994, with a Secretariat now located at the Bank for International Settlements (BIS) in Basel, Switzerland. The IAIS promotes principles and standards on insurance supervision, together with training, textbooks, case studies, and issue papers. IAIS tries to collaborate with the IMF, World Bank, and International Accounting Standards Board. Recent topics for discussions have been natural catastrophes, terrorist disasters, growing litigiousness, capital adequacy, insolvency, bankruptcies, reinsurance, money laundering and e commerce. As of this writing, more than 200 jurisdictions are represented in the IAIS, constituting 97% of the world's insurance premiums. Their impact, along with IOSCO, the BIS, IMF, and World Bank will be gradually to improve accountability, responsible performance, and resiliency in global insurance markets. (The NAIC in the United States actively promotes and encourages these IAIS developments.)

The recent financial crises, with extensive losses in banking, securities, and some aspects of insurance, have posed serious challenges. Urgent Federal assistance, bailouts, guarantees, and lending were needed to prevent a broader financial and economic breakdown. Great uncertainties aggravated these problems, with "toxic" assets that are hard to evaluate. Risks of default on counter party obligations complicated things. A big surge in securitized obligations and derivatives had been issued, some of which could be very costly and disruptive. Many new "quasi-insurance" products were sold in recent years that, in retrospect, created more risk liability than could be covered by the premiums, reserves, and capital provided to back up these obligations. Big losses and failures threatened financial markets in many countries. Financial conglomerates like AIG, Citigroup, and Bank of America (which took over Merrill Lynch) were "too big to fail," and needed better government surveillance, supervision, and support.

More dramatic responses at the federal level need to be explored, but these have been slow to materialize. The Dodd-Frank Act established the Federal Insurance Office (FIO) within the Department of the Treasury and vested FIO with the authority to monitor all aspects of the insurance sector, monitor the extent to which traditionally underserved communities and consumers have access to affordable non-health insurance products, and to represent the United States on prudential aspects of international insurance matters, including at the International Association of Insurance Supervisors. In addition, FIO serves as an advisory member of the FSOC, which has the authority under the act to designate large insurance companies, among other non-banking financial institutions, as systemically significant financial institutions subject to Federal Reserve supervision. (There are no current designations as of this writing.) The FIO also has the authority to recommend and approve the resolution of a troubled insurance company under the "orderly liquidation" authority of the FDIC. So, for the future at least, there are practical options available for the Federal Government to exert authority over the insurance sector.

3. BANKING AND INSURANCE CONTROVERSIES

Recent OCC rulings attempted to widen bank powers and allow more insurance activities by banks. U.S. Supreme Court decisions like *NationsBank v. VALIC* in 1995, where the court allowed banks to sell annuity insurance policies, and *Barnett Bank v. Nelson* in 1996, where the court overruled a Florida law that limited bank sales of insurance in small towns (in conflict with an older federal statute), illustrated how a gradual opening of insurance markets could occur by regulatory and court decisions. A complication for the insurance industry was that no strong federal regulatory agency (like the Federal Reserve, OCC, or SEC) existed to represent their interests; those Federal regulators allowing banks to expand into insurance activities were the *banking* agencies (especially the OCC, and to a lesser extent, the Federal Reserve).

Why did some banks and BHCs want insurance underwriting or marketing authority and powers? Many banks feared consolidation, retrenchment, and digitalization pressure, and believed that financial service operations could be leaner with fewer employees. Accordingly, some banks favored expansion into insurance as an offset growth channel, even though this came at the expense of insurance agents (and, to some extent, insurance companies). In addition, some banks saw economies of integration for banking, asset management, and customer services (including insurance). While most smaller banks would get little growth from insurance, a sizable number of large BHCs could make profitable mergers with insurance companies as financial service holding companies.

However, most independent insurance agents fear that many ordinary auto, home, life, and health care policies could be sold in bank lobbies. Over time, traditional independent insurance agents could be marginalized and replaced by insurance policies sold in bank lobbies or on bank websites, or tied in with bank loans, title insurance, checking account, annuity sales, and mutual fund services offered by banks. For these reasons, independent insurance agents (hundreds of thousands of them) resisted any Glass-Steagall reforms that allow banks to enter freely and take over insurance marketing. From their viewpoint, such a banking takeover could mark the end for viable independent insurance agents. Life insurance sales slowed in recent years, and banks were less suited for sophisticated business and estate planning arrangements that need to be carefully tailored for client needs. For group life policies, margins are thinner, and group policies are often packaged with health insurance for larger employers (and often tied in with HMOs). These areas may be less appropriate for bank marketing, although some BHCs might find profitable mergers with selected life insurance companies. Nonetheless, annuity policies and investments were becoming attractive sales vehicles for large banks in the insurance area. In the diverse network of property and casualty insurance, with many specialized lines of insurance and thinner markets, banks would not find many large scale markets. Only the auto and home insurance markets offer major marketing opportunities for standardized policies, and plenty of insurance competition already exists in these areas. Thus, it would seem that the main potential for BHCs in the insurance industry is not so much large sales increases for policies, but rather in selected merger opportunities with stronger insurance companies (or alternately, underpriced insurance companies with low stock prices that allow profitable mergers). From this perspective, however, financial service holding companies could be formed just as well by strong insurance companies acquiring BHCs.

Finally, with respect to socialized insurance, transfer payments, and "excessive" spending outlays, these are big federal budget and tax policy issues. Almost 10 percent of the U.S. gross national product is now involved in government or "socialized insurance" programs in one form or another. The proper guideline for any government outlay, regulation, tax subsidy, insurance or guarantee program is that net social benefit should result, and that government intervenes only when it improves the marketplace. The political process is supposed to resolve these questions responsibly, but the disorderly, sometimes incomplete compromises of recent years are disturbing. Unfortunately, there are major, unresolved budget problems for the United States with respect to long-term Social Security and pension funding, government subsidized disability insurance, nursing homes, Medicare, Medicaid, and overall health care and its insurance. These budget and financing issues are dealt with also in the next two chapters.

CHAPTER VIII

PENSION FUNDS, RETIREMENT ACCOUNTS AND SOCIAL SECURITY

Pension funds, retirement accounts, and Social Security benefits are an increasingly important part of the economy. From relatively modest beginnings with private pensions before the Social Security system was established in 1935, the benefits paid under these arrangements have grown, as a share of U.S. GNP, from .6 percent in 1940 to 3.9 percent in 1960, reached 8.2 percent in 1980, and have continued to grow over time. Reserve assets held for pensions and retirement accounts are growing substantially, and pension funds (in one form or another) are major financial intermediaries. In 2007 private, state and local government pension funds held about $17,600 billion in assets. If Social Security were funded comprehensively, its current benefits might need another $10,000 billion in assets (but Social Security is financed mainly with current payroll taxes, and only limited trust fund reserves). Thus, the collection of funds for pensions, retirement, and Social Security are major elements in the network of financial intermediation and saving for prosperous industrial societies like the United States.

A. HISTORICAL DEVELOPMENT

The broadening of pensions for the elderly reflects increased affluence among industrial societies, a shift from rural living toward more dispersed urban families, and greater longevity. Before the last 60–100 years, pensions were limited, and considered a reward for special services, such as successful military leaders, injured soldiers and sailors, or others deserving favor. Individual family resources were the principal means of support for older people in traditional societies, which prevailed until the last several generations.

In the United States, pensions were first developed as compensation for war veterans, starting after the Revolutionary War, and major wars thereafter. Some government officials and judges also received pensions, but they were not extended to the majority of government employees until the last several generations. Private pensions were pioneered by a few large corporations in the later Nineteenth Century, with American Express and a few large railroads as leaders. Early company pensions were often disability related, or restricted to long-term, senior and "deserving" employees and executives. Because companies frequently used them against unions (and limited access to union members), the American Federation of Labor tended to resist company pensions in this period. Unions tried to develop their own pension and death benefit plans in the early Twentieth Century, but union benefits were usually modest.

Meanwhile, social insurance and old age assistance was introduced by Bismarck, the conservative German leader in the 1880s. Bismarck's program included sickness insurance 1883, accident insurance 1884, and old age and disability insurance

1889, financed by contributions from employers and employees. Such social insurance programs became a standard package of legislation sought by social democratic and liberal reformers throughout most of the world in the last several generations.

In the United States, however, there was greater resistance, which lasted for a longer period. The traditions of voluntarism were well established. Higher wages prevailed, farms were larger, and there were more business opportunities. The federal system made it difficult for individual states to experiment with more expensive forms of social insurance, such as old age pensions, because the necessary payroll taxes would handicap their state's employers against those in other states.

Workers compensation laws for industrial accidents were the only type of social insurance to be widely enacted in the United States before the Great Depression. They began with Maryland 1902 and a limited federal law in 1908. Courts declared most early laws unconstitutional, but successful enactments followed rapidly in 26 states between 1911–1914. Private liability insurance quickly developed for employers, and they soon preferred the definite and limited costs of scheduled workers compensation laws to the indefinite risk of unlimited tort liabilities. These laws ultimately spread to all states.

During the 1920s private pension plans proliferated, especially those offered by large corporate employers. By 1929, 3.7 million American workers were covered by nearly 400 company plans (roughly 10 percent of the non-agricultural labor force). More trade unions also developed pension plans, though with less resources. Although company pensions became common for larger employers, early vesting was rare, 20–25 years' service was usually required, and only one tenth of the employees got benefits. Most plans were financed entirely by the employers, with no employee contributions. Financing was from current company revenues in the majority of plans, and only a minority of plans collected serious reserves in advance for potential obligations. By this time pensions were established for the military services, the federal civil service, some state and local government workers, many schoolteachers and university faculties, and some of the clergy. Company stock-option plans were also common, and served some retirement purposes, though mainly for higher salaried executives.

The Great Depression greatly weakened this budding pension movement. Unemployment reached one fourth of the workforce, many businesses and farmers suffered reduced income, and family resources to cushion adversity and old age were reduced. Many companies and governments were forced into retrenchment, and they found their pension obligations very expensive. A large number of pension plans failed, and many were discontinued.

This emergency of widespread economic distress and reduced income for many families and older people brought three Congressional responses, which greatly expanded American social insurance: (i) unemployment compensation; (ii) federal support for the railroad industry retirement system; and (iii) Social Security (old age and survivors insurance). Only sickness or health insurance failed of enactment at this stage, with weaker support and strong opposition from the medical profession.

For unemployment insurance, Congress established as part of the Social Security Act of 1935, a federal payroll tax, minimum standards, and administration for unemployment compensation insurance. Every state has its own plan under this framework, with some more liberal than others. Experience ratings are used, so that employers with lower layoff rates pay less in payroll taxes.

With growing affluence, Congress felt greater benefits were desirable and affordable, even though payroll taxes had to be raised to some degree. Over the years survivor and dependent benefits were added, along with disability insurance. Earlier retirement was allowed for women, and then for men also. Eventually, in the late 1960s, Medicare (health insurance) benefits for older people were tacked on with a separate trust fund. The Social Security system was extended to cover farmers, domestics and the self-employed, and became nearly universal. The net result has been a substantially increased level of basic old age pensions for almost all citizens.

In addition, state and local government pensions, along with private employer, union, and self-employed plans, grew substantially to supplement the rising "floor" of basic Social Security benefits. Increased profits and wages during World War II encouraged employer pension plans, especially because war-time excess profit taxes and wage restraints could be avoided this way. Since income taxes remained higher in the post-war era, sustained by bracket creep, these incentives continued to encourage company pension and stock-option plans, especially for upper-level executives and technical talent. Corporate contributions to such plans were deductible business expenses, and the income earned by these accumulations normally was sheltered from taxation against the recipients until benefits were withdrawn. Unlike Social Security, most company pension plans provided benefits closely related to individual contributions, so that high salary employees could gain substantial tax savings this way.

The stronger unions also sought pension plans from employers as fringe benefits and wage hikes in the years right after World War II. Many multi-employer and company plans were established because of collective bargaining pressures. The National Labor Relations Board and the courts strengthened the pension movement by requiring employers to bargain in good faith over demands for pensions and related fringe benefit packages under Section 8(a)(5) of the National Labor Relations Act, 29 U.S.C.A. § 158(a)(5).

State and local governments also broadened pension plan and other fringe benefits in this postwar era. Some plans remained independent of Social Security, while others merely supplemented Social Security benefits. But many state and local pension programs built up considerable reserve funds, like the stronger private pension plans.

As this movement for pension plans gathered momentum, Congress provided for the self-employed to receive tax sheltering opportunities through H.R. 10 or Keogh plans in 1962. Insurance companies also developed tax deferred annuity (and variable annuity) policies for the self-employed market, along with high salaried employees. Mutual funds began to encourage special investment accounts for this purpose. The tax laws were revised to facilitate supplemental contributions to company and government pension plans, and in 1974 individual retirement accounts (IRAs) were authorized under ERISA to provide wider opportunities for tax sheltered savings for many taxpayers. Additional liberalization of Keogh plans and IRA tax sheltering opportunities followed in 1976, 1978, and with the Economic Recovery Tax Act of 1981 (ERTA). The Tax Reform Act of 1986 cut back on the deductibility of IRA contributions for higher income participants in employer pension plans. However, the Economic Growth and Tax Relief Reconciliation Act of 2001 scheduled increases in the amount of IRA contributions allowed, with inflation adjustments.

The cumulative result of this pension and retirement account movement was to create supplementary pension income, above and beyond Social Security benefits, for the majority of workers. Roughly half the private sector employees obtain such pension benefits. While government Social Security programs provide the bulk of benefits paid to ordinary retired people with limited incomes, these additional private, state and local government pension funds and retirement accounts have expanded greatly. Hence, the private and public pension funds are important financial intermediaries with large funds to invest.

B. PENSION PLAN AND FUNDING REGULATIONS

Early regulation of pension plans involved compliance with Internal Revenue Act requirements or tax qualification. Since the early 1920s, employer contributions to trusts for stock-bonus or profit-sharing plans were deductible expenses, and not income for the beneficiaries until actually received by them. Similar deductibility for employer pension fund contributions was later allowed, and insurance annuity policies established by employers received comparable treatment. Some restrictions were placed on these arrangements, however, because of their potential for corporate and executive income tax evasion. Firm commitment or irrevocability was required. The Revenue Act of 1942 added further regulations, because heavier war-time income and excess profits taxes made these "tax loopholes" very attractive for business. The new requirements included at least gradual vesting of pension benefits, participation by 70 percent of the employees in a pension plan (except for temporary and seasonal workers, and those with less than 5 years seniority), and non-discrimination in favor of executives (although contributions and benefits proportionate to compensation were permissible). Subsequently the vesting of benefits was required before plans could be terminated. Apart from these tax qualification requirements, the only other significant law regulating pensions was the law of trusts in each state for funds taking the form of legal trusts, and state insurance law for insurance contract plans developed by insurance companies. Note that commercial banks and trust companies commonly serve as trustees for pension plan trust funds, and banking law indirectly affects their activity.

The Welfare and Pension Plans Disclosure Act of 1958, with substantial amendments in 1962, provided for pension plan participants and employees to receive information about their plans. This was intended to discourage malpractices and fraudulent administration. The Secretary of Labor received investigation and anti-fraud enforcement authority. However, instances of funds misuse, particularly concerning union pension and welfare funds, aroused continued public controversy. Improved remedies for breach of fiduciary duties were needed for pension funds generally.

Many funds lacked sufficient funding or reserves, and when a company went out of business or its plan terminated, this could leave many workers with greatly impaired pension benefits. Other problems concerned delays in vesting benefits. Job changes, layoffs, mergers, or other breaks in pension accrual could substantially reduce pension benefits. In contrast, the early vesting and full portability of the Teacher's Insurance Annuity Association (TIAA) pensions for college, university, and private school faculties and staff, stimulated criticism for the delayed vesting in many company plans, and the lack of "portability" in most private plans. Other complaints developed about incomplete participation, and workers left out of tax qualified plans.

These problems and complaints led Congress to enact the Employee Retirement Income Security Act of 1974 (ERISA), 29 U.S.C.A. § 1001 *et seq*. ERISA increased private pension and benefit plan reporting and disclosure, improved vesting and employee participation standards, strengthening funding and fiduciary discipline, created more retirement opportunities for the self-employed and a new individual retirement account (IRA), and established the Pension Benefit Guaranty Corporation (PBGC) to ensure that vested benefits would survive plan termination. The Internal Revenue Service (IRS) continued its regulatory role, but with new responsibilities for enforcement of the enhanced participation, vesting, and funding requirements. The Labor Department received responsibility for enlarged pension plan supervision, reporting and disclosure, and fiduciary oversight. The impact of ERISA has been to strengthen substantially private pension plan benefits and their reliability.

1. PARTICIPATION AND VESTING

Eligibility was broadened under ERISA, so that new employees must be allowed to participate and accrue benefits after only one year of employment. 29 U.S.C.A. § 1052(a)(1)(A)(ii). Only two major exceptions are now allowed: (i) employees under 21 may be required to wait until that age, *id.* § 1052(a)(1)(A)(i); and (ii) a two-year waiting period can be imposed if benefits are vested 100 percent after that time. *Id.* § 1052(a)(1)(B)(i). Older workers may not be excluded from pension plans on the basis of age. Id. § 1052(a)(1)(B)(ii).

Vesting was substantially improved and accelerated for many employees by ERISA. Under many employer pension plans vesting had been delayed until 15–20 years' service, and/or reaching the age of 45–50 (or some combination along these lines), and some plans delayed even further. Under ERISA a pension plan must vest 100 percent of the employee's contributions immediately, and the employer's contributions originally had to vest at least as early as one of the following:

(i) A 10 year vesting schedule, after which all accrued benefits are 100 percent vested; [This was most widely accepted for convenience, and referred to as the "10 year cliff", because many employers required the full period before complete vesting occurs.]

(ii) A 5–15 year vesting schedule, with 25 percent vested after 5 years' service, 50 percent after 10 years, and 100 percent after 15 years; or

(iii) A rule of 45 vesting schedule, under which benefits were 50 percent vested, when employees with 5 years or more of service reach a combination of age and years of service equal to 45, and another 10 percent vests each year for the next 5 years.

Some critics wanted full portability for pension plan benefits, but ERISA did not go that far. ERISA merely encouraged portability by allowing 60 days within which an employee could transfer or "rollover" his lump sum distribution of vested benefits to an IRA, if the new employer would not accept these benefits under its plan (or if the employee became self-employed).

Vesting was liberalized substantially and made more rapid by the Tax Reform Act of 1986, partly to help women and minority employees (who had higher turnover and less frequent vesting). The new vesting regime (in effect since December 31, 1988) provided only two alternatives: (i) 5-year cliff vesting (for multiemployer plans, 10 years of service allowed for employees covered by a collective bargaining agreement); or (ii) graded vesting, 20 percent per year after the second full year (so that full vesting is completed after 7 years).

2. FUNDING REQUIREMENTS

The requirements for funding are most demanding for "defined benefit" plans, *i.e.*, where the pension liability of the employer, union, trust, or insurer is expressed in specific amounts for retirement, survivor's benefits, etc. Before ERISA it was sufficient to pay current pension liability, plus interest on unfunded accrued obligations. This meant the capital base or reserves need not be provided in advance for the larger part of potential liabilities, and that something close to "pay as you go" financing was allowed. Under ERISA, pre-1974 plan obligations must be funded with additional contributions to amortize them over a 40 year period; for new plan obligations additional contributions must be amortized over 30 years. Reasonable actuarial procedures and estimates must be used for these amortization programs, taking into account projections of asset values and fund portfolio earnings.

For "defined contribution" plans, no additional outlay is required by ERISA, *i.e.*, where a specific amount is vested or set aside for each employee's account. In these pension, stock purchase, or profit-sharing plans, there was little problem of misrepresenting the adequacy of plan reserves to achieve certain benefit goals, and the employee's account merely grows to the extent of such defined contributions. Many of these plans were better funded, though, because sponsors and participants often selected contribution levels in competition with defined benefit plans, so that some comparability in yield would result for plan beneficiaries. ERISA merely requires defined benefit plans to cover their obligations with 30- to 40-year amortization programs, and appropriate levels of funding and contributions.

Expanded participation and earlier vesting requirements have funding implications for many pension and benefit plans. To the extent additional employees are included, greater contributions have to be made by employers (and perhaps employees).

Furthermore, where vesting occurs earlier for many employees, this increases the pension plan's liability exposure, and enlarges funding requirements for pension and benefit plans.

Where business conditions impose hardship on employers in making their plan contributions, the IRS may waive funding requirements. However, no more than five waivers in 15 years are allowed, and underpayments should be made up in not less than 15 years.

To enforce these funding obligations, substantial excise taxes may be imposed (up to 100 percent of the accumulated deficiency), and in extreme situations a pension or benefit plan could be forced into termination by the PBGC. If a plan is terminated, the PBGC may enforce a lien to the extent of 30 percent of an employer's net worth, in order to reimburse the PBGC for satisfying deficiencies in vested pension funds. If an employer decides to terminate an under-funded pension plan, this may be allowed, but only subject to PBGC reimbursement (*i.e.*, up to 30 percent of the employers' net worth in meeting vested deficiencies).

Congress relaxed and modified ERISA, to some extent, in the Multiemployer Pension Plan Amendments Act of 1980, affecting some 2,000 plans and 8 million covered workers. This gave some relief to multiemployer plans developed by labor unions, and was designed to ease burdens for declining industries with special difficulties in meeting ERISA funding requirements. This legislation relaxed some funding obligations, allowed for hardship withdrawal by employers (and fair share contributions thereafter), provided for reduction of certain benefits to prevent plan insolvency, attempted relief of plans with overloads of retiring employees, made "unavoidable insolvency" an insurable event for PBGC assistance, and authorized premium increases for PBGC insurance coverage. However, financial distress continues to be a problem for private pension plans generally, with awkward financial dilemmas, affecting many individual employer plans, as well as union-developed and other multiemployer pension and benefit plans. Because of recently increased premium charges for the PBGC, a surplus of some $7 billion accumulated by early 2000. Some years before the PBGC was forced to increase annual premium charges from $2.60 to $19 per participant to cover PBGC deficits in the late 1980s to early 1990s. As of this writing, the per-participant flat premium rate for plan years beginning in 2015 is $57 for single-employer plans (up from a 2014 rate of $49) and $13 for multiemployer plans (up from a 2014 rate of $12).

3. INVESTMENT REGULATION

Three kinds of managers are used by private pension funds. (1) A large number of plans are "insured" and managed by insurance companies, with up to one-fourth of the private pension assets, including many smaller plans. State insurance regulation applies to this sector, with restrictions upon assets, bonds, mortgages, equities, and loans. (2) Banks manage a large portion of the majority of other private pension trust funds, and handle many of the bigger plans. The national and state banking laws, together with the state law of trusts, provide guidelines and prudential regulation for investment management. (3) Many remaining private pension funds involve mutual funds, or perhaps union collective bargaining trusteeship arrangements, where there was sometimes a lack of guidelines or investment standards for pension fund managers.

ERISA mandates fiduciary responsibility for investment managers, trustees, or any other person with control over the pension plan or its assets. The standard for investment is the skill and diligence of a prudent person, loyal to the plan, and without significant conflicting interests. Reasonable diversification is required, and no more than 10 percent of a plan's assets should be invested in securities of the employer for defined benefit plans. Fiduciaries are liable to the plan for losses resulting from breach of fiduciary duties. Some civil penalties apply with respect to prohibited transactions, mostly involving self-dealing practices. Suits to enforce these fiduciary liabilities may be brought by the Secretary of Labor, plan participants or beneficiaries, or other fiduciaries. Remedies may include damages or injunctive relief, and attorney's fees may be obtained. Criminal penalties may also be applicable for intentional or willful violations of ERISA requirements.

Thus, ERISA broadens and complements the fiduciary responsibilities already existing for many pension trusts, and extends these fiduciary liabilities to employers, pension plan managers, trustees and others controlling such funds. Remedies and relief for breach of these duties have been strengthened. Significant litigation since 1974 has applied ERISA to a variety of pension and benefit plan arrangements, including insurance contracts, and has enforced fiduciary duties against employers, managers, trustees and others with responsibilities for such funds.

Generally speaking, ERISA provides that pension fund managers, trustees, or officials with control over such funds must be bonded. Specific exemptions, however, apply to bonding for insurance company, bank, and trust company fiduciaries, but their executives are often bonded anyway, and these financial institutions would be liable themselves for any breach of fiduciary responsibilities.

4. REPORTING AND DISCLOSURE

The reporting and disclosure obligations for pension and benefit plans were substantially enlarged by ERISA. This information provides the basis for IRS, Labor Department, and PBGC supervision, and allows participants, beneficiaries, and other fiduciaries the opportunity to protect their interests. Plan summaries must be given to all participants. Every plan should be audited by independent accountants annually, with annual reports (including actuarial certification if appropriate). Participants must have at least annual access to accrued benefits. Most reports to the IRS or Labor Department are public information, except benefit data on particular individuals. Civil penalties apply to plan administrators failing to make specified reports, and there are criminal liabilities, fines or imprisonment for knowing or willful violation of these disclosure and reporting requirements. The Secretary of Labor is primarily responsible for enforcing these obligations, but participants or beneficiaries also may obtain disclosure or reporting relief where appropriate.

5. PENSION BENEFIT GUARANTY CORPORATION

ERISA created the PBGC as an insurance agency within the Department of Labor to protect vested pension benefits. If a pension plan is terminated, the PBGC guarantees the payment of most basic, vested benefits (*on defined benefit plans*) to appropriate participants or beneficiaries, up to a certain limit of monthly benefits, based on a complex formula factoring in age of the beneficiary and whether the plan is a single-life annuity or a joint and survivor annuity. PBGC insurance does not apply to defined contribution plans. The PBGC allocates assets available upon termination of a plan according to priorities, but it pays off deficiencies in satisfying the basic benefits which have vested (within the specified limits). Most pension plan terminations are voluntary, and generally these plans have been financially sound.[1] Mergers, reorganizations, plant closings, liquidations, or the cost of making contributions are normal reasons for voluntary plan

[1] Voluntary terminations totaled more than 100,000 between 1975–1995, and normally the benefits are annuitized or paid off as lump sums to beneficiaries.

termination. However, where plan assets are insufficient, or when termination is sought by the PBGC to protect the interests of plan participants and beneficiaries, a sponsoring company (or companies) will be liable for up to 30 percent of their net worth. Stock-market values, earnings, or, if necessary, the equity for a bankruptcy proceeding, can be used to calculate the sponsor's net worth.

Unfortunately, when a sponsoring company becomes insolvent (in a balance sheet sense, *i.e.*, liabilities exceed assets), net worth is normally negative or non-existent. In these circumstances, the PBGC's lien on 30 percent of net worth would be useless. In effect, other corporate creditors have priority over vested pension participants and beneficiaries when balance sheet insolvency occurs. Strictly speaking, it would be wise for the PBGC to intervene before actual insolvency, and get some net worth for reimbursement. Thus far, however, it has not been PBGC practice to monitor potential employer (or multi-employer) business failures, and precipitate insolvencies in order to get the maximum reimbursement value. Almost all plan terminations have been voluntary (often involving mergers, closings, or changes in business organization). Between 1975–1995, for example, only 2,100 distress or involuntary terminations occurred, requiring trusteeships for insufficient plan assets.

The PBGC, while comparable to the FDIC, NCUSIF, and SIPC as a financial institution insurance agency, is weaker than most of these other agencies. It does not have as active a monitoring role for financial soundness of pensions, partly because the IRS has some of this financial responsibility. It does not have comparable corrective order authority, and limitations with respect to the 30 percent lien on net worth constrain its use as corrective leverage. Nor does the PBGC guarantee all pension benefits; it merely insures basic benefits up to the monthly limits, and covers only "defined benefit" plans, not "defined contribution" plans.

C. INDIVIDUAL RETIREMENT ACCOUNTS

In 1962 Congress enacted the Self-Employed Individuals Tax Retirement Act of 1962 (more commonly known as H.R. 10 or the Keogh Act). This legislation allowed self-employed people, professionals, and proprietors to establish tax-deferred retirement accounts for themselves and their employees. It was intended to "equalize", somewhat, the opportunities for tax-sheltering through pension and benefit plans already enjoyed by corporate leaders, high-salaried executives, and their employees. H.R. 10 originally authorized defined contribution "Keogh" plans for the self-employed (and their employees) under which tax-deductible contributions could be made amounting to 10 percent of annual (earned) income up to a maximum of $2,500 each year. Such sheltered accounts could accumulate income free of income tax until drawn upon for retirement many years later. As amended, the legislation increased the deduction for contributions to a defined contribution plan that is a profit-sharing plan to a maximum of 15 percent of a participant's compensation, and as much as 25 percent for a contribution plan that is a money purchase pension plan.

ERISA increased these contribution limits substantially in 1974, so that Keogh plan participants could enlarge annual contributions. ERISA also authorized a new individual retirement account (IRA). The IRA allowed individual workers not covered by pension plans to set aside income for similar tax-sheltering and retirement purposes. (Participants in terminated pension plans also could convert their lump-sum benefits into IRAs.) Originally, the annual limits on IRA contributions were $1,500 or 15 percent of earned income, but these have been increased legislatively from time to time. More importantly, ERTA generalized access to IRAs by allowing all employees under 70½ years of age to open such accounts, including people already covered by existing employer, union, government or Keogh plans. Thus, IRAs are available now to most of the working population (instead of merely the 35–40 percent not previously covered by private or government employee pension plans), and to most low- and middle-income employees in the country. As a result, major new funds have flowed into IRAs. The Tax Reform Act of 1986, however, cut back heavily on IRA incentives for upper-, middle- and high-income families participating in employer pension plans. Although all the profits from IRA and Keogh accounts remain sheltered from income taxes, full deductibility on contributions is retained only for $25,000 individual incomes or those without pensions. (For participants in pension plans, deductibility is phased out entirely for individuals earning $35,000 adjusted gross income (or $50,000 for joint returns. This somewhat reduced the rate of growth in IRAs.)

Important limitations apply to Keogh and IRA plan accumulations, though, with respect to early retirement. Substantial tax penalties are imposed on premature distributions or withdrawals before age 59½ (unless one is disabled or transfers benefits due to divorce). This tax penalty is 10 percent of the premature distribution, which eliminates a considerable part (if not most) of the tax benefits received.

In addition, participants in many established pension plans can make substantial additional contributions to their retirement accounts for tax-sheltering purposes, often referred to as supplemental retirement annuities (SRAs). *See* Internal Revenue Code §§ 401–404A, 406–415, 26 U.S.C.A. §§ 401 *et seq*. Many of these additional contribution options have existed for years, but the spread of IRAs make this concept more widely known. SRAs offer advantages, including greater convenience, avoidance of IRA fees and charges, earlier withdrawal, and broader options to purchase annuities on retirement. Hence, SRAs and related supplementary benefit plan contributions should be considered as part of the expanded scope for tax-sheltering of retirement income in recent years.

The economic significance of self-employed, individual retirement accounts, and supplementary retirement options is substantial. These accounts broaden the access to retirement savings among financial intermediaries, and allow more competition for these funds. Banks, MSBs, savings associations, insurance companies, mutual funds, and money market funds compete for these funds, along with many established pension plans (through SRAs and related options), and securities brokerage firms offer "self-directed" Keogh investment accounts for stocks, bonds and other securities. More savings may result from Keogh, IRA, SRA and related accounts, although funds in this category may have less liquidity, and are often subject to financial institution management and service fees. The widening of access to these tax-sheltered savings and investments may be influential politically. This may prove to be a popular, broadly desired tax concession for many families. Conceivably, the taste for "individualized" pension plans could alter group pension and benefit plans for employers, unions, and government (including some elements of Social Security).

Another legislative development, the Tax Equity and Fiscal Responsibility Act of 1982 (TEFRA), was important for executives, professionals, and small business pension plans. For high-income earners, the constraints upon tax sheltering through Keogh plans had encouraged incorporation. Although ERISA set some limits on annual contributions to pension plans for high-income "employees", these limits were not very low. Thus, there were tax incentives to use the corporate form, and substantial differences in access to tax-sheltering. TEFRA achieved more equal treatment for contributions to pension plans, and reduced the limits on tax-sheltered plans for high income earners (whether or not they are self-employed or "corporate" employees.) Some corporate plan participants complained that "equity" had been achieved by reducing their access to tax sheltering, but Congress felt this was desirable, and that high income tax sheltering could be cut back somewhat. This basic approach was reinforced by the Tax Reform Act of 1986, which expanded the application of the minimum tax, both as to corporate and noncorporate taxpayers, by retaining the existing alternative minimum tax for individuals, with specified modifications, and replacing for corporations the prior law add-on tax with an alternative minimum tax, similar to the individual minimum tax, but with a different rate structure.

D. SOCIAL SECURITY, PENSIONS AND FUNDING CONFLICTS

Although the United States evolved a general system of Social Security pensions and disability insurance (OASDI) for most people, supplemented by expanding private pensions and retirement accounts, many aspects of funding and tax support remain controversial. Four issues have provoked conflict: (i) the extent to which progressive taxation and transfer payments should be built into the system, or the degree to which benefits are linked to an individual's contributions; (ii) the role of government old age and disability insurance and pension benefits versus private pension plans; (iii) the scale of benefits and sources of tax support for the "socialized" or government portion of pensions; and, (iv) the proper response to recent strains upon Social Security financing, including the increasing proportion of older Americans within the population,[2] health care inflation, immigration flows (including illegal immigrants), and the risk of slowed economic growth, enlarged unemployment, and less prosperity than had been expected.

Social Security and disability insurance in the United States represent a compromise achieved by Congress, worked out over the years. Most politicians accept the established momentum of a socialized insurance system for the elderly, which includes a basic floor of benefits, together with additional private benefits reflecting individual earnings, savings, and retirement plans. Congress has been generous in both directions, with budgetary support for Social Security, and tax subsidies to private pensions, insurance, and retirement accounts.

Naturally, there has been dissent. From conservative viewpoints, we have proposals to reduce the socialized, transfer payment element, and narrow the scope for progressive taxation in Social Security payroll taxes. Some conservatives suggest privatizing a large part of Social Security, retaining only a residual safety net of assistance for the elderly. One method frequently mentioned is to convert Social Security for "younger" people into retirement bonds, allocated according to earnings. Poverty relief

---

[2] For example, in the mid-1930s when Social Security was established, the average U.S. life expectancy was 64 years; a 65-year-old was only expected to live another 12 years. In 2001 the average U.S. life expectancy was 77 years; a 65-year-old was expected to live another 18 years. Thus, longevity has increased dramatically.

or a negative income tax could take care of the less fortunate. A complication with such conversion plans, however, is the lower wage earner, a rather numerous category. Under present Social Security arrangements their basic pensions are subsidized through progressive taxes. How would this continue? If the lower wage earners should lose net pension benefits, are such reforms politically realistic? One answer, suggest many conservatives, is to substitute "more productive investments" (with little or no income tax, such as private pensions) for the current employer-employee payroll taxes, so that greater yield results. But these extra investment earnings would go predominantly to the higher-income workers, still leaving many low wage people with reduced pension benefits (unless supplemented by progressive tax-transfer payments in some fashion).

A collateral question is the efficiency and productivity of private pensions versus Social Security taxes and disbursements. Private pensions can attain higher yields with investment portfolios (with some variance in success), but management fees and profit margins for private entrepreneurs must be included. Social Security has been operated primarily as a current cash flow system (with less interest income), but its administrative costs have been low. Administrative expense for combined OASDI operations has been less than one percent in recent years, an impressive achievement for a system of its size and complexity. Some complain of mistakes and confusion by Social Security in individual cases, but no system can be perfect, and the appeal and hearing procedures improve performance considerably.

There are limits, of course, to the extent that the Social Security tax burden is bearable. Many believe Social Security taxes have reached (or exceeded) this limit already, and that any further retirement income gains must come from increased personal saving and investment (mainly from more prosperous citizens). Because of constraints upon Social Security payroll taxes, some liberals believe general tax revenues should be used to help support Social Security (and related social insurance and health care). But business interests, the insurance industry, most financial institutions, and, thus far, the majority of Congress have resisted this idea. They argue that Social Security disbursements cannot be properly disciplined (and limited) unless they are tied to some self-contained payroll-tax contribution mechanism like the present system. At issue is the basic level and distribution of pension and retirement benefits that society believes it can afford.

With this background on the funding controversies for Social Security and private pensions, we should review recent concerns for the "adequacy" of Social Security finances. Social Security benefits and administrative expenses have exceeded interest income since 1940, and their trust fund reserves were never intended to fully support disbursements. Current cash flow or "pay as you go" became the primary method of Social Security financing.[3] But

---

[3] One might question whether this is actually a Ponzi scheme, legitimized by federal statute, where payments to

trust fund assets for OASI (and later DI) were built up considerably, for a while, as a partial revenue source, and as a contingency reserve. The OASI trust fund assets reached $17.4 billion in 1952 (for $2.2 billion benefits), but grew more slowly thereafter. Benefits grew faster than reserves in subsequent years, financed out of current Social Security taxes. In 1974 the combined OASDI trust funds peaked at $45.9 billion (but benefits of $58.5 billion exceeded reserves). By 1981 the OASDI trust funds had fallen to $24.5 billion (with benefits enlarged to $139.4 billion). Between 1974–1981 OASDI trust fund contingency reserves had been substantially depleted to low levels (barely sufficient to cover the next monthly benefits). Temporary borrowing from the health insurance and supplementary medical insurance trust funds (with some $26 billion in assets in 1982) helped ease immediate difficulties, but this situation could not go on much longer.

A "short-term crisis" in Social Security finance grew from the fact that annual benefits slightly exceeded Social Security tax revenues, a condition

---

beneficiaries are actually drawn from the contributions of current working participants. A "Ponzi scheme"—named for Charles Ponzi, a Boston financial adviser who ran such a scheme in the early 1900s—is an extended securities fraud, in which an investment adviser promises very high "returns" on investments, which are actually paid from the funds contributed by newer investors, and these high returns seem to confirm the legitimacy of the adviser's promises. (In fact, there are no investments; the adviser is simply recycling a small portion of new investments to benefit earlier investors, while draining off most of the money for herself.) For background and explanation of Ponzi schemes, see *In re Lake States Commodities, Inc.*, 253 B.R. 866, 869 n.2 (Bankr. N.D. Ill. 2000).

persisting between 1974–1981. The gap each year was not very large (in most years), but this violated the "pay as you go" principle of Social Security finance. What produced this gap? Most commentators emphasized three factors: (i) an overly generous indexing formula to offset inflation that added somewhat to benefits; (ii) unexpected rates of inflation for the later 1970s and early 1980s; and (iii) reduced levels of Social Security tax revenue caused by increased unemployment and slowed economic growth. In other words, if the economy had enjoyed full employment, healthy growth, and low inflation, there would have been no short-term financing crisis for Social Security in 1974–1981.

While this realization helps understand the problem, the financing gap had to be closed. The short-term crisis could only be relieved by reducing benefits, increasing Social Security taxes, or taking money from general tax revenues. None of these options were popular in Congress or the Administration. But some solution had to be found. Borrowing from health and supplementary medical insurance trust funds could only be a temporary expedient.

Meanwhile, a "long-term crisis" in Social Security financing was developing for the years 2012–2035 and beyond. The projected deficits in "pay as you go" financing became substantially larger as the "baby boomers" of the 1940s–1950s reached retirement age in the next century.[4] This problem is demographic,

[4] Meanwhile, between 1995–2010 Social Security "surpluses" were generated. Fewer babies were born 1930–1942,

reflecting greater longevity and an increasing proportion of the elderly in the population. Thus, "promised" benefit streams (with inflation indexing) exceed Social Security revenues generated by projected tax rates. Social Security financing assumptions are too optimistic, and require more economic growth, improved productivity, and employment than the economy actually generates. Various stop-gap measures have been enacted to adjust the assumptions.

In any event, Social Security finance needs continued attention.

---

because of the Depression; and many of these were retiring later. Thus, benefit payout burdens were eased for 1995–2010.

PART D

EMERGING ISSUES IN THE LAW OF FINANCIAL INTERMEDIARIES

CHAPTER IX

CONTROVERSIES AND PROSPECTS

Banking and financial institutions law is an evolution of compromises. The development of money and banking law, banking market regulation, international banking, thrift institutions, securities markets, insurance companies, pensions and Social Security funding was set forth in previous chapters. But a number of important issues continue to be controversial, and are being dealt with by the Executive Branch, Congress, and the regulatory agencies. While outcomes cannot be predicted with certainty, the issues and arguments can be summarized. This provides considerable insight into the challenges for banking and financial market regulation in the coming years.

A. CURRENT CONTROVERSIES

Current controversies and challenges for bank and financial institutions regulation include: (i) the need for harmonized rules in an increasingly transnational market; (ii) the impact of digital currencies and transactions on regulatory policy; and, (iii) the threat of international crises to a stable banking and financial market. These controversies are in addition to the perennial problems of government deficits and monetary policy. The interests affected, public and private, are struggling over these policies. Significant changes in financial institutions law and policy were enacted in 2010, with far reaching consequences for the economy and politics, but implementation of these changes has lagged.

Monetary, banking, and financial institutions policy should promote healthy economic growth, ample savings and productive investment, full employment and low inflation. Interest rates and financial service charges should be adequate, but not excessive or discriminatory. Competition among financial institutions is essential, with relatively easy entry, but participants should be responsible and properly capitalized. Large multinational institutions are desirable for many purposes, yet we should avoid excessive concentration or dominance by these firms. Institutions that are "too big to fail" pose awkward "moral hazard" problems. Decentralized enterprises and healthy local institutions are important in a federal democracy, and their vitality should be encouraged.

A continuing flow of international trade, investment, credit and financial services is necessary for world prosperity. Adequate liquidity, access to borrowing, reliable debt service, and responsible national economic policies should be linked together. Financial policies, therefore, of the more important countries are interdependent, and should be harmonized. The benefits of productive financial intermediation should be spread more widely among developing countries. Healthy economic growth, with low inflation, and a minimum of disruption or defaults is desirable for the community of nations.

Regulatory authorities should work to achieve these objectives. Continued integrity of financial institutions and public confidence is indispensable. Equitable treatment of customers and institutions has been established as legal policy, and this should be maintained. Institutions must be carefully supervised, with appropriate disciplines for accountability (including their international activities). Gaps in supervision can be dangerous. Regulatory organizations, legislative oversight, and executive coordination should function smoothly and expeditiously to achieve these ends.

Obviously, problems arise in implementing these general goals. Even these relatively straightforward objectives are controversial to some participants in financial markets, and for other nations (particularly debtor countries wanting generous renewal of credits and foreign assistance). Most banking and financial trade associations have more specific agendas of financial gain, relief, and "turf protection" against each other. There are real, important, and unavoidable conflicts of interest in framing monetary, banking, and financial institutions policy.

B. GOVERNMENT DEFICITS, FINANCE, AND MONETARY POLICY

The Great Recession of 2008–2013 hit the United States, EU member states, and many other nations with marked severity and led to a widespread renewal of Keynesian deficit spending. Economic slumps had substantially reduced employment, tax revenues, and prosperity. Many jobs were lost. U.S. federal budget deficits increased markedly, along with budget deficits and borrowing for many state and local governments. Sadly, the rate of recovery in the Great Recession has been slower than any other economic recession since the Great Depression of 1929–1938.

In the Reagan years, 1981–1988, U.S. federal budget deficits averaged $200 billion annually. Gross federal debt, as a share of GDP, rose from 33 to 53 percent between 1981–1988. Under George H.W. Bush, between 1989 and 1992, deficits declined somewhat; but gross federal debt still increased from 53 to 60 percent. Under Clinton, 1993–2000, federal deficits were gradually eliminated, and a moderate surplus emerged. Federal debt as a share of GDP declined to 57 percent. But under George W. Bush, 2001–2008, deficit spending resumed, with gross federal debt reaching 70 percent of GDP. Then under Barack Obama, 2009–2016, federal deficits grew even faster. Federal deficits went from $458 billion in 2008 to $1.4 trillion for 2009 and remained above $1 trillion for the next three year, dipped to $679 billion in 2013 and continued below $600 billion throughout the rest of the Obama presidency. On the other hand, gross federal debt rose to $19.5 trillion by 2016. With the incoming Trump Administration in 2017, economic conditions began to worsen, with a $665 billion deficit in 2017 and $779 billion in fiscal year 2018. Gross federal debt continued its increases to $21.5 trillion by 2018.

A major complication in the last decade was health care spending and conflicting reform proposals. Most experts agreed that U.S. overall health costs were excessive (at 18 percent of GNP). The problems were how to get the cost reductions, and implement broader coverage. In a largely private health insurance system, poor people and younger workers did not earn enough to afford adequate coverage. Obama's Affordable Care Act (ACA) of 2010 tried to increase taxes for health care, and to enforce near universal coverage. But many resisted individual and employer mandates. During 2011–2014 the U.S. health care controversies over the ACA, tax revenues, and federal spending were deeply entangled in the overall fiscal stalemate and other policy disagreements.

Meanwhile, monetary policies in the United States, EU member states, and other countries had to be coordinated with fiscal, tax, and deficit spending. The Great Recession of 2008–2013 had created a big and lengthy slump, major unemployment, and excess capacity. This allowed an extended period of very low interest rates, together with fiscal and monetary stimulus. But why was the recovery so slow and incomplete? (1) Losses from the financial crisis, bad loans, and toxic securities (including derivatives) were unusually severe. (2) Business confidence eroded in the United States and parts of the EU (especially Greece, Ireland, Portugal, Spain, France, and the UK). (3) The U.S. health care overhaul controversy brought disruptions, risks, and uncertainties to 18 percent of the U.S. economy. For many small- and medium-sized companies, projected health insurance costs, premiums, and taxes threatened to rise substantially. Increased health costs and premiums reduced incomes. This discouraged hiring in many sectors, and these problems were likely to continue. The harshly divided political situation, typified by closely contested presidential and congressional elections between 2000–2016 and beyond, was a difficult environment for business planning, in the United States, EU, and some other markets.

Improving job growth and broader prosperity is clearly a U.S. priority. In recent years, the U.S. Federal Reserve added significant "Quantitative Easing" (Q.E.)—big purchases of bonds and other securities by the Fed—to add liquidity and stimulus in the economy. While this was accepted by many as an additional tool in the mix of fiscal-monetary easing, some worried that excessive flooding of cheap liquidity could be addictive. Some other countries, nonetheless, began to use Q.E., following the Fed's policy, as a further instrument of monetary policy.

In deeply divided countries like the United States, fiscal and tax policies were hard to "fine tune," so that Q.E. also represented a more flexible, incremental form of monetary policy. But could slowdowns be "tapered downward" through Q.E.? This problem was a cutting-edge issue in Obama's second term. More incremental flexibility was desirable, both for monetary easing and stimulus. However, would expanded debt loads be dangerous, slow long-term growth, and weaken the dollar in exchange rate rivalries? These problems persist, and only time will tell whether the current administration has anything new and effective to contribute to economic policy.

C. INTERNATIONAL BANKING AND FINANCE

Over the last 50 years the global economy has generally prospered with greatly enlarged international trading activities and capital movements. But there have been stressful difficulties. During the 1970s a surge of price inflation hit most global markets. Oil prices trebled (OPEC I, 1973–1974) and trebled again (OPEC II, 1978–1979). Food and many other commodity prices more than doubled. A wage-price spiral of "stagflation" ratcheted upwards in most countries. And inflation hit countries quite unequally. Non-oil nations generally suffered, but oil rich exporters often prospered. Big petro-dollar profits, especially from the Persian Gulf, had to be recycled through leading international banks. These banks, flush with swollen liquidity, loaned generously to multinational corporations (MNCs) and many less developed countries (LDCs). Debt loads for many developing nations built up rapidly. And yet, the global inflation was deeply worrisome to most countries. Most economists felt that inflation had to be disciplined and brought under control somehow.

By the early 1980s all this led to a crackdown on inflation among the leading banking nations (including the United States, Germany, the United Kingdom, Japan, Switzerland, and others). A major global recession and slump followed for many countries, along with high interest rates, serious debt servicing strains, and an extended debt rescheduling crisis. This required a stretch-out of international financial obligations for more than 60 countries during the 1980s, together with tougher fiscal discipline and slowed growth. Slumps followed for many LDCs around the world, but Japan, Taiwan, South Korea, and most of the countries in the Association of South East Asian Nations (ASEAN) group prospered. The United States mainly prospered, though some of its "rustbelt" and manufacturing areas slumped. Europe prospered unevenly, too, with a mixture of slumps and progress. But Latin America and Africa, for the most part, failed to match East Asian and Indian growth rates. Through it all, however, most multinational banks did well, and the global economy was growing faster than most nations.

In contrast, in the late 1980s the USSR's communist economic-political system broke down in the late Gorbachev years. Liberalization and "market oriented" reforms followed (at least to some extent) for Eastern Europe and the former USSR. China moved more successfully toward market decentralization, although democratic reforms were resisted. Meanwhile, the European Economic Community deepened their market integration. Most of Western Europe joined the Maastricht 1992 treaty arrangements, and formed a wider European Union (EU) that began admitting central European states into closer linkages with the EU.[1] Since then,

---

[1] A much stronger, long-term economic performance for democratic Western Europe, and most of Asia, than the USSR and its East European satellites, was decisive in the collapse of centralized communism as a political-economic system. Decentralized, market incentives and greater personal freedoms

however, the EU is facing the exit of the United Kingdom (the so-called "Brexit") as a result of a British plebiscite, but EU-UK negotiations towards an orderly separation have been inconclusive as of this writing.

By the early–mid-1990s, a movement toward more open, integrated world markets achieved great momentum. Multinational companies (MNCs) now invested more widely in developing countries, with encouragement and legal safeguards from their governments. Privatization and market-oriented reforms became fashionable. The Uruguay Round of multilateral trade negotiations and the establishment of the World Trade Organization (WTO), pursuant to the WTO Agreements of 1994, offered more support to open markets, although not to the same degree everywhere (significant asymmetries remained a serious problem). "Emerging markets," many of which suffered painful slumps in the 1980s, now welcomed foreign direct investment. Unfortunately, speculative euphoria got out of hand in some countries, *e.g.*, Mexico (1994) and some Asian countries (1997–1998), with nasty banking and currency devaluation crises. And although there were widespread complaints about the "excesses" of globalization, few believed that any broad breakdown or general retreat from world markets was likely or desirable.

On the other hand, frequent adjustment strains, devaluations, and threats to jobs and incomes in

---

had brought broader growth and prosperity to most Western countries.

many countries brought concerns about appropriate "limits" to globalization. Thus, when an ambitious effort at a new WTO millennium trade round was launched at Seattle in 1999, these meetings broke down. Also, the WTO Doha round progress was slow. Most developing nations want to limit further market opening, and many LDCs want relief from commitments to stronger intellectual property rights and investment protection for MNCs and the advanced countries. On the other hand, many agriculture, business, labor, and environmental interests in advanced countries also felt that global market integration had gone too far, and needed stronger limits, reciprocity, and safeguard relief. The United States, the EU, and Japan bickered among each other, as well.[2]

Meanwhile, in the world's financial markets the recent crises brought painful lessons for many countries. Stronger regulation, capital adequacy, prudential supervision, and transparency were essential safeguards for both public and national interests. Weak regulation, corruption, and poorly informed markets were major elements of fragility that made the global economy more vulnerable and dangerous. Speculative excess, unsound loans and investments, panics, and disruptive capital flows were aggravated by inadequate regulatory supervision. These lessons applied all through

[2] The WTO dispute settlement process, celebrated by some as a means to global harmony and enforcing free trade more fairly, was becoming a new source of stubborn trade conflicts. Little agreement seemed in sight on "completing" an equally open world trading system.

banking, securities, and insurance. Widespread mistakes, fraud, and cronyism were suffered in many nations. If the shortcomings in global financial markets are not dealt with effectively, confidence in global trade and finance could be undermined. Sound financial institutions benefit from healthy competition and market reinforcing supervision that enforces responsibility and common-sense prudence.

Governments often play a key initiating role in fostering the growth of finance, banking, corporations and securities markets, and various branches of insurance coverage. In crises governments are crucial to relief, reform, and rebuilding healthy finance. But as major nations progress, become highly industrialized and prosperous, the role of governments shifts more to maintaining healthy regulation, surveillance, and corrective action to prevent or limit serious problems.

Meanwhile, international financial market coordination has provoked controversy. The IMF plays a central role in assisting countries to ease their balance of payments problems. The IMF encourages governments toward more responsible and sustainable economic, fiscal, and monetary policies. As a result, countries can live within their means, and engage the global marketplace more successfully in investment and trade activities. The World Bank and regional development banks supplement the IMF's role with longer-term lending assistance for infrastructure, education, technology, and the environment so as to promote healthy economic development. In many ways these efforts were quite helpful over the last 40–50 years, but many nations suffered difficulties and did not do so well, or bridled at restrictions on their economic policies imposed by the IMF or other multilateral lenders. How to improve the less successful nations is a major challenge.

Capital markets have broadened and deepened in many ways. But better statistics, transparency, and risk assessment are needed. Improved market supervision, accounting, and regulation for financial markets is important. But implementation is a continuing challenge.

Less complete are the multilateral institutions for regulating and supervising international trade in goods and services. Although the WTO evolved from eight successive rounds of multilateral trade negotiations under the General Agreement on Tariffs and Trade (the GATT, from 1947–1994), the new WTO is suffering serious difficulties. There is a conflict over voting and decision-making. Major asymmetries and lack of reciprocity, which fosters extensive free-riding and limits on further trade opening measures are a problem. Finally, the scope for national regulation in all forms of trade in goods, services, capital, and financial flows is extremely broad. This greatly complicates decision-making at the multilateral level. For these reasons, many nations are going forward with regional and bilateral trade arrangements.

One of the toughest challenges for financial market regulators is the trend towards wider financial conglomerates (banking, securities, and insurance), along with an increased number of multinational enterprises in these financial sectors. We have learned through many institutional failures (*e.g.*, the 1991 collapse of the Bank of Credit and Commerce International) that good accountability, comprehensive reporting, reasonable transparency, and sufficient capital are essential for sound finance. Mergers across national boundaries make this supervision more difficult, and multinational financial conglomerates even more so. Thus, stronger collaboration regimes (including "source of strength" doctrines) must be established among financial regulators (banking, securities, and insurance), but also across international boundaries. Thus, the Basle Concordat regime sponsored by the BIS to establish basic principles for responding to liquidity and insolvency problems in global banking could be extended in some form into a multi-dimensional grid of supervision for international finance (banking, securities, and insurance). This is a key priority for global financial markets.

An important development in global capital markets is also forcing this trend. Already substantial cross-investments are occurring by pension and mutual funds through international boundaries. Thus, the pension and investment intermediaries of the world are already investing into international markets. This is occurring among OECD countries, but also into developing country securities and investment opportunities. International trade in goods and services promotes global commerce, but a lot of this is relatively short-term. But international investments by pension and mutual funds is a longer-term network of financial "marriages" and interdependence. When countries commingle their pension fund investments (not unreasonable from a diversification viewpoint), their need for mutual trust is greatly enhanced. Through joint supervision of international pension assets many nations are more closely bound to each other. Implementing this responsibility is a major institutional challenge; it should lead to an important strengthening of international financial supervision, mutual disclosure and accountability.

In the wake of the capital markets crisis of 2008–2013, the Dodd-Frank Act contains some modest provisions encouraging greater international coordination in formulating responses to any future crisis. For example, section 175 of the act authorizes the president to "coordinate . . . similar policies as those found in United States law relating to limiting the scope, nature, size, scale, concentration, and interconnectedness of financial companies, in order to protect financial stability and the global economy." Similarly, the act directs the Financial Stability Oversight Council to "consult with the financial regulatory entities and other appropriate organizations of foreign governments or international organizations on matters relating to systemic risk to the international financial system." However, "consultation," without further specification, is likely to be a soft process.

More concrete results may be expected from the mandate in section 752 of the act that the Commodities Futures Trading Commission (CFTC), the SEC and other agencies make specific harmonization efforts toward the establishment of "consistent international standards with respect to the regulation (including fees) of swaps, security-based swaps, swap entities, and security-based swap entities." The section specifically authorizes federal agencies to conclude agreements for "such information-sharing arrangements as may be deemed to be necessary or appropriate in the public interest or for the protection of investors, swap counterparties, and security-based swap counterparties." In addition, the CFTC is required to "consult and coordinate" with non-U.S. regulators in establishing "consistent international standards with respect to the regulation of contracts of sale of a commodity for future delivery and options on such contracts." The CFTC is also authorized to conclude agreements deemed necessary or appropriate in the public interest to protect users of commodity futures contracts.

D. RESTRUCTURING FINANCIAL MARKETS

Until recently each major field in the spectrum of U.S. financial institutions—commercial banking, thrift associations (MSBs, S & Ls, and credit unions), securities marketing firms, and insurance companies—was almost entirely specialized to itself. There was little diversification or cross-ownership between these financial industries, and not much ownership of significant financial enterprise (in any of these channels) by outside industrial companies. Each financial sector was supervised mainly by its own regulatory agency or agencies, usually sympathetic to industry needs, along with more general public and consumer interests. Within their respective channels, banks, thrifts, securities firms, and insurance companies performed their intermediation roles, served depositors and customers, and grew within the latitude allowed for their industry. (See Chart IX-1, infra, for traditional market participation among financial institutions.) Chartering policies, fiduciary responsibilities, business custom, and historical evolution strengthened this pattern. So did the Glass-Steagall Act of 1933, which separated commercial banking from securities marketing and underwriting, and subsequent court interpretations of that legislation. The Bank Holding Company Act amendments of 1970, which kept commercial banking largely confined to this field, were another important strengthening of this momentum. The traditions of dual regulation, federal and state, for banking and thrift institutions, along with state regulation of insurance, also fostered a conservative view of financial market boundaries.

Growing rivalry, however, began at the borderlines between these industries. Commercial banks and thrift institutions always took some savings deposits from consumers in competition with each other. And, to a limited extent, their lending activities overlapped (more so recently). Meanwhile, securities marketing firms sold bonds, stocks, and notes to customers as saving and investment alternatives in partial competition with deposit taking institutions. Mutual funds were developed as a more convenient means to investment accounts, with flexibility and liquidity more like savings accounts. Insurance companies developed life insurance contracts with investment features, and added variable annuity policies close to mutual funds in character. Banks developed pooled trust investment accounts in response to mutual funds. In another area, commercial banks, insurance companies, and labor organizations (along with other professional groups) took active roles in developing pension funds and their management. All this reflected some competition among financial institutions, even though considerable product and service differentiation partly separated banking, thrifts, securities marketing, and insurance companies.

Chart IX-1
Traditional Market Participation Among Financial Institutions

Type of Intermediary		Market Structures
I. Deposit Taking Institutions		
Commercial Banks—		
(Generally restricted to single states under established law)		Competitive national banking market serves large customers
		Local oligopolies serve small businesses and families
Thrifts—		
MSBs S & Ls	Expanding to commercial banking	Competitive alternatives to commercial banking, with special role in housing finance
Credit Unions	More limited services, mostly	Limited competition for banks, other savings institutions

	for employee members	
II. Securities Marketing Institutions		
Brokerage Firms, Mutual Funds and Investment Companies Underwriters	Often integrated, national enterprises	Loose oligopoly of nationwide firms, with competitive fringe of smaller and local firms
Issuers (Corporations, Partnerships)		Includes all enterprises issuing securities
III. Insurance Companies		
Life, Health Insurers		Loose oligopolies of nationwide firms, with smaller and local firms as competitive fringe
Property, Liability Insurers		Loose oligopolies of nationwide firms, with smaller and local firms as competitive fringe
IV. Pension Fund Managers		
Commercial Banks Insurance Companies Labor or Professional Organizations		Loose oligopolies of nationwide firms, with smaller and local firms as competitive fringe
V. Social Insurance System		
Federal Social Security		Unitary nationwide system
Other Federal Insurance		
State and Local Government Social Insurance Activities		State (or Municipal) programs

Chart IX-2
Potential Restructuring of Market Participation Among Financial Institutions

	Type of Intermediary		Market Structures
I.	**Deposit Taking Institutions Commercial Banks**		
	(Nationwide enterprises with unrestricted branching and diversification activities)		Nationwide oligopoly of conglomerates, with some local banks surviving as limited competition
	MSBs SBs S & Ls	Close to commercial banks, but usually smaller	Limited competition, mainly in local areas
	Credit Unions	More limited services, mainly for employee members	Limited local competition
II.	**Securities Marketing Institutions**		
	Brokerage Firms	Nationwide diversification allowed	Nationwide oligopoly of financial conglomerates, and weak competitive fringe of smaller firms
	Mutual Funds & Investment Companies		Closer links between major financial conglomerates and leading corporations
	Underwriters		
	Issuers (Corporations, Partnerships)		
III.	**Insurance Companies**		
	Life, Health Insurers Property, Liability Insurers		Nationwide oligopoly of financial conglomerates, and weak competitive fringe of smaller firms

IV.	**Pension Fund Managers**	
	Commercial Banks	Nationwide oligopoly of financial conglomerates, and weak competitive fringe of smaller firms
	Insurance Companies	
	Labor or Professional Organizations	
V.	**Social Insurance System**	
	Federal Social Security	Unitary nationwide system
	Other Federal Insurance	
	State and Local Government Social Insurance Activities	State (or Municipal) programs

In the mid-1970s through 1980s, this rivalry among financial intermediaries increased. MSBs and S & Ls began offering NOW accounts, with consumer convenience close to that of bank checking accounts, but paying interest to depositors as well. In the late 1970s, when Regulation Q limits kept savings account interest rates substantially below rising money market rates, the securities industry responded with money market mutual fund accounts. The MMMFs offered higher interest rates, almost the same convenience, and added limited check writing privileges. Merrill Lynch introduced cash management accounts (CMAs) for large deposit customers with unlimited check writing, followed by other securities brokerage firms. Gradually, commercial banks and thrifts accepted the need to meet this deposit competition, with lower denomination certificates of deposit. Finally, the Garn-St. Germain Act of 1982 mandated money market accounts for banks and saving institutions. These developments substantially increased deposit account rivalry among commercial banks, savings institutions, securities marketing firms and mutual funds.

Meanwhile, savings institutions received broader lending latitude (especially S & Ls, whose charters had limited them mainly to real estate loans). The DIDMCA of 1980 and Garn-St. Germain were particularly significant (see Chapter IV, *supra*). Thus, deposit taking institutions became more competitive with each other, and experienced greater competition with the securities industry.

These developments combined with a more free-market, relaxed, and permissive attitude toward mergers and conglomerate business growth held by leaders in the Reagan-Bush-Clinton-Bush administrations. This encouraged inter-market diversifications and related acquisition moves in the financial sector. And the Glass-Steagall Wall between banking and securities was significantly eroded by administrative and judicial interpretation, and in 1999 the Gramm-Leach-Bliley Act eliminated significant parts of the Wall, at least as to affiliations between banking and securities operations. Following the market collapse of 2008, however, the Dodd-Frank Act did repair part of the Wall by restricting, but not eliminating, proprietary securities trading by banks.[3]

---

[3] For discussion of the restriction—known as the "Volcker Rule," for former Federal Reserve Chairman Paul Volcker, who pushed for the restriction—see pages 127–129, *supra*.

Many observers viewed this trend of diversification as moving toward nationwide financial conglomerates. Early leaders in this structural transformation were the largest U.S. commercial banks, Citicorp, Chase, and Bank of America, Merrill Lynch (strongest in the securities industry), Sears'-Allstate-Dean Witter-Coldwell Banker (an early nationwide-retailing-insurance-securities-real estate brokerage conglomerate), Shearson-American Express (brokerage, credit cards, and travel services), and Prudential-Bache (a major insurance securities combination). A continuation of this merger trend and diversification movement, if unrestricted, could produce, within a number of years, a restructuring of U.S. financial markets. (See Chart IX-2, *supra*, for potential restructuring of market participation among financial institutions.) What had been separate financial industries, broken down into loose oligopolies, with many small and local financial institutions, could essentially become a much more concentrated, nationwide oligopoly of financial conglomerates, with substantially weaker competition.

The ultimate results could substantially weaken competitive rivalry for small business, consumer, and individual family accounts. Only larger business and wealthy individual accounts would be likely to bargain with enough clout to get the lowest possible rates or good service from giant financial conglomerates. Corporate headquarters for these financial conglomerates would be concentrated into fewer states, and many communities would lose significant financial leadership talent. Such a radical, structural transformation of the financial organization of American society would constitute a major break with past legal and business traditions. The theme of federalism, which dominated the financial development of this republic, would no longer be influential.

To what extent is such a structural transformation of U.S. financial markets at hand? Would new legal constraints be required to limit this transformation and increased concentration in financial markets? To what extent, if any, should the Bank Holding Company Act be modified? Should new limitations be applied to cross-industry penetration (or large mergers) in the financial sector? Should large companies from other industries be allowed to acquire major banks? and establish big financial conglomerates? Can antitrust enforcement be relied upon to set proper limits on the expansion of financial conglomerates? Or should free market forces, unrestricted merger activity, and expansion of financial conglomerates be allowed to proceed without any legal regulation or constraint whatsoever?

These are important issues on the horizon, but one should recognize that substantial increases in aggregate concentration have already occurred within U.S. financial markets. Between 1980–2003 the share of domestic commercial bank deposits held by the largest 100 U.S. BHCs grew from 46 to 72 percent. The assets of the top four BHCs reached 64 percent of total BHC assets in 2008. The number of commercial banks declined from 14,600 to 7,300. S &

Ls and savings banks declined from 5,000 to 1,260; thrift institution assets declined substantially relative to commercial banks, and these trends continue apace. Credit unions declined from 21,000 to 8,300 although their assets are still growing somewhat. Consolidation and concentration increased as well in the securities industry, among mutual funds, and in the insurance industry. By 2007 the top 12 securities firms had 89 percent of the industry's capital (and six of these were affiliates of multinational banks.)[4] The top 25 life insurers had more than two thirds of their industry's revenues, while the top 25 property-casualty insurers had more than 60 percent of their industry's revenues. These other branches of the financial sector were always much more nationally concentrated than commercial banking (or depository institutions), and further consolidation occurred in the 1990s–early 2000. More consolidation is likely in the 2008–2010 global recession, unless limited by government policies.

During the 1990s the U.S. Congress and bank regulatory agencies had greatly relaxed the limitations on financial concentrations. The key steps were Riegle-Neal in 1994 (allowing interstate bank branching), and Gramm-Leach-Bliley in 1999 (allowing financial holding companies (FHCs) across banking, securities, and insurance). By 2003, 630

4 The six multinational bank affiliates were: Citigroup; Credit Suisse; Deutsche Bank; J.P. Morgan Chase; UBS; and Wachovia. In addition, by the year 2003, among 630 FHCs, 26 FHCs did insurance under-writing, 165 did insurance agency activities, and 57 did securities underwriting and dealing.

FHCs had been formed in the U.S.; these FHCs controlled 78 percent of the BHC assets in the U.S.

This illustrates a market transformation of financial institutions toward very large, nationwide, and heavily diversified enterprises. But as Congress largely eliminated the Glass-Steagall Wall, there were still concerns about competition, financial concentration, and limiting conflicts of interest. Various proposals for "firewalls" between banking and securities (or other) affiliates, separate capitalization requirements, anti-tying restrictions, and limits on dealings between affiliates have been under review. But Gramm-Leach-Bliley left a lot of this follow-up work to the bank, securities, and insurance regulatory agencies, and especially, to the Federal Reserve as lead FHC regulator.

Many of those believing in broader latitude for financial consolidation expect that a lot of the smaller firms will have to merge into larger institutions or fall by the wayside. This outlook assumes substantially increased economies of scale and integration for financial institutions, based on increased electronic funds transfer and computerization. Others are not so sure that large numbers of smaller banks, thrifts, insurance companies, or securities firms need leave the marketplace. In any event, many people still trust the "market," more than "regulation," as the better decision-making process. Of course, some surveillance, supervision, and supervision constitute sound, traditional regulation, to help markets perform responsibly.

The smaller banks, securities firms, and insurance companies (and independent insurance agents) still muster considerable political strength. And many consumer advocates, academic experts, and public-minded legislators are worried that too drastic a reduction in competition has now occurred in the U.S. financial sector. From their perspective the public and consumer interests in a wide array of competitive choices, and the need for preserving a strong role for smaller banks, securities firms, and insurance companies scattered through most of the 50 states, have been neglected. The predominant regulatory agencies (Federal Reserve, OCC, and SEC) are wedded too closely to the outlooks of large institutions. The smaller, more local banks, S & Ls and savings banks have been greatly weakened; many of their thrift survivors are regional or state-wide chains. Only credit unions (there are still well over 5,000 of them) remain substantially decentralized, or confined to the employees of particular companies, government agencies, or local communities. In the securities field smaller, regional brokers have not been that strong since the 1980s, although new entry may not be that difficult. (Capitalization for local brokers is not that burdensome.) And in the insurance sector (especially some branches of property-liability coverage) a significant range of smaller-medium sized companies has been able to survive (especially when "protected" by state insurance rate bureaus that kept premiums at "adequate" levels).

When competition among financial institutions is weakened too much there is a direct impact on the rates, charges, fees, interest rates, and yields available to consumers and small business. Already in many cities and states the deposit interest rates have declined for ordinary consumers, while the margins charged by the largest institutions have widened. Only the biggest depositors and borrowers are able to get better deals, *i.e.*, better competitive pricing for many kinds of financial services. If the Federal Reserve, OCC, and SEC are not aggressively supervising the adequacy of financial competition, this responsibility must be taken up by Congressional committees and their investigations. State agencies might do some work on these lines, too, but it is much harder for state regulatory agencies to investigate and get full information from interstate financial institutions.

Unfortunately, the trend toward giant and conglomerate financial institutions aggravates the problems of supervision and surveillance for firms "too big to fail." Firms with divergent mixtures of banking, investment banking and securities, and various insurance activities are not easy to manage or supervise. And yet, the biggest and leading giants, like Citigroup, Bank of America, Merrill Lynch, AIG, or UBS, cannot be allowed to fail—the national and international effects are too disruptive. Even their own private managements have difficulty guaranteeing success in their stressful rivalries. With the market collapse of 2008, increasingly vocal critics expressed the belief that such "too big to fail" giants should either be broken into more viable pieces, or more closely supervised as quasi-public utilities.

The response of the Dodd-Frank Act—still in the process of implementation—is to attempt both the threat of break-ups and the establishment of closer supervision. The act established the Financial Stability Oversight Council (FSOC) to identify systemic risks, to promote market discipline, and to respond to emerging threats to the U.S. financial system. The FSOC has the authority to designate large non-banking financial institutions as "systemically significant," which would place them under the supervision of the Federal Reserve. The act also gave the FDIC authority to supervise the resolution of any financial crisis—or "orderly liquidation"—with respect to any systemically significant financial company. No such designations are currently in place.

E. CHANGING REGULATORY ORGANIZATION AND FRAMEWORK

In a period of controversy over monetary, banking, and financial institutions policy, we often hear proposals for change in regulatory organization, consolidation of agencies, and the framework for decision-making. When monetary management, interest rates, and their relation to fiscal policy are in dispute, proposals to change the decision-making structure of the Federal Reserve are frequently heard, or at least there are concerns over methods of appointment and selecting Fed leaders (and other regulatory heads). While the Fed's substantial independence seems reasonably well-established, critics sometimes raise this issue, perhaps hoping to influence its course of decisions.

Among the possible restructuring options were consolidation of most federal bank regulation activities (other than Federal Reserve monetary policy) into a new agency. This could be called the Federal Banking Commission (FBC) or a broadened OCC-FDIC. Crucial questions would be its leadership, responsiveness to different elements of the banking industry (multinational banks, regional banks, and independent banks), thrift institutions, and broader public interests. Some proposed reducing (or "weakening") the Bank Holding Company Act's regulation along with such a change, although this is controversial. Few seemed to favor including the NCUA in such a consolidation, at least initially.

Merger policy would be controversial, especially if independent Justice Department review under the Bank Merger Act were altered in any significant way. Because of so many unresolved controversies, many observers of financial market regulation had not expected any really major legislative developments during 1985–1999.

But the FSLIC recapitalization of 1989, and the enactment of FIRREA in August 1989, did lead to some restructuring of bank and thrift regulation. The Home Loan Bank Board was abolished, and most of its regulatory and supervisory responsibilities were transferred to a new Office of Thrift Supervision (OTS) in the Treasury. Meanwhile, FSLIC was absorbed by the FDIC, and the insurance funds were divided into the Bank Insurance Fund (BIF) and the Savings Association Insurance Fund (SAIF). This left the NCUA intact as credit union regulator, along with its NCUSIF. In other respects, the financial institutions regulatory structure remained essentially unchanged in recent years.

After Gramm-Leach-Bliley, which allows FHCs to operate in banking, securities, and/or insurance, the problems of conglomerate financial oversight must be faced more realistically. The Federal Reserve has been the primary regulator of bank holding companies; its staffing and expertise have been stronger. This is why the Federal Reserve became the primary regulator for FHCs. The SEC, on the other hand, had built a strong tradition for quality supervision of securities disclosures. Nevertheless, the SEC failed to supervise adequately investment banks that became over-leveraged. Also, the SEC showed great negligence in not catching Bernard Madoff, the perpetrator of an outrageous securities firm "Ponzi scheme" fraud before he diverted some $50–60 billion from clients. And various derivative securities, collateralized credit obligations, and swaps have not been adequately supervised in recent years. By contrast, insurance regulation in the United States has been almost entirely left to state insurance commissions, with a mixed performance—excellent in some states, not so effective in others. Recently, after investigative probing by congressional committees and the General Accounting Office, the National Association of Insurance Commissioners (NAIC) has become somewhat more active, responsible, and important as a serious regulatory institution. A crucial question is whether or not the NAIC can rise to the level of an equal partner to the Federal Reserve and SEC in the supervision and regulation of financial holding companies. If so, fine; if not, many (from both within and outside the insurance industry) will urge the need for a federal insurance regulatory agency.

In this context, it should be emphasized that U.S. banking and financial market regulators and industry experts are becoming more aware, interested, and knowledgeable about banking and financial market regulation in other advanced industrial countries, especially Europe and Japan. In these other countries, banking, securities, and insurance regulation has some similar characteristics. Each nation has a Central Bank and Finance (Treasury) Ministry for monetary and fiscal policy. Banking market supervision and detailed regulation is either the central bank's responsibility, or delegated to a banking commission or similar agency. Insurance might be regulated by the Finance Ministry or an independent agency, while securities are regulated by the Finance Ministry or independently. Merger activity is closely supervised, along with significant international bank branching in their territories. Exchange and credit control authority is commonly established, though not used often by moderate and conservative governments. Foreign exchange markets are supervised more carefully (with significant intervention or support by many countries.) Reporting and auditing disciplines are roughly comparable, and guidelines for capitalization and reserves are receiving greater attention. In the EU countries, in particular, there has been an effort toward harmonization of banking supervision and regulation of financial markets. Greater collaboration efforts through the Bank for International Settlements (BIS), the G-12 countries, and annual IMF meetings are evident. An important step was the agreement on risk-based capital requirements in late 1987 among the G-12 nations (the United States, Japan, the United Kingdom, West Germany, France, Italy, Switzerland, the Low countries, Sweden, and Canada), which moved international banking toward a more level playing field. A further step came from the Basle Committee on Bank Supervision at the BIS, which established stronger minimum standards to prevent another BCCI failure. The new minimum standards provide: (i) All international banks should be capably supervised by a home country authority with consolidated accounting; (ii) Host countries should impose restrictive measures on unsound operations in their territories that are not well supervised.

Finally, everyone should realize that bankers and financial leaders around the world have become more international minded over the last generation. There is a large functioning market for liquidity and capital that encompasses most of the globe. National economic policies are more interdependent than ever, and the dimension of international finance must be taken into account for many aspects of financial market regulation. There has been a trend of greatly increased mutual contacts and shared insight that includes regulatory leaders and key staff experts. The global economy is becoming a broadly shared field of market experience. This development will enhance mutual understanding and sophistication, and may help ease the economic strains and conflicts that arise inevitably among nations.

INDEX

References are to Pages